More Than Our Pain

SUNY series in African American Studies

John R. Howard and Robert C. Smith, editors

More Than Our Pain

AFFECT AND EMOTION IN THE ERA OF BLACK LIVES MATTER

Edited by

Beth Hinderliter and Steve Peraza

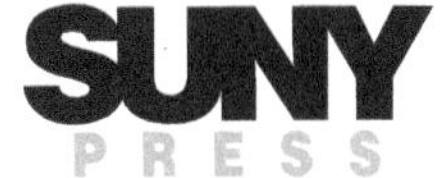

Cover image: Jon Henry, *Untitled #31*, Wynwood, Florida. © Jon Henry.

Published by State University of New York Press, Albany

Printed in the United States of America

For information, contact State University of New York Press, Albany, NY
www.sunypress.edu

Library of Congress Cataloging-in-Publication Data

Names: Hinderliter, Beth, 1973– editor. | Peraza, Steve, editor.
Title: More than our pain : affect and emotion in the era of Black Lives Matter / [edited by] Beth Hinderliter, Steve Peraza.
Description: Albany : State University of New York Press, [2021] | Series: SUNY series in African American studies | Includes bibliographical references and index.
Identifiers: LCCN 2020029175 | ISBN 9781438483115 (hardcover : alk. paper) | ISBN 9781438483122 (ebook)
Subjects: LCSH: Black lives matter movement. | African Americans—Psychology. | Affect (Psychology)—Social aspects—United States. | Affect (Psychology)—Political aspects—United States. | Emotions—Social aspects—United States. | Emotions—Political aspects—United States. | African Americans—Social conditions—1975– | United States—Race relations—Psychological aspects.
Classification: LCC E185.615 .M627 2021 | DDC 155.8/496073—dc23
LC record available at https://lccn.loc.gov/2020029175

10 9 8 7 6 5 4 3 2 1

Contents

Part II
Shaping Collective Protest and Speech through Affect and Emotion

Part III
Moving Forward: Overcoming Fatigue with Rage and Joy

Illustrations

Acknowledgments

Lauren Alleyne's "Heaven, *for Sandra Annette Bland*" and "Elegy, *for Tamir Rice*" were previously published in Lauren Alleyne, *Honeyfish* (Kalamazoo, MI: New Image Poetry and Prose, 2019); "The Hoodie Stands Witness, *for Trayvon Martin*" was first published in Lauren Alleyne, *Difficult Fruit* (Leeds: Peepal Tree Press, 2014); "Poetry Workshop after the Verdict, *For the Trayvons*" appeared in *One* 6 (August 2015); and "Post-Verdict Renga, *for Trayvon*" appeared in the *Los Angeles Review of Books*, April 29, 2014, lareviewofbooks.org/article/national-poetry-month-post-verdict-renga-trayvon

Shanna Benjamin's "The Uses of Anger: Wanda Coleman and the Poetry of Black Rage" was previously printed in *Hecate* 40, no. 1 (2014): 58–79.

Dominique Christina's poem "In response to the Question 'If 2017 was a poem what would it be called?'" previously appeared in "34 Poets of Color Summarize 2017 in Verse," *Huffington Post*, February 28, 2017, www.huffpost.com/entry/poets-of-color-2017-title_n_58b07eb6e4b060480e079dbf

Javon Johnson's "Black Joy in the Time of Ferguson" was previously published in *QED: A Journal in GLBTQ Worldmaking* 2, no. 2 (Summer 2015): 177–183.

Introduction

More Than Our Pain: Affect and Emotion in the Era of Black Lives Matter

BETH HINDERLITER AND STEVE PERAZA

In 2013, following the acquittal of George Zimmerman in the killing of Trayvon Martin, the Black Lives Matter Global Network coalesced as a call to action demanding justice for Black Americans killed by police and vigilantes. As videos of black death scrawled across device screens in what felt like an unending feedback loop, more violence unfolded as protestors in the streets of Ferguson, Missouri, in 2014 were targeted with tear gas, rubber bullets, fists, batons, and tanks. The protestors' grievances were largely dismissed in mainstream media coverage of the events. Black anger and hurt was manipulated in the nightly news as outpourings of collective anguish, grief, and righteous rage became media stories of individual looting and greed.

Using tactics to spectacularize death and criminalize victims and protesters, the media avoided root problems of racialized violence in the United States. As Brittney Cooper wrote in August 2014, "Nothing makes white people more uncomfortable than black anger. But nothing is more threatening to black people on a systemic level than white anger. It won't show up in mass killings. It will show up in overpolicing, mass incarceration, the gutting of the social safety net, and the occasional dead black kid."[1] Black Lives Matter activists and protesters called for an emotionally honest accounting of the racism and harm that African Americans face. Moreover, they provided a space for mourning and healing denied by the national media.

This volume *More than Our Pain: Affect and Emotion in the Black Lives Matter Movement* explores expressions of grief and rage as well as love and joy central to the movement from 2013 forward. In the streets, outpourings of grief met with collective indignation, a solemn funeral send-up, a registering of centuries of grievances, and a wave of love—these emotions knitting a shattered community together (see figure I.1). Black joy and love brought communities together when the weight of trauma, pain, and murder—historical and contemporary—was too much to bear. As poet Dominique Christina laments in part III of this volume, "I have forgotten how to cry in this country, I open my mouth, I capsize. I barely woman. I barely human. I wolf or something like it. I sugarcane and long memory.

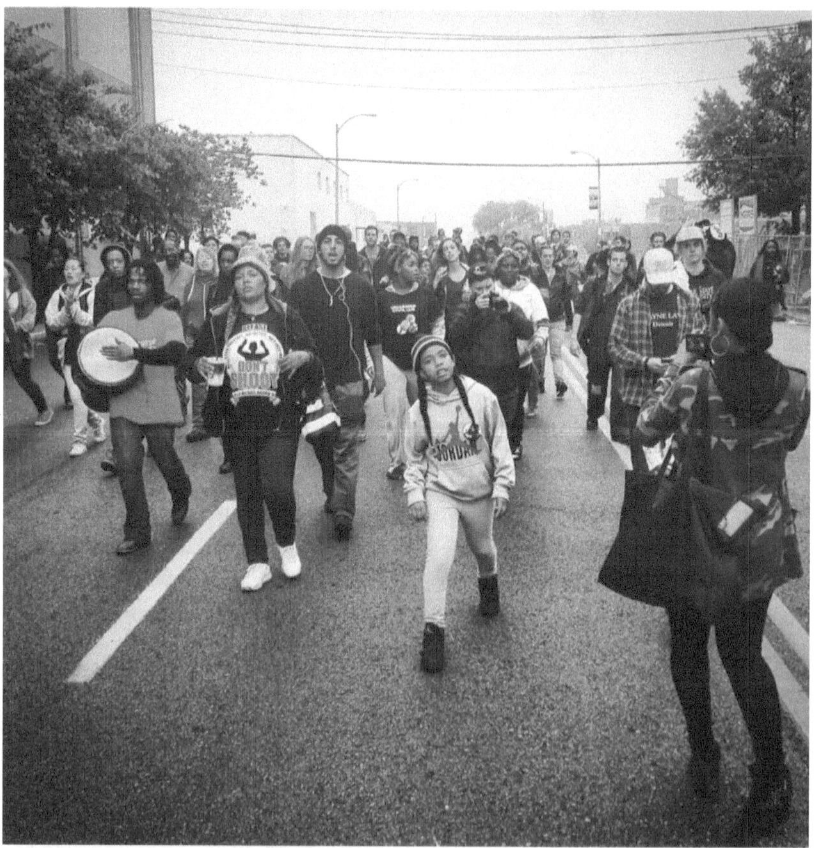

Figure I.1. Andrew Padilla, Mike Brown protests led by a young girl in St. Louis, October 2014. © A. Padilla.

I cotton field and long blade. I eulogy. I suicide note. I manifesto. I rage. I grief. No tears left."

The plurality—as well as the potency—of these emotions calls into being important forms of national and international solidarity. Critical also at this moment was the work protestors and activists did to bring attention to the specific affects and emotions that pervade white supremacy, which largely presents them as rational and neutral. As detractors of the Black Lives Matter movement sought to dismiss its grievances and demands, the gap between differing emotional worlds, or what B. Cooper called *sentient knowledges*, became abundantly evident. How can a single event provoke such profoundly different emotional responses amongst different individuals and groups? As Erin Stephens writes in her chapter in this volume, Black Lives Matter organizers cultivated emotional resources for movement work, attempting to mitigate the ability of "White emotion" to undermine legitimate grievances and claims of social injury.

During the Ferguson protests in 2014, activist Deray McKesson tweeted a reminder that "we are more than our pain."[2] McKesson's words pushed back against the flattening of emotions and the distractive and race-baiting logic of the media, which labeled the uprising as a riot, thereby conjuring stereotypes of black criminality. Taking inspiration from this phrase, *More than Our Pain* asserts that affect and emotion have been central to the organizing and uprisings seen across U.S. cities such as Ferguson, Baltimore, and Charlotte (and many more) since 2014. The sentient knowledges unleashed during these moments have been central to the many artists, writers, and cultural producers who have given them visual, verbal, and political form. Many of them ask a shared question of how can one artistically represent a life that has been severed from political representation? Feelings are not psychological states beyond social meaning, as Sara Ahmed points out. Rather, they are social and cultural practices deeply related to the power structure of society. They are a form of meaning-making whereby both self and society are constituted.[3] *More than Our Pain* takes Ahmed's claim as central to our work of grappling with whose grievances are registered on the national political stage. Where—in what spaces—do we live our emotional lives in their fullest or in their most reduced capacities? How do we do the work of re-humanization when our emotions are erased or delegitimated? As Yomaira Figueroa-Vásquez and Jessica Marie Johnson write in their chapter in part I, "We need new words for what we do, for how and why we stay, for the labor of making black love and black joy and black pleasure in a world of this."

More than Our Pain: Affect and Emotion in the Black Lives Matter Movement offers multiple viewpoints on how affect and emotion are key to Black Lives Matter Global Network's radical modes of collective assembly and protest. The authors in community in this volume assert the Black Lives Matter movement as a human rights movement, rather than a civil rights movement, which has relied on the foregrounding of emotions erased from the public sphere by acts of violence and deliberate political exclusion as well as those forged in the bonds of communal protest. It should be remembered that the movement itself originated in an act of love when co-founder Alicia Garza, following the acquittal of George Zimmerman in the killing of Trayvon Martin, penned a love letter declaring "black people. I love you. I love us."[4] *More than Our Pain* centers and supports these emotions and affects unleashed by the Black Lives Matter movement in order to reclaim their misuse in the media, propel their resistance into the future, and honor the spirit in which Black Lives Matter organizing has transpired.

Affect and Emotion in Social Justice Activism

In adopting multiple affective strategies (rage-filled raucous voices, sagging pants and hip-hop ethos, belligerent refusals to be forgotten, high-fiving and hip-shaking practices of freedom and joy), Black Lives Matter actors marked a clear break from the civil rights–era activists. When conservatives and reactionaries in the 1950s and 1960s identified civil rights activism with rage and rebellion, many black leaders trained activists to dress in Sunday clothes and turn the other cheek; that is, they countered false narratives about protesters as thugs and criminals with images of God-fearing, disciplined young black Americans. As the wisdoms of Black Feminism have shown, there are steep costs to suppressing the intense feelings that result from racial discrimination, as internalized rage results in self-destructive behavior, an inability to display vulnerability, and lashing out at others who care most about you.[5] In contrast, the Black Lives Matter movement in the early twenty-first century makes no qualms about black rage and the prospects of rebellion. Affect and emotion—no longer the antithesis of rationality as traditional political theory presents it—have moved from the margin to the center of the movement. Accordingly, *More than Our Pain* explores how affect and emotion have driven collective action in the face of this *new nadir* in twenty-first-century race relations in the United States.

Like Black Lives Matter activists today, leaders of the modern Civil Rights Movement channeled emotion strategically in the social justice campaigns of the 1950s and 1960s. Specifically, they proved adept at training activists to show love and, at times, sadness to achieve moral suasion. The affective power of grief, for example, galvanized the Civil Rights Movement following the open-casket funeral of Emmett Till, in which the mutilated body of a black teenage boy showed the horrors of Jim Crow terrorism to the world (see figure I.2).[6] Louis Till, the young child's father, communicates dismay and tragedy as he stares at the viewer. He also stands firm, clutching his wife Mamie Till, mother of the slain boy, whose catatonic

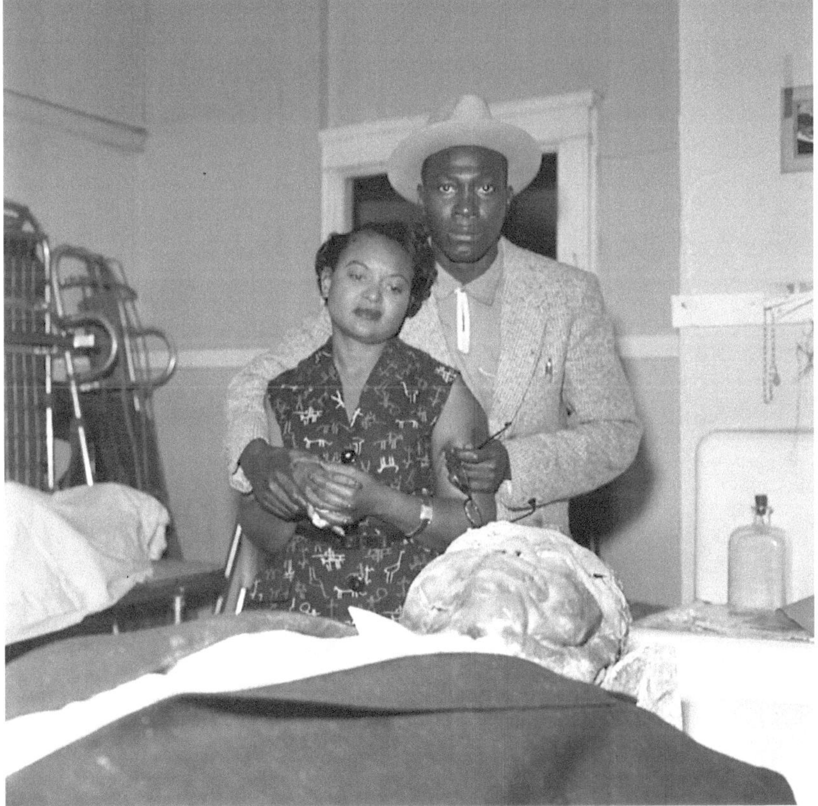

Figure I.2. David Jackson, *Emmett Till*, 1955. Printed in *Jet Magazine*, 1964. "Just like mothers before her, choked, hurt Mrs. Mamie Bradley viewed gory features of her son, Emmett, for last time."

glance at her son's defiled body belies the deep grief that occasioned it, the incomprehension family and friends feel when someone they love dies (or gets murdered) inexplicably.

The emotions of love and joy, on the other hand, were perhaps best captured in a photo taken after the Brown vs. Board of Education of decision in 1954 (see figure I.3).[7] A dignified mother sat beside her daughter on the U.S. Supreme Court steps, her arm drawing the young girl near, as she appeared to explain the decisions that banned racial segregation in public schools. Social justice campaign leaders carefully curated these signs of affect and emotion to showcase the humanity and peacefulness of civil rights protesters, who were defying racial stereotypes of black Americans as criminals and rabble rousers. Expressions of anger and rage found no place in these strategies; to show the full spectrum of black American emotional responses to Jim Crow may have risked reifying racial prejudice.

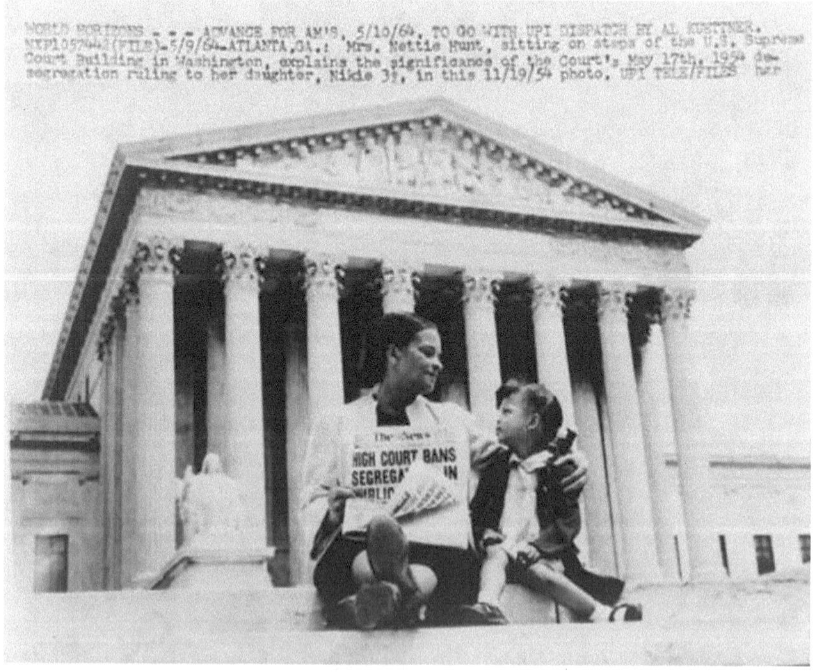

Figure I.3. Mrs. Nettie Hunt and daughter Nikie on the steps of the Supreme Court, 1954. Gelatin silver print. © New York World-Telegram & Sun Collection, Prints and Photographs Division, Library of Congress (97) Digital ID #cph 3c27042.

Fear, anger, and disgust were emotions expressed in private, not in public, and certainly not as the political message intended by direct actions; civil rights activists hoped to inspire righteous indignation in onlookers and bystanders rather than unleash their own that ostensibly fueled the social justice protest. Activists planned and practiced nonviolent direct actions precisely so they would not devolve into expressions of emotions, especially anger, which could feed popular stereotypes that black Americans were rabble rousing and disturbing the peace criminally. The dramatization of Jim Crow terrorism in the 1950s and 1960s required activists to show stoicism as victims of heinous racial attacks, so that other U.S. citizens could witness how viciously Jim Crow sympathizers treated black Americans for trying to desegregate public spaces and to vote in U.S. elections. Expressing anger, in their eyes, would have weakened the moral impact of watching black Americans get dehumanized without any provocation or physical retaliation.

In contrast, Andrew Padilla's photograph of the 2013 #Hoodiesup protest for Trayvon Martin in the Bronx shows a mother holding her child in a loving embrace while raising her in a defiant black power salute (see figure I.4). The photograph reveals the interconnected nature of defiance and love during a moment of intensified public conversations about the fears

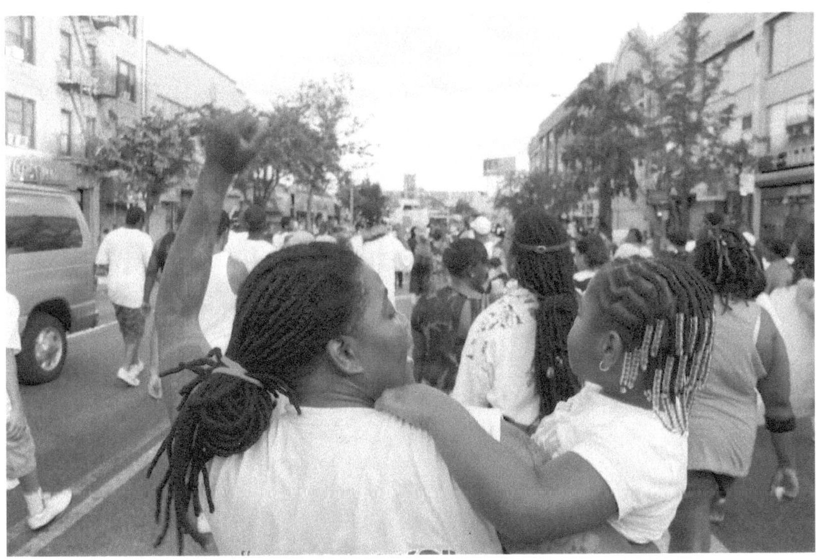

Figure I.4. Andrew Padilla, NYC #Hoodiesup protest for Trayvon Martin in the South Bronx, summer 2013. © A. Padilla.

that black parents have for the safety of their children. BLM activists were redefining rage as a righteous response to the derogation of human rights. By deploying this emotion in protest tactics and rhetoric, they carved out a space for the articulation and dramatization of anger, disgust, and rage in nonviolent direct actions. More important, as in this photography, they elicited affect and emotion to catalyze allies; the goal is not only to trigger empathy but to provoke action. Another photograph taken by Padilla during this protest reveals the strength and dedication of committed activists, who drew on their emotions as a source of energy during the march, demanding the gathering audience to witness their pain (see figure I.5). Righteous rage, when harnessed by social justice activists, can impassion communities and inspire an international human rights campaign by spotlighting the tragedies of injustice and fueling protest with indignation that follows.

More than Our Pain examines the strategic deployment of affect and emotion in the mobilization efforts of the Black Lives Matter Global Network. This volume insists that the intentional deployment of affect and emotion in the political mobilization efforts of BLM activists marks an innovation of the nonviolent direct-action strategies of the modern Civil Rights Movement. *More than Our Pain* advances the important work of scholars

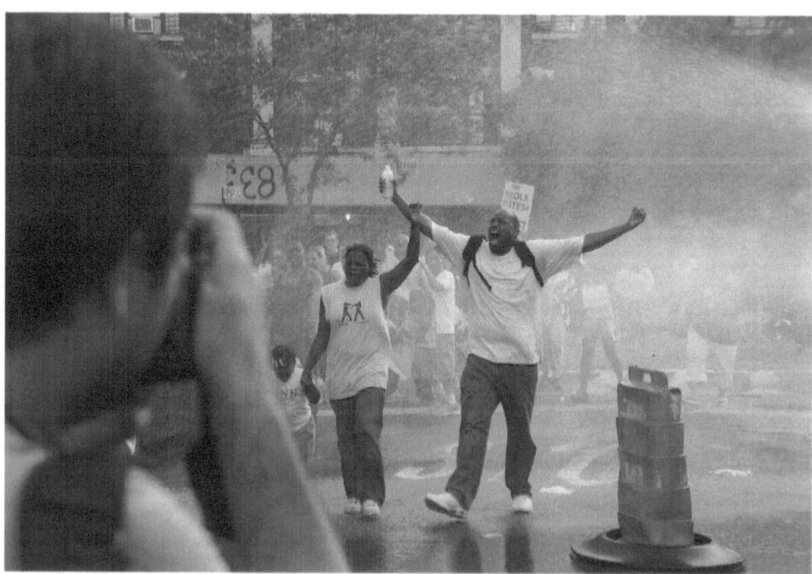

Figure I.5. Andrew Padilla, NYC #Hoodiesup protest for Trayvon Martin in the South Bronx, summer 2013. © A. Padilla.

who are identifying continuities and discontinuities between the BLM and other social justice campaigns in the black liberation struggle. As historian Jeanne Theoharis explains, much of the early work on the Black Lives Matter movement analyzed the campaigned comparatively, noting similarities and differences with the modern Civil Rights Movement:

> Key similarities exist between the civil rights movement and BLM—from the forces they are up against to the criticisms they encounter to the expansive vision of justice they seek. Like the young activists propelling BLM, civil rights activists were regarded as dangerous and reckless by many and as downright desirous by others. The movement was pushed forward by young people, who made many people nervous sixty years ago, just as they do today. Thus, substantively considering new movements for racial justice in the context of the civil rights movement means seeing the ways they are tied to, rather than set apart from, this longer movement history.[8]

More than Our Pain aims to show, however, that Black Lives Matter activists have innovated new strategies and tactics to advance social equality, specifically innovations in technology and protest strategy that distinguish them from the modern Civil Rights Movement.

For example, *More than Our Pain* contributes to an increasingly nuanced investigation of the historical contingencies of the Black Lives Matter movement. One nuance receiving considerable investigation is the use of social media technologies. Historian Barbara Ransby has called social media the site where Black Lives Matter was "incubated": "Social media is the place where news of outrageous injustices is disseminated and people are called to action. It is the soapbox and public square of this generation, where many of the debates about strategy, tactics, and ideas are argued out in sound-bite form, for good or ill. In many ways, it is where [the Black Lives Matter movement/Movement for Black Lives] was incubated."[9] The use of platforms like Twitter and Facebook have facilitated the international Movement for Black Lives, "a critical and important tool for publicity and for creating a forum for debate and politicization."[10]

Sociologists and communications scholars have also conceded that social media transformed the social justice campaigns of the early twenty-first century. Ray, Brown, and Laybourn, for instance, have studied the social media data to understand the ways that "the evolution of social movements and the sustainability of collective identities."[11] The innovative use of social media to mobilize a social justice campaign both national and internationally reveals the historical contingencies that differentiate Black Lives Matter from other black liberation struggles. "Social media provide," Ray and colleagues concluded, "a portal to combine theoretical frameworks in identity formation and collective action with methodological advances in technology to capture the creation and sustainability of social movement narratives as they are occurring."[12]

Innovative use of affect and emotion joins technological evolutions as defining characteristics of the Black Lives Matter movement. The murder of Trayvon Martin is widely held as the clarion call to protest. This was a moment of national outrage in black American communities nationwide, captured powerfully by Patrisse Khan-Cullors, one of the movement's founders:

> I read that a white man—that's how the killer was identified and self-identified until we raised the issue of race—had killed a Black boy and was not going to be charged. . . . I start cursing. I am outraged. In what fucking world does this make sense? I put out a call: Have people heard about 17-year-old Trayvon Martin? I have loved so many young men who look just like this boy. I feel immediate grief, and as my friends begin to respond, they, too, are grief stricken. We meet at my house. We circle up. A multiracial group of roughly 15 people dedicated to ending white supremacy and creating a world in which all of our children can thrive. We process. We talk about what we've seen and experienced in our lives. We cry.[13]

Khan-Cullors gave voice to anger and frustration when confronted with vigilante, Jim Crow justice. This was not the blind rage that devolved into riots and chaos but, rather, the righteous rage that convened a meeting of mourners to remember the dead and to plan for "a world in which all of our children can thrive."

Moreover, *More than Our Pain* reveals how the Black Lives Matter slogan affirms black humanity in part by echoing affect and emotion on a wide range from joy to rage. Black Lives Matter activists insist that black Americans live complex, feeling lives that get reduced to stereotypes and devalued by state institutions. The stereotype that black Americans are predisposed to criminality and violence has helped police officers kill unarmed black Americans without repercussion and municipalities finance the prison industrial complex with impoverished black populations. So, quite reasonably, the slogan responds defiantly to the wanton destruction of black life in the hands of police, prisons, and vigilantes: a sarcastic reminder that life should be honored at all times, even when the person is perceived racially as black. This is one half of the work "Black Lives Matter" does as political rhetoric.

The other half of the work is valorizing black American culture and community. Black Lives Matter activists deploy the slogan as an affirmation of what matters to black Americans—life. Black Lives Matter *because* Black Americans love; they treasure family, friends, community, and nation; they fear state-sanctioned terrorist acts from police brutality to mass incarceration; they mourn the men and women, young and old, whose lives have been harmed and terrorized; and they protest and persevere in the face of racism and oppression. The "Black Lives Matter" slogan thus demands the re-humanization of the black American interpersonal experiences.

In turn, Black Lives Matter activists have innovatively integrated affect and emotion in their protest tactics. They have used anger, joy, fear, love, and other emotions in their direct actions and writings to dramatize for local and national audiences that *black lives matter*, for being complicated, feeling members of U.S. civil society, and thus not a myth whose transhistorical racial stigma has rendered expendable. Black lives matter because the black American men and women losing their lives were sons and daughters, husbands and wives, fathers and mothers; because they belonged to and were beloved in their communities; because they were loved; because their death devastated those left in the wake. The affect and emotion incorporated in Black Lives Matter tactics enriches the meaning of the slogan and suggests a fruitful approach to studying the social justice campaign.

Shaping Collective Protest and Speech through Affect and Emotion in this Book and Beyond

Defining affect as the capacity to affect and to be affected, authors in this volume analyze three main emotions that BLM activists have used to mobilize the movement: grief for the injured and lost, rage at many forms of violence visited upon black and brown life, and the joy of celebrating the vitality of black life in the face of those who would harm it. Grief articulates rage, which, in turn, catalyzes collective action. Indeed, as Lauren Alleyne crafts her "Elegy, for Tamir Rice," she begins by invoking that it was going to be a curse poem, hexing the man who killed Rice with "an unchained melody of rage" that would haunt his nightmares. However, she charts another course to redeem Rice's suffering through writing a prayer poem instead. In it, she constructs a radical freedom, where freedom is a verb conjugated by the power and beauty of black life. Like Alleyne, Shanna Benjamin also expounds on the radical possibilities of black rage. In her chapter "The Uses of Anger: Wanda Coleman and the Poetry of Black Rage," Benjamin reveals how anger is a useable art. Anger affirms our presence in the world, asserts our subjectivity despite persistent erasure or stereotyping, and expresses vulnerability even as it might be misunderstood by most. Benjamin portrays the poet Wanda Coleman as a mistress of black rage whose careful attention to poetic form provides an opportunity for our catharsis while also critiquing racist inequities. But anger alone cannot heal the Black community.

Beyond mounting mourning and grief as a collective loss, the Black Lives Matter movement embodies other emotions in the struggle against injustice, such as anger, fear, resentment, but also joy in shared communion of resistance. By asking other questions as well about how, for example, black excellence and joy is often distorted and turned into pathology, and why rage, instead of being seen as righteous insurgency, is more often represented as criminality, the Black Lives Matter Global Network puts affect at the core of contemporary failures of democratic values, but also uses it as the precondition of future change. Emotions can come from an individual, but they are also the fabric that holds the social body together. Javon Johnson writes in his chapter "Black Joy in the Time of Ferguson" that "our bodies harbor knowledge, and in these moments every smile, head nod, hip shake, and high five is an exchange of embodied truths that black joy is phenomenally transformational." Johnson's chapter extols the healing beauty of black joy.

In appeals to "stop killing us," BLM activists demand the most basic of human rights. They recall Third World Feminist organizing in the United States and the 1979 march in Boston against the murders of Black women. "We cannot live without our lives" read one banner held during the march. Here the emotional appeal is most urgent and emphasizes how deadly and dehumanizing our contemporary formations of power and capital are. In part II of this book, authors examine how affect and emotions shape collective action. The urgency of affect within the Black Lives Matter movement gained traction in a moment of the rise of post-truth politics where a speaker's emotion is vaguely, if at all, linked to reality or the verifiability of their speech. The balkanization of media consumption amidst assertions of "fake news" created a moment in which people increasingly choose their own set of facts, most often associated with their preferred set of "cultural values."[14] As affect is still increasingly presented as anchorlessly adrift from factual reality, the power of the Black Lives Matter movement's use of affect is rooted in techniques of witnessing. Witnessing records not only the devastation of violence within the community, but also calls attention to the specifics of how this violence is absorbed into mainstream news narratives—making these crucial actions invisible even when conducted in a sphere of total visibility. Robin Kelley has written about both the importance and trauma of this witnessing. "While every generation of black Americans has experienced unrelenting violence," Kelley writes, "this is the first one compelled to witness virtually all of it, to endure the snuffing out of black lives in real time, looped over and over again, until the next murder knocks it off the news. We are also talking about a generation that has lived through two of the longest wars in U.S. history, raised on a culture of spectacle where horrific acts of violence are readily available on their smartphones."[15] Witnessing, under the conditions of spectacularization, erasure, and gaslighting, makes this task all the more critical, yet difficult to bear.

We must at times, as Yomaira Figueroa-Vásquez and Jessica Marie Johnson tell us in their chapter "Hoodrat Praxis in a Time of Love and Fury" refuse to bear witness. We cannot participate in the narratives and discourses that erase us. "Black diasporic women have spent centuries cultivating an insurgent, femme-loving, audacious practice of freedom whose roots lie in creative and defiant resistance to their own enslavement," they write. We are united with our *forefemmes* in a refusal to submit and our belligerent fight for our kin. Similarly, Erin Stephens reminds us that Black women's strength, born in pain and struggle, is not magical, nor endless. Black women's emotions are likewise not a commodity to be consumed at will. Witnessing to this strength and pain is a labor of both love and fury. Poet Lauren Alleyne witnesses in this hoodrat praxis that they speak of. In her "The Hoodie Stands Witness, *for Trayvon Martin*," Alleyne has Martin's sweatshirt tell his story, from the banal objects held in its pockets to comfort it gave Martin as the bullet ripped through them. Alleyne conjures the fabric as a bandage, a second sweaty skin, that held him in his last moments.

More than the Pain also contends that a grammar of the body—dominant bodies and stigmatized bodies, armored bodies and bodies in pain—lies at the core of the twenty-first-century black freedom struggle. The Black Lives Matter movement proceeds from the point of asking whose life counts as a life that is protected, cared for, and grievable. Emotional rejections of extrajudicial violence and dehumanization surface as powerful weapons that *body* forth political representation in spaces where black humanity is marginalized, if not erased. Derek Conrad Murray's chapter "Bodies That Matter" makes this point forcefully in his discussion of vulnerability in the over-determined realm of black visuality, the image of blackness.

Locating the source of Black Lives Matter activism in body and affect sheds new light on the movement's innovative protest strategies, which challenge the erasure of Black life with *embodied* politics. At die-ins, protesters form a collective corpse by lying on the ground for four minutes—a metaphor for the four hours Michael Brown's lifeless body lay on the Ferguson, Missouri, street. Their collective rebirth at the end of the performance is a statement of the strength of collective action in the face of its erasure. Similarly, when BLM supporters raise their hands and chant *hands up, don't shoot*, they enact an affective form of political speech. As protesters face down a riot squad with military grade weapons, *hands up, don't shoot* counters an armored fascist body with the fragility of painfully exposed flesh.

Affect and emotion offer productive insights into how black social justice activists mobilize for change. For example, Siona Wilson's chapter " 'I can't breathe': Resistance between Body, Word and Image" points out that the phrase *I can't breathe* used by Black Lives Matter activists became more than a reference to Eric Garner's death in 2014: it was also an expansive metaphor for the feelings of exasperation and despair at the failed criminal justice system in the United States—a call to unify in mourning for the men and women whose lives have been hurt and/or lost due to police brutality. Affective work also addresses the denial of racial injustice implicit in phrases like "all lives matter." Joseph Flynn's chapter "Puzzle Pieces on the Floor" offers practical steps for overcoming what he calls "white fatigue" with issues of racism and social justice. This fatigue makes it difficult if not impossible to see how the long history of racial violence and stereotyping affects society in all aspects, especially the criminal justice system.

Finally, the goal of *More than Our Pain* is to show how affect and emotion are implemented as strategies for successful collective action and protest. The volume's contributors explore grief, rage, love, and joy as responses and resistance to lethal police violence in order to uplift, unite, and form a contemporary praxis of assembly, protest, and self-care. *More than Our Pain* also condemns the ways in which the mass media has represented, defanged, and sold black affect in their coverage of the Black Lives Matter movement. Examining black rage as a righteous force for change and black joy as a shield against oppression, *More than Our Pain* offers a space where the black radical tradition is celebrated and where the next steps toward an equitable, democratic, and just society will be inspired.

PART I

AFFECT AND EMOTION IN THE ERA OF BLACK LIVES MATTER

Chapter 1

Emotional Work and Care Labor in the Art and Politics of Black Lives Matter

BETH HINDERLITER

Poet Dominique Christina, grieving those slain in United States in 2017 by vigilante and police violence, laments, "I have forgotten how to cry in this country, I open my mouth, I capsize. I barely woman. I barely human. I wolf or something like it. I sugarcane and long memory. I cotton field and long blade. I eulogy. I suicide note. I manifesto. I rage. I grief. No tears left."[1] Her words pour forth emotions that exceed the confines of one body with its limited pool of tears. If 2017 were a poem, this is how it would feel. Rage and grief meet a love and joy that eulogize and seek to soothe this trauma. Christina's words echo the sentiments of many Black Lives Matters activists who, in the years following 2013, made affect and emotion central to movement work, rather than the stuff of private lives to be dealt with solely inside the walls of one's own home. "We are more than our pain," DeRay McKesson tweeted during the uprising in Ferguson, Missouri, where the streets were full of outpourings of grief, righteous rage, recognition of collective and individual hurts, but also the love and joy of shared fellowship.[2] These emotions brought people together into the streets as the community sought to grapple with its pain. What emerged were new activist strategies seeking human rights that put emotion and emotionality at their core. As Yomaira Figueroa-Vásquez and Jessica Marie Johnson demand,

"We need new words for what we do, for how and why we stay, for the labor of making black love and black joy and black pleasure in a world of this."[3]

Stressing the work of care as labor is one way to avoid naturalizing the relation of violence to suffering. The images of suffering bodies saturating our visual realm from the nightly news to visual arts museums and galleries obscure the violence of the perpetrator, often miring us in a spectacularized pain that fails to make the structural conditions of white supremacy and imperialist patriarchy visible.[4] As detractors of the Black Lives Matter Global Network sought to dismiss its grievances and demands through distractive and race-baiting logic deployed in the media that conjured up stereotypes of black criminality, the gap between differing emotional worlds, or what Brittney Cooper has called *sentient knowledges*, became evident. To what extent are these knowledges shared or sharable under the current circumstances of racial capitalism that extracts value from this knowledge, while also debasing the conditions of life that gives rise to them? Important conversations around this have called for opacity to protect the vulnerable and for more work on how white supremacy codes specific white emotions and affects as universal, rational, and neutral. Erin Stephens, in particular, has focused on how Black Lives Matter organizers cultivated emotional resources for movement work specifically to mitigate the ability of "White emotion" to undermine legitimate grievances and claims of social injury.[5] All too often in the years following the formation of the Black Lives Matter Global Network, both the dismissal and the co-optation, or colonization, of emotions have taken place requiring Black activists and movement leaders to continually reassert that black pain is not for profit. Within these conditions, co-conspirators to the antiracist work of BLM actors must address how their work does not amplify original violence, but dismantles structural injustices while sheltering those harmed from further exposure.

The embodied knowledge created during these moments has been central to the many artists, writers, and cultural producers who have turned to affect as a means to bring into focus those lives severed from political representation in the United States. Feelings are not psychological states beyond social meaning, as Sara Ahmed points out, but are social and cultural practices deeply related to the power structure of society.[6] However, this view has been largely pushed aside in the mid–twentieth Century as the influence of B.F. Skinner's behaviorism—and his view that emotions were only fictional causes of behavior—came to dominate many areas of thought. The supremacy and elitism dominant in academic spaces also impact movement work spaces as well, leaving many feeling that their emotions have been censored, controlled, or mediated in some way. For many BLM activists, the demands that rage and its many ancillary emotions be witnessed as righteous marked a clear break from the civil rights–era politics of respectability. If conservatives and reactionaries in the 1950s and 1960s identified civil rights activism with rage and rebellion rather than reason and reform, many Black leaders, in turn, trained activists to dress in Sunday clothes and turn the other cheek largely to counter these false narratives that painted protesters as thugs and criminals. However, the Black Lives Matter movement in the early twenty-first century makes no qualms about black rage and the prospects of rebellion. Collective rage, as Barbara Ransby reminds us in her book *Making All Black Lives Matter: Reimagining Freedom in the 21st Century*, can "simply be the refusal to tolerate the intolerable."[7] Black Lives Matter actors have simply demanded, "stop telling me how to feel" and are using these emotions to as a basis for their work.

How do we do the work of making structural violence visible when our emotions are erased or delegitimated? Consider, for example, how activists in the Black Lives Matter movement (and the artists inspired by them) have acted as affective geographers, mapping the spaces where we live our emotional lives in their fullest and also in their most diminished capacities. Signs by artist Kameelah Janan Rasheed placed in differing public spaces and galleries in 2015–2016 demand that viewers "lower the pitch of your suffering!" Invoking public responses to BLM activists' complaints written off as impermissible by a larger public, her work reveals the nature of emotional labor brought forward by the Black Lives Matter movement. According to Rasheed, her work examines "superhuman restraint" in repressing anger. She reveals that in the face of state-sanctioned murder, barricades, handcuffs, and tear gas are not the only forms of discipline but, rather, smiles, tears, and anger. Our "compulsory affective labor of smiling through the pain," Rasheed writes, "so as not to make others uncomfortable persists as a way to maintain social order."[8] As the mainstream media strove to delegitimize protestors' rage, Black Lives Matter activists were constantly being told to manage their emotions, to turn away from the pain, and to smile. However, as bell hooks and others have pointed out, the suppression of feelings that arise from experiences of racism has many undesirable outcomes, including misdirected anger, self-destructive behavior, and a fear of intimacy.[9]

Activists within BLM have stressed the need for self-care as emotions rage in us and as traumas tear us apart. In initiating a new conversation around the modes of self-care, BLM organizers and protestors reveal that care of the self is also care of the collective. That is, without intentional and intensive attention to care of the self, agents working against a logic of disposability and incarceration can often internalize and reproduce dominant white supremacist affects such as suspicion of the other or the need to attack or tear down illusory threats. As BLM co-founder Alicia Garza has commented, "our focus on care and caring for each other has to go beyond the way we talk about it—it's very individual. It's always like "take a day off." It always involves capitalism . . . What we need to do to interrupt the logic of capitalism is invest in collective care, as much as self-care. And do a little bit of a deeper dive around healing trauma . . . we're not as depthful as we could be around what it takes to address harm, and what we do to address trauma, and how we do that in a way where we don't throw each other away but we build each other up."[10]

Self-care in the age of Black Lives Matter involves emotional care—individually and collectively. As AD Win, a social justice and public health advocate notes, "like many black children, I was told of the impending racism awaiting me in the world. Many of us are instructed to be resilient, dignified, and above all, strong. However, we are not taught that the assessment of our strength shouldn't rest on a steely capacity to endure racism without emotional fallout."[11] However, caring for our emotional fallouts is often overlooked as what happens in our private lives, at home, away from movement spaces. We live in a white supremacist colonial cissexist ableist patriarchy that oppresses us in multiple ways, and the care labor that hold our communities together is so often overlooked, gendered as women's work and erased. "Far too often," Leah Lakshmi Piepzna-Samarasinha reminds us, "the emotional labor we do isn't seen as labor—it's seen as air, that little thing you do on the side. Not real organizing, not real work, just talking about feelings and buying groceries. Not a real activist holding a big meeting stuff."[12] BLM activists remind us that emotional healing is part of movement work: care labor cannot be erased and must be consensual so that everyone gets the care they need.

The framing of self and collective care initiated by Black Lives Matter has become a topic for artists and writers who extend activism beyond its traditional spaces into museum and gallery spaces and community spaces to develop new sensorial modes of engaging audiences. For example, artist Simone Leigh has elucidated the discourse of self-care and community care and the healing of trauma initiated by Black Lives Matter in her recent installations and art projects. Given the complex and important nature of her work and her involvement with the Black Women Artists for Black Lives Matter group, I will explore her projects at greater length here.

In September to October 2014, Leigh established a *Free People's Medical Clinic*, a performative and environmental art project that ran a month-long series of events, performances, and activities. Events at Leigh's *Clinic* addressed medical discrimination and health disparities within historically black neighborhoods in Brooklyn. Part of a larger curatorial project titled "Black Radical Brooklyn," Leigh's work responded to curator Rashida Bumbray's celebration of the Weeksville area in Brooklyn, a community founded by free Blacks ten years after emancipation in New York State—as an intentional place of refuge and Black power. Leigh's contribution focused on the history of Black nurses within the community. Her installation was located at Stuyvesant Mansion, a house formerly owned by Dr. Josephine English, the first African American woman to establish an OB/GYN practice in New York state (who delivered all six of Malcolm X and Betty Shabazz's daughters). The project also drew upon the legacy of the United Order of Tents, a group of Black nurses operating continuously since the era of the Underground Railroad, as well as the Black Panthers Party Free People's Medical Clinics that fought against medical disparities in African American health care. During its month of existence, Leigh's *Free People's Medical Clinic* offered health and wellness classes and activities, including self-knowledge classes led by a master herbalist from the United Order of Tents, massage and acupuncture sessions, HIV screenings, wellness and OB-GYN care from Ancient Song Doula Services, as well as Black folk dance and a version of Pilates that Aimee Meredith Cox, an anthropologist and former dancer for Alvin Ailey's dance troupe, calls *afrocentering*.

Administering to an audience partly from the surrounding community and partly from the art world, the *Free People's Medical Clinic* drew on the historical legacies of black health care and healing while also responding to the contemporary moment within BLM activism, which has revealed the need for self and collective care to heal the trauma of police violence, including the trauma inflicted from watching videos of police violence. Leigh, who started a group of Black Women artists for Black Lives Matter, has in all of her work focused on the textures and concerns of black women's lives and identities. For *The Free People Medical Clinic*, she targeted the long heritage of black nurses after being surprised to learn about the Order of the Tents, which owned and operated a care clinic out of a brownstone building in the Weeksville neighborhood.

"Black women," Leigh remarks, "have been containers of this kind of knowledge [of care and healing] and have passed it down from one generation to the next."[13] Yet much of this knowledge, she finds, occurs in private spaces and doesn't enter into larger public frameworks, leading not only to a threatened loss of this knowledge but a loss of its history altogether. This dynamic structured much of the participatory sessions in Leigh's clinic: some classes and workshops, which otherwise would happen in a separate room, were brought out into the large open "waiting room," which pulsed with the beat of house music provided by a resident DJ. On the other hand, certain sessions were closed events and offered only to specific visitors, such as a yoga class for South Asians and a workshop for those who identify as queer and/or transgender. "A lot of black life, for practical reasons, happened in secret," Leigh has detailed. "If you can't be completely human in public, maybe you can do that privately. It peeks out every now and then. But in these private rooms, a lot of culture is developed. All of this informs, I think, this project and the need, at times, for separatism."[14] Her strategies of opacity both resist any expropriation of labor while honoring the culture of dissemblance, which as Darlene Clark Hine reminds us, has been used by Black women to deflect the structural and interpersonal violence of white supremacy. Leigh's focus on care as a critical mode in which to move through the world seeks to reduce trauma and its repetition, and therefore reject the politics of respectability, long criticized for its blaming of people as deficient, rather than dismissing the structures of oppression and power. In doing the emotional work around criticizing respectability politics, Black Lives Matter Global Network activists broke with an older generation of civil rights activists like Jesse Jackson and Al Sharpton—and their model of charismatic male leadership. From the exterior perspective, the movement felt leaderless by many who did not recognize anything beyond the framework of the older familiar styles of leaderships of the charismatic male. So much of how the BLM movement *feels* different from past freedom movement spaces is how the leadership of Black, Queer-centered, decolonial women are bringing their whole selves into these spaces in ways that simply were not legible before.

Self-care is another critical component here, as it recognizes how we must learn to walk through a world that is constantly impressing on us the infinite ways it can create immanent harm at any moment. It resists the older framework of empathy—that we are supposed to identify with or feel the pain of others, when so many from the movement have been trying to point out that this is itself a part of the problem of racism, this smothering presumption that emotions are visible/recognizable/accessible/transferable. Empathy often proceeds from the perspective that people themselves are damaged, rather than highlighting the institutions that actually do the harm. Instead of presuming an empathetic ability to share personal triggers or traumas, this approach calls on people to reduce harm by locating its enactment in the social-cultural landscape. This demands a form of emotional realignment through the senses.

While Jesse Jackson has claimed that there is no difference between today's freedom struggles and the civil rights struggles of the 1950s and 1960s (and that they are all part of a continuous struggle), younger activists in the streets in Ferguson challenged him, demanding that he leave upon arrival in the city. This frustration with Jackson came at a time when right-wing commentators like Fox News personality Bill O'Reilly, attempting to normalize racial profiling in the wake of the uprisings in Ferguson, pointed to Jackson's now famous comment from 1993, "There is nothing more painful to me at this stage in my life than to walk down the street and hear footsteps and start thinking about robbery. Then look around and see somebody white and feel relieved." For Black Lives Matter activists, such comments had long revealed the problems inherent to respectability politics. However, within the context of Fox News, Jackson's comment was twisted out of context to justify racist fear and prejudice. This was only part of the larger coverage given to Black Lives Matter by Fox News in 2014 and 2015, as they tried to stir up racial bias and fear and to demonize the Black Lives Matter movement.

"Sad to say," O'Reilly spewed in December 2014, "the overt impression formed about young black males who act and speak in a certain way is negative; it may not be fair, but it's reality."[15] In this atmosphere of respectability politics turned against itself, Al Sharpton delivered a eulogy for Michael Brown after he was shot six times by policeman Darren Wilson in Ferguson, Missouri, on August 9, 2014. Starting his thirty-minute speech with an indictment of the militarization of policing in America, he shifted to condemn the rebellions that took place in the streets of Ferguson after Brown's murder. Sharpton lamented that Michael Brown's parents should have to break their mourning to ask people to stop rioting. "We have to be outraged," Sharpton argued, "by our disrespect for each other, our disregard for each other, our killing and shooting and running around gun-toting each other [*sic*]. So that they are justifying trying to come at us because some of us act like the definition of blackness is how low you can go."[16]

Yet this is precisely the logic that many of the new voices in political activism have opposed. Respectability politics cannot account for how the simple act of walking while Black becomes, as Garnette Cadogan writes, a "pantomime undertaken to avoid the choreography of criminality."[17] Looking respectable, driving a nice car, living in a suburban community, attending college, growing up in a middle-class family, being a child of a doctor—none of these things prevented Prince Jones, a young African American from Maryland, from being gunned down by Maryland police, as Ta-Nahesi Coates recounts in *Between the World and Me*. Similarly, poet Claudia Rankine notes, "When blacks become overwhelmed by our culture's disorder and protest . . . the wrongheaded question that is then asked is, What kind of savages are we? Rather than, What kind of country do we live in?"[18]

Dismissing the uprisings in Ferguson as a "ghetto pity party," Sharpton foregrounded the emotionality of protestors, basing his comments on classic political theory that discounts emotions within the realm of civic engagement. The respectability politics to which he subscribed admonished activists in the streets of Ferguson, at least those with sagging pants, XXL white t-shirts, and loud voices, suggesting they were not worthy of protection under democratic laws and institutions because of their unwillingness to conform to purportedly mainstream styles, vocabulary or comportment. "Blackness has never been about being a gangster or thug," Sharpton commented, "you lost where you came from."[19] As Brittney Cooper, part of the Crunk Feminist Collective, argued only days after the eulogy, Sharpton had tried to placate the people of Ferguson by "ostensibly affirming their sense of injustice, while disaffirming their right to a kind of righteous rage in the face of such injustice."[20] Let's highlight here the emotional work of Cooper's writing—she not only acknowledges rage, but frames it as righteous.

Elsewhere in the media, respondents continued to transcribe righteous rage as thuggery, an interpretation confirmed by veteran civil rights activist Barbara Reynolds in the *Washington Post* on August 2015:

> The baby boomers who drove the success of the civil rights movement want to get behind Black Lives Matter, but the group's confrontational and divisive tactics make it difficult. In the 1960s, activists confronted white mobs and police with dignity and decorum, sometimes dressing in church clothes and kneeling in prayer during protests to make a clear distinction between who was evil and who was good. But at protests today, it is difficult to distinguish legitimate activists from the mob actors who burn and loot. The demonstrations are peppered

> with hate speech, profanity, and guys with sagging pants that show their underwear. Even if the BLM activists aren't the ones participating in the boorish language and dress, neither are they condemning it.[21]

Is it the sagging pants or the riotous acts that are illegitimate in this view? By such logic, partisans of respectability politics turn a deaf ear to even Martin Luther King, who called out the 1967 riots across American cities as legitimate, deeming them to be "the language of the unheard." Yet, here too activists in the BLM movement break with the past by refusing to adopt the term "riot" or play into the media's dismissal of righteous rage as illegitimate violence. As Marc Lamont Hill writes in *Nobody: Casualties of the War on America's Vulnerable, From Ferguson to Flint and Beyond*, "even calling the actions 'riots' rather than 'rebellions' or 'uprisings' obscures the principled outrage that animated many acts of resistance."[22] Indeed, a large part of the work that Black Lives Matter activists and allies did in the aftermath of Michael Brown's murder was to challenge the media obsession over the black rage unfolding in the streets, pointing instead to white anger, the rage of white supremacy that structures the contemporary landscape of segregation, mass incarceration, failing schools, and extraordinary inequality.

Respectability politics silences righteous rage, making it invisible by calling it illegitimate. Black Lives Matter activists have taken this logic to task by dismissing the idea of what is legitimate or illegitimate in appearance and what condones respect or dismissal. The arrest of esteemed Harvard professor Henry Louis Gates in 2009 made this point abundantly clear. After a neighbor called the police when she saw a black man entering a nearby house, Gates was subsequently arrested by the Massachusetts police. Responding to the event by questioning the logic of the policeman in conducting the arrest, President Obama later walked back his comments after much media attention and criticism. As comedian W. Kamau Bell quipped in response, "Man, America took it to a new level on this one . . . we will invent some new crimes for Negroes, won't we? Arrested for being in his own house . . ."[23] Gates, commenting on his own arrest, said how it made clear to him the vulnerability of Brown, Black and poor people in America to "capricious forces like this rogue policeman."[24]

Within the United States, we need to come to terms with how vulnerability is dismissed and ignored by being presented as superhuman strength and capacity. President Obama, often chastised by the mainstream media were he to make comments on race or racial politics during his time in office, defined the phrase Black Lives Matter as referring to "the specific vulnerability for African Americans that needs to be addressed"[25] Yet it is this vulnerability that the detractors of the Black Lives Matter movement in the media specifically seek to challenge and obscure as victims are continually portrayed as attackers. Freddie Gray's confrontation with the Baltimore police began with a simple look, making eye contact with an officer, yet it ended with his death. Gray's spinal cord was 80 percent severed during a "rough ride" in the police van after his detention. Eric Garner was portrayed as having acted aggressively toward the Staten Island Police. And Michael Brown's size was reported to be threatening. Recall the harangue of conservative pundits like Megyn Kelly, who in her attacks on the Black Lives Matter movement on the Fox News network condemned Al Sharpton for his supposedly "unethical" comments that an unarmed Mike Brown didn't use "deadly force" against officer Darren Wilson. "This community doesn't need an authority figure like Sharpton telling them that," Kelly argued with Bill O'Reilly, both of whom repeatedly asserted that Brown was a criminal and that he brought on his own demise. We can recall that as she asserted Michael Brown to be the aggressor at the time of his murder, Kelly was herself filled with anger, which she wielded to turn black vulnerability into superhuman strength.

The desperation to spin the tables and turn victim into assailant, to render invisible the pain of victims, and to cloak murder by rhetoric of self-infliction are also matched by the longstanding fetishistic obsession with Black bodies in pain in the United States. In his testimony to the grand jury, Darren Wilson represented that Michael Brown had the "most aggressive face . . . like a demon." His description of Brown focused on his large hulk-like body, insensate, hardened, demonic, but also inanimate. "I don't know how many [rounds] I shot," Wilson recalled. "I just shot *it*."[26] To see Brown's pain would be to see him as human, not as a demon or an *it*. To see his pain is to recognize his vulnerability. Wilson noted he saw at least one bullet hit Brown from his first round of shots and that in his memory Brown's body "twitched"—visibility can also be invisibility. As Javon Joy tells us, "the in/visibility and in/audibility of black pain are often one and the same, establishing orders and essentially communicating/dictating place and boundaries in service of the nation-state that uses anti-black racism as the foundation for white supremacy."[27] Within the racist matrix that sees black skin as superpowerful and weaponized, mourning and anger become irrational rage. The media erases the collective body of assembly, countering black rage at social injustice and our new contemporary form of extrajudicial killings with its own rage over lawless looting.

The Black Lives Matter movement has unleashed new forms of collective assembly and protest, which challenge the erasure of Black life with new means of embodied politics and affective vitality. At die-ins, protesters form a collective corpse by lying on the ground for four minutes, a metaphor for the four hours that Michael Brown's lifeless body lay on the Ferguson street. The silence of the four minutes is a shroud that hangs over the group body. Their collective rebirth at the end of the performance is a statement of the strength of collective action in the face of its erasure. Donna Austin shared the experience of a 2014 die-in, stressing the enormity of the shared emotions of the moment: "Dying put me back in touch with the sheer physicality of my body, and enabled me to reach both hands through the numbness and feel my emotions as they moved between my fingers. Empowered by my renewed sensuality, for the first time in I don't know how long, I just *felt*."[28]

Similarly, when Black Lives Matter supporters raise their hands and chant *hands up, don't shoot*, they enact an affective form of political speech. As protesters face down a riot squad with military grade weapons, *hands up, don't shoot* counters an armored fascist body with the fragility of painfully exposed flesh. That such bare human exposure has been repeatedly met with teargas, nightsticks, tasers, rubber bullets, and real bullets reveals the lengths to which militarized police forces will go to ensure its dominance over public space. *Hands up don't shoot* is political speech made by subjects denied political representation—the body's inherent vulnerability met with state force.

Black Lives Matter as both a statement and a movement rejects respectability politics for its role in confirming both the visibility and invisibility of black pain. Rather, by emphasizing vulnerability, the movement challenges the erasure of black life with new means of affective politics and embodied vitality. As the Black Lives Matter movement proceeds from the point of asking whose life counts as a life that is protected, cared for, and grievable, it mobilizes affect and emotion as powerful weapons that body forth political representation in the space of its denial. As media outlets obsessed over the looting that took place in Ferguson rather than report on the killing of Mike Brown, emphasizing vulnerability via identification with the murdered, beaten and repressed was one means for activists to forge a counternarrative. Even Fox News pundits who after the events of Ferguson largely sought to discredit Black Lives Matter activism, noted the penchant of the media for spectacle. According to Howard Kurtz, host of Fox News *Media Buzz*, the media were like "paratroopers [who] invaded the Missouri suburb for the nightly clashes, their cameras drawing outside troublemakers, exacerbating the tensions and, of course, lifting ratings."[29] Following the militarization of the police, so too the media became weaponized in the rhetoric that painted them as colonial stabilizers of chaotic foreign territory.

Vulnerability in *hands up, don't shoot* stressed dispossession—not that of objects and property but, rather, of the body. *Hands up, don't shoot* showed that at any moment, even if you were football players from the St. Louis Rams entering the field with your hands raised, or Congressional representatives like Hakeem Jeffries, Al Green, Yvette Clark and Sheila Jackson Lee, whose raised hands protested racial terror to congress, Black and Brown people face being gunned down in the street by killers assured impunity. As Ta-Nahesi Coates warned his son in *Between the World and Me*, "your body can be destroyed. The destroyers will rarely be held accountable . . . Mostly they will receive pensions."[30] This vulnerability must also, however, be seen in relation to the rage issued against dispossession. Two of the best-known images from Black Lives Matter activists depict both the vulnerability of protestors and their righteous rage. Some might point to the breathtaking calm demeanor of activist Iesha Evans as she was arrested in Baton Rouge, Louisiana, on July 9, 2016. With chaos erupting around her, Evans calmly held out her wrists to be handcuffed. Yet this image stood in contrast to other images of activists that were widely circulated, like Edward Crawford, who was photographed throwing a can of tear gas away from himself and other protestors, an act widely seen as a rejection of the militarized war waged on civilians by police. As Evans's photograph spread across the internet and news outlets, her calm demeanor became emblematic of the dignity of direct action and resistance, revealing the vulnerability of protesters, in contrast to the body armor and military equipment of the forces deployed in Ferguson.

As tactics of nonviolent protest and strategic rebellion held sway in the events unfolding in the streets of Ferguson, many activists and writers spoke about their fury and bitter anger at being told by President Obama to "respect the rule of law" or hearing the attorneys for the Brown family admonish protesters to become "dignified and disciplined." The discourse of the uprising in Ferguson used the righteousness of protestors' rage as a means to reveal the foundational violence at the core of American society. Brittany Cooper, for example, writing after the refusal of the grand jury to indict Darren Wilson on November 24, 2015, commented that with the failure of justice for Mike Brown there could be no "dignity" expected from protestors. "Do you feel the struggle in these words?" she asked. "The utter inadequacy of them? The struggle to contain and train my rage on the proper (white) people, and not all of them? The challenge of trying to narrate black rage, and black pain, and black fear, and black freedom dreams deferred—*again*—in hopes that white folks would really understand? The resentment at my failure? The rage at my having to do so in the first place?"[31] The media largely avoided the kinds of challenges that Cooper articulated, focusing instead on the few who directed their rage at store windows or car windshields. The media's spectacularization of rage turned audience attention away from core dynamics of white supremacism, which overpolices in order to demonize and disinvest in Black American communities. The righteous rage revealed in Ferguson and elsewhere became likened to James Baldwin's fire next time, a fire that Cooper called a "sentient knowledge, a kind of black epistemology."[32]

We are reminded of Baldwin's words that "to be a Negro in this country and to be relatively conscious is to be in a rage almost all the time."[33] Yet, as he also lamented, one had to be very careful in the ways one dealt with that rage: that it wasn't packaged to be consumed innocuously by whites. Xandria Phillips suggests that "Black people are too often expected to consolidate and distribute their pain in a marketable way. In these situations, it is not nuance within Black experiences that is called for, but pain packaged for non-Black consumption."[34] As she details in an issue of the web magazine *Winter Tangerine* titled "Love Letters to Spooks," she aims "not for non-Black people to gain proximity to Black experiences, but for Black folks to have access to themselves free of non-Black projections. Not all deaths that Black people endure are physical. Pain exists that can only be detected and interrogated by Black consciousness. Not all grief is grace."[35] Black epistemology calls for empathy and respect from others who cannot sense this pain and have not lived through this pain.

Beyond the fire of black rage, the BLM movement points to white anger as a system of terror rendered invisible by normative daily structures. In pointing to White rage in the face of media obsession over Black uprisings, they have sought to show that one uprising can cloak another. As Carol Anderson has argued, White rage works in the court systems, legislatures, and in government bureaucracies to counter Black advancement—its efficacy fueled by rhetoric that blames the victim.[36] When the media engages in long debates over the justification of the use of deadly violence simply because a killer felt (but did not prove) they were threatened, they advance rhetoric that turns prey into a predator. This affective work makes White rage visible, belying its neutral background.

One particular moment at a community discussion in Los Angeles revealed this dynamic between White anger and Black rage. Describing a panel on the topic of "What is contemporary?" at the Museum of Contemporary Art Los Angeles, art historian Helen Molesworth noted a moment in the audience conversation where one audience member's anger and rage created a moment of tension and apprehension amongst the white people in the room. The moderators of the event, Patrisse Cullors and Tanya Lucia Bernard, gave the floor over to the audience, inviting them to speak about their current experiences and feelings. It was the week of the murders of Alton Sterling and Philandro Castile. One man asked why white people were occupying most of the seats in the room. As the conversation turned from the spaces of the streets outside to the interior of the room itself and the bodies inhabiting it, Molesworth noted Cullors's remarkable leadership skills in moderating conversation. Cullors acknowledged the standing man's "righteous rage" and commended him for his honesty and vulnerability in speaking publicly about his feelings. For Molesworth, the brilliance of Cullors's acknowledgment was how it assuaged the tension in the room. "In this one linguistic, affective moment of pure genius, she reframed his rage—and all of its implicit and attendant fear and violence and its potential for confusion and miscommunication—as the very attribute that makes us most human: vulnerability."[37]

Does rage need reframing? What about Cullors's careful and circumspect description that his rage was righteous—not confusing or prone to miscommunication? As Judith Butler has written, vulnerability has the critical capacity to reveal a person as both agentic and receptive at the same time.[38] Yet, as she warns us, it is not sufficient to just embrace vulnerability as this act somehow renders you authentic. Authenticity, then, becomes the opposite of agency. As Cullors acknowledged the vulnerability of speaking in public, particularly to a largely white audience, she did not diminish the speaker's rage, which originates from outside the meeting space. We should acknowledge that at the core of Molesworth's reflection is a question about how and for whom such reframing is done. For whom and for what purposes do we see rage being reframed? What if, instead of relying on the moderator to ease tensions, White people had stood up and moved from their chairs? What else could have been done to see rage, acknowledge it, and offer care at that moment?

What are the techniques for realizing a community of care called for by the Black Lives Matter movement? Returning to Simone Leigh's work here can help clarify this point. Drawing on the legacy of the Black Panther's Free Medical Clinics, Leigh established her clinic as an aesthetic project that takes its very existence as political. She is treating a community under siege; her clinic opened just two months after Eric Garner had been killed by New York City police officer Daniel Pantaleo. Leigh also details how much of her work meditated on the death of Esmin Elizabeth Green at the Kings County Hospital in Brooklyn in 2008, after she collapsed on the floor of the waiting room following a twenty-four-hour wait for care. Three of the four area hospitals had recently been closed, and waits at emergency rooms at this remaining hospital are the longest in the country. This is the same neighborhood where Black Panthers piled sandbags at the entrance to their free medical clinic to provide safety against deadly police raids, such as the Chicago raid that killed Fred Hampton and Mark Clark and the raid of the LA headquarters in December of 1969, which was the first deployment of a SWAT team in police history, complete with a tank, helicopters and 400 Los Angeles police officers. Leigh describes being moved by the visit of two former doctors at the Brooklyn Black Panther Party Free People's Medical Clinic who described to her the embattled conditions of the clinics, "so besieged with direct conflict from the police that the facade of the building was covered in sand bags. . . . It was much more like a bunker than a hospital."[39]

In her subsequent project, an installation titled *Waiting Room* (2016), Leigh stacked sandbags as an homage to the work of the Panthers against the gallery wall of the New Museum of Contemporary Art in New York City. She created space for healing, community building, and celebration of the multiplicity of women's identities, including a herbarium that draws on the history of African American hoodoo and conjure. *The Waiting Room* builds a refuge, however temporary, that can heal people terrorized by state violence and those who feel particularly vulnerable over their safety. Leigh reminds us that not all violence is quick. Medical disparities, the privatization of public schools, hospitals, housing, transit, and other public resources, the dismantling of a welfare safety net, and the militarization of the civilian police force are all forms of a slower but nonetheless deadly violence. But most of all, *The Waiting Room* demands an end to the eternal waiting for the minimum conditions of existence to be met.

On the opening night of *Waiting Room*, Leigh invited the Black Women Artists for Black Lives Matter group to the museum to perform, demonstrate, and take over the museum with their art. The women, who had been meeting weekly over the summer, arrived dressed in red, holding flags that read "Joy" and "Grief," and read the Black Lives Matter policy platform. As LaTasha N. Nevada Diggs recalls, "we were a congregation of red-beaded necklace adorners, velveteen ushers, rattlers, and clenched-fist praise dancers. We were holy ghosted, mounted, released, & made well. Joyful & grieving."[40]

Among the videos, performances, and other art works, the BWA for BLM created a digital altar as a catalyst for black joy. Snapshots of happy moments shared with family and friends flashed across the screen in the museum's theater, recalling that in the face of state-sanctioned terrorism, the affective nature of Black Lives Matters politics negotiates the question of care as a form of activism. Black joy has emerged as a means of healing in the face of trauma, of building up in the face of state-sanctioned violence and destruction. Joy is intimate and familiar, but carries within it the imprint of the institutional structures and barriers it has overcome on its path to existence and expression. As Javon Johnson writes in "Black Joy in the Time of Ferguson," "our bodies harbor knowledge, and in these moments every smile, head nod, hip shake, and high five is an exchange of embodied truths that black joy is phenomenally transformational."[41] In the form of an altar, this catalyst for black joy resources images of families and friends to resist the myriad ways that Black family life has been represented as "a tangle of pathologies" since Daniel Patrick Moynihan's report "The Negro Family" offered that diagnosis in 1965. Moynihan's report had not only overlooked both the joy of family life in all their forms and shapes, but also its internal binding force to resist anti-black racism within the public sphere. It erased the distinct paths and life trajectories of Black women who have historically assumed both economically productive roles (in labor of all kinds) while also fulfilling domestic roles as well. As Deborah King detailed in her canonical text "Multiple Jeopardy, Multiple Consciousness: The Context of a Black Feminist Ideology," the survival of Black women in the United States has long depended on her ability to use all the economic, social, and cultural resources available to her. Funneled through Moynihan's mono-focal lens, this resourcefulness is stigmatized as pathology, and those who have historically profited from exploiting Black women's labor are not held to account. "The legacy of the political economy of slavery under capitalism is the fact that employers, and not Black women, still profit the most from Black women's labor," King argues. "And when Black women become the primary or sole earners for households, researchers and public analysts interpret this self-sufficiency as pathology, as deviance, as a threat to Black family life."[42]

The critical capacity of black joy, as Gina Dent has written, lies in its capacity to cut across the twentieth-century American color line, revealing the constructed and oppositional nature of double consciousness about which W. E. B. Du Bois spoke. "The experience of joy," Dent writes, "provides another context for these oppositions; remaining alternative and outside, it signals our more democratic hopes and dreams for the future."[43] Joy is thus intimate and familiar, but carries within it the imprint of the institutional structures and barriers it has overcome on its path to existence and expression. From Carrie Mae Weems's *Family Pictures and Stories* (1981–1982) to the series of family and friendship photographs that scroll up the screen at the end of *13th*—a documentary on race, justice, and mass incarceration directed by Ava DuVernay (2016), images of black joy have been bodied forth by artists and filmmakers to counter the stereotype of the pathological disrepair of the Black family spread by Moynihan.

More than simply presenting emotions that have been silenced, such as joy or rage, the Black Lives Matter movement asks us what we will do with these feelings. As Sara Ahmed has written, "Justice is not simply a feeling. And feelings are not always just."[44] Finding allies or an empathetic audience is not the same thing as finding justice. Nor does finding justice end pain and suffering, though it may go a long way in the process of healing. Too many activists who have expressed their rage, anger, and resentment in the streets have not found the relief from suffering: three of the organizers from Ferguson—De Andre Johnson, Darren Seals, and Edward Crawford—have since passed. Erica Garner, daughter of Eric Garner, died in December 2017, reminding us of all the ways in which the stresses of racism are killing African American women. Others are noting the physical demands of emotional turmoil and stress. Self- and group care has become a political necessity as the movement continues.

For example, *Harriet's Apothecary*, a group of liberation-focused healers based mostly in Brooklyn, travel to different community-based events and conferences to offer massage and acupressure treatments, counseling sessions, guided meditation, herbal medicines, aromatherapy, Indigenous sound healing, embodied movement, and healing justice workshops. Taking inspiration from freedom practices of elders such as Harriet Tubman, they seek to end cycles of illness and violence through holistic practices that create spaces of community and shared healing from trauma. As Adaku Utah, one of the founders of the group, has remarked, "If you are invested in a system of liberation, then your self-care won't only end at yourself."[45] Similarly, New Orleans–based Black Feminist Future has offered visioning salons led by Paris Hatcher, who sees the salons as intentional spaces of collective engagement where Black women and girls meet to work through the difficult emotions—ambivalence, disgust, outrage—of being rendered invisible in the political status quo and to activate their political power.

In the work of Leigh and other artists who take inspiration from Black Lives Matter activism and who center healing, we are reminded that "we are, and always will be, more than our pain."[46] Artists, moved by the affective politics of the Black Lives Matter Global Network, have sought to channel emotions and mobilize audiences to the work needed to build a more just future—one anchored in beauty and joy. Affect has been used to deflect the spectacularization of death and violence, to re-humanize a de-humanized people, and to challenge audiences to discern whose pain is felt and how. Channeling rage, processing grief and trauma, overcoming fatigue, and also positing joy, they have reaffirmed one of the goals of the Black Lives Matter network—resilience in the face of deadly oppression.

Chapter 2

The New Nadir

Decline and Despair in U.S. Race Relations

STEVE PERAZA

In 1954, U.S. race relations continued to languish nationwide even as resistance to racism was on the rise. That year black American historian Rayford Logan published *The Negro in American Life and Thought*, which some have labeled "the overall framework" for understanding the post-Reconstruction era in the United States.[1] Between 1877 and 1918, the United States experienced "the nadir" in race relations, a low point when the United States betrayed black Americans with false promises of liberty and equality.[2] "The South," Logan wrote, "sought to have the Constitution interpreted, federal laws repealed or rendered innocuous and Northern public opinion made amenable to the end that Negroes should become what were later called second-class citizens."[3] Meanwhile black and white American racial justice advocates had just won the first major battle in the nascent social revolution of the period. In the *Brown v. Board of Education, Topeka* decision, the U.S. Supreme Court ruled against racial segregation in public schools, overturning *Plessy v. Ferguson* and the Separate but Equal doctrine that sanctioned Jim Crow laws nationally.

The United States appeared to be rectifying its wrongs in 1954, a fact Logan noted in his study. "The Negro in the United States has achieved today the highest status in his history," Logan explained, "more American people than ever before are participating in movements to encourage, consolidate and accelerate his progress."[4] Indeed, the Civil Rights Movement—inaugurated by the1954 *Brown v. Board of Education* decision segregation in public schools, galvanized by the 1955 Montgomery Bus Boycott dismantling segregation in Alabama's public transportation system, and encapsulated in the Civil Rights Act of 1964 and Voting Rights Act of 1965 that turned segregation and restrictions on the voting rights of black Americans into violations of federal law—lifted the United States out of the nadir. One might imagine readers of Logan's book sensing some relief that the betrayal of black Americans had not continued in full force, that the "American Creed was dormant at the end of the century but it was not dead and buried."[5]

Today, Logan's cautious optimism seems naïve at best. The American Creed rings hollow because de facto segregation, legal disfranchisement, and racial terrorism continue to affect black American communities nationwide. Despite the successes of the Civil Rights Movement, race relations have hit a new low. Not even the 2008 presidential election—when black and white voters joined forces to elect Barack Obama as the first black American president in U.S. history—brought economic and political relief to black communities. In fact, President Obama's administration helped expand the wealth gap between black elites and the black middle and working classes by bailing out financial institutions like banks and stock markets but not the people that these institutions exploited.[6] Perhaps worse, his regime failed to address the systemic racism of the prison industrial complex and seemed unwilling to condemn murderous police officers who killed unarmed black Americans seemingly without provocation. If black Americans had reached their highest status in 1954, as Logan asserted, then they were stuck in a cycle decline of decline not unlike that which Logan described at the end of the nineteenth century.

We are living in a new nadir, a new low point in race relations, when U.S. society seems to be questioning the value of black American life while progressively limiting black Americans' access to the American franchise. Since the late 1960s, the legal and political status of black Americans has been on decline. Racial inequalities have persisted not only in the economy but also in law enforcement. This toxic blend of poverty and prison has mischaracterized black citizens as "visibly lawless" and therefore subject to aggressive policing and, at times, extrajudicial killing. Felony convictions have also served to restrict black American participation in state and national elections. Black American communities are thus in economic and political crisis; they are victims of what legal scholar Michelle Alexander calls a "racial caste system" that discriminates and disfranchises black Americans in ways not unlike previous systems of racial oppression like U.S. slavery and Jim Crow.

Despite its similarities to old racist regimes, the new nadir has three distinct characteristics. First is the persistence of extrajudicial killings, especially at the hands of state institutions.[7] These include police killings for which officers have received no penalty as well as murders committed by white vigilantes who fatally attack black Americans for passing through their neighborhoods. Second is the persistence of colorblind laws, which do not target race expressly but are enforced in ways that disproportionately impact nonwhite racial groups. Finally, there is a crisis in black leadership. Despite an unprecedented growth in the number of black elected officials as mayors, governors, congressmen, and even president, black political leaders have not produced nationwide improvements in black communities. Moreover, they have called for a repression of the "righteous rage" that many black Americans experience in response to continued oppression.[8] As a result, many black Americans have begun to distrust U.S. politics as a means to effect social change, especially as their communities remain riddled by high rates of poverty and incarceration. The electoral success of black leaders has backfired such that some black Americans are less likely to participate in politics now that black leaders have held office and done little to help.

From this declining faith in black American political leadership has arisen an international movement born of black American indignation over dehumanization by state and municipal authorities. Leading this movement are young, passionate black Americans—many of whom are radical black feminist and queer thinkers and doers—who constitute the Black Lives Matter movement or the Movement for Black Lives. Their righteous rage has fueled protests, lawsuits, and policy initiatives following the murders of Trayvon Martin, an unarmed seventeen-year-old black child killed in Florida by a white vigilante in 2012, and Michael Brown, an unarmed eighteen-year-old black teenager killed in Missouri by a white police officer in 2014. They have written a new chapter in the black liberation struggle, one still being drafted by activists, journalists, and scholars as this chapter goes to print.

This struggle is one in which I have a personal stake as a black man, husband, and father in the United States. I recall the despair I felt in 2012, when the Florida court exonerated George Zimmerman for the murder of Trayvon Martin. I still fear that Stand Your Ground laws, which allowed U.S. citizens to use fatal force in self-defense if they perceived themselves to be in danger, facilitate extrajudicial killings of black Americans. "It's open season on black and brown people," I told my wife in 2012. Today I feel much the same way. People who shoot and kill black and brown Americans seem to get a pass in city and state courts, as they have in Buffalo, New York, where I reside. Most recently, Buffalo police officers have been cleared of all charges in the fatal shootings of Wardel Davis in 2017 and Jose Hernandez-Rossy in 2018.[9] I roil with anger when I consider that the men and women whose protection I pay for with income and sales taxes may one day threaten my own or my children's lives and face no repercussions.

Perhaps my biggest concern, however, is that even this new movement and its brilliant leaders may not have found a way to catalyze conversations across racial divides and heal the wounds that racism has caused United States citizens. The Black Lives Matter movement is an important first step toward lifting the nation from the new nadir. Deep divisions remain, as distinct racial, ethnic, and sexual identities pursue social transformation, often in ways that compete against one another's interests. Perhaps a rehabilitation of the idea of integration, as theorized by Dr. Martin Luther King Jr. and James Baldwin, can inspire greater unity among historically marginalized groups. The most essential step toward breaking down racial barriers, I conclude, is the propagation of a new ideology of social equality, a humane vision of cross-racial solidarity that demands an end to inequities in U.S. society.

Cycles of Despair

In recent years, historians and legal scholars have marked the decline into a new nadir in compelling studies of mass incarceration, white reactionaries, and the #blacklivesmatter movement. Michelle Alexander's *The New Jim Crow* has revealed how and why the War on Drugs and the criminal justice system have restored the very racial caste system that the Civil Rights Movement fought valiantly to dismantle. Carol Anderson's *White Rage* has shown that white American reactionaries in cultural, political, and legal institutions have fought aggressively and successfully to stem black American progress in the United States. Finally, Keeanga-Yamahtta Taylor's *From #Blacklivesmatter to Black Liberation* locates that current social justice campaigns in the black community are responding to persistent racial inequality and terrorism in the United States. Collectively, these studies suggest that the United States has once again betrayed black Americans by not protecting the privileges and protections afforded them by federal law. They find themselves trapped in a cycle of decline leading to a new nadir like that of the post-Reconstruction era.

The cyclical interpretation of Black History has gained significant traction in recent years, as historians seek to explain the reincarnation of racial oppression following the Civil Rights Movement. Perhaps the most compelling work in this new scholarship has been Michelle Alexander's 2010 monograph *The New Jim Crow*, which explored the evolution of mass incarceration in the United States and the racial caste system it buttressed. Alexander employed a cyclical framework to highlight how and why a new racial caste system emerged at the end of the modern Civil Rights Movement. "Since the nation's founding," Alexander explained, "Africans Americans repeatedly have been controlled through institutions such as slavery and Jim Crow, which appear to die, but then are reborn in new form, tailored to the needs and constraints of the time."[10] This recycling of racial oppression set the stage for the current moment in which poverty, police brutality, and mass incarceration are devastating black communities nationwide.

Alexander described in detail how black freedom struggles have been followed by periods of regression, when reactionary forces besieged the political gains black Americans won. The first example was in the mid-1800s. The Civil War and Reconstruction helped transform black Americans from slaves to citizens, but soon after southern white lawmakers and residents "reacted with panic and outrage." They in turn created and sustained a new social order that rolled back the civil and political rights won during the war. "The backlash against the gains of African Americans in the Reconstruction was swift and severe," wrote Alexander. Southerners systematically segregated and disfranchised. Despite the deliberate violation of blacks' constitutional rights, the federal government and northern lawmakers did very little to support them. Moreover, vigilantes ensured that the new laws and racial customs were enforced: "[The] campaign to 'redeem' the South was reinforced by a resurgent Ku Klux Klan, which fought a terrorist campaign against Reconstruction governments and local leaders, complete with bombings, lynchings, and mob violence." Jim Crow was born soon after slavery died in the war.[11]

The second example took place in the mid-1900s. While the modern Civil Rights Movement galvanized the nation in the 1950s and 1960s, calling on the U.S. government to protect black southerners' civil rights by force if necessary, white lawmakers on the federal and state levels created new criminal laws that would inspire a "new" Jim Crow system. These new laws were "colorblind"—that is, they did not expressly target black Americans in the letter of the law, even if the law in actions was enforced in a racially discriminatory way. Such was the matrix of laws constituting Nixon's and

Reagan's wars on drugs. This domestic "war" in the 1970s and 1980s helped militarize local police forces and authorized long prison sentences for first-time drug offenders. The net result was the mass incarceration of young black American men and women caught in a dragnet that disproportionately targeted their communities. The collateral consequences of incarceration ensured that black Americans were segregated in prisons, thereby splintering families in black communities, and restricting ex-felons' voting rights, weakening their power to shape politics in their neighborhoods. A new racial caste system thus replaced the old one facilitated by Jim Crowism.

Michelle Alexander was not the only scholar who utilized a cyclical approach to explain the contemporary problems in Black America. Carol Anderson's timely monograph *White Rage* also integrated this interpretation to show how and why moments of political success for black Americans were so short-lived. Anderson began by questioning why politicians and pundits continued to characterize black communities as angry and violent whenever they protested police killings. Anderson noted that this focus on black "rage" veiled a persistence push among white Americans to stall, if not prevent, black social and political gains. "The trigger for white rage," Anderson argued, "is black advancement."[12] Her monograph unfolds an historical trajectory that moves in a spiral rather than a straight line. *White Rage* traces white reactionary responses to black advancement following the Civil War, the Great Migration, the Civil Rights Movement, and the election of President Barack Obama. The story seems to repeat itself even though conditions black Americans in each epoch have changed. What she calls "black ambition"—signs of progress for black Americans—is met consistently by "[a] formidable array of policy assaults and legal contortions [to punish] black resilience."[13]

Unlike Alexander and Anderson, historian Keeanga-Yamahtta Taylor applies a revisionist approach to her study of the #blacklivesmatter movement and the conditions that caused it. In *From #Blacklivesmatter to Black Liberation*, Taylor aims to correct misconceptions about postracialism, black political achievement, and criminal justice. A major premise of her work, however, is that "there are . . . periodic ruptures in the US narrative of its triumph over racism as a defining feature of its society."[14] These ruptures are, in fact, cyclical and imply a decline from a time when the United States seemed poised to exorcise race from the national zeitgeist. The police brutality and murder that plagues the black community casts a long shadow on the racial progress of the Civil Rights Movement. Extrajudicial killings by police officers have inspired black Americans to protest the derogation of their civil and human rights. "Today, the birth of a new movement against racism and policing," Taylor argued, "is shattering the illusion of a colorblind, postracial United States."[15] Myths of colorblindness and postracialism have veiled the cycle of decline leading to the new nadir; Taylor's monograph lifts that veil.

Shifting Interpretations of Black History

The cyclical interpretation of Black History is one of many. In his 1982 essay, "Coming of Age: The Transformation of Afro-American Historiography," historian Robert L. Harris identified five general interpretations of Black History and suggested how and why historians transitioned from one dominant interpretation to another. The interpretations of Black History included: revisionism, which aimed to correct white American misconceptions about Black life and history; the hidden-hand approach, which explained the black past through the lens of Christian determinism; contributionism, which highlighted the achievements of black men and women in spite of oppression; the cyclical approach, which viewed the black past as unfolding in cycles of success and failure; and liberalism, which described Black History as a progressive march toward freedom and equality.

Until the 1960s, the most prevalent interpretations were the contributionist and liberal approaches, largely because they sought to cultivate race pride and show how black Americans helped advance U.S. society. Historians who adopted the contributionist approach created studies "to demonstrate black participation in the development of America."[16] They focused on exceptional individuals who accomplished extraordinary feats for the black community and for the United States as a whole. These studies challenged stereotypes about the alleged inferiority of black people and the presumption that they had not advanced human civilization in any meaningful way. Contributionist historians cultivated race pride, informed black activists how their ancestors overcame oppression, and taught white Americans about racism and black American resiliency.[17]

The contributions of exceptional black Americans facilitated progress in the black community, an idea that liberalist historians championed. According to this interpretation, black Americans have marched in a straight line from slavery to freedom. In the process, they obliged the United States to honor its values of liberty and equality. In this approach, Black History is synonymous with "progress." Not only were black Americans working diligently to ensure they would enjoy the rights and privileges afforded by the U.S. Constitution, but they were also showcasing the exceptionalism of United States democracy, a nation-state capable of transforming from the perpetrator of racial slavery to the standard-bearer of freedom worldwide.[18]

The contributionist and liberalist approaches prevailed before the 1960s largely because they did not threaten the racial status quo in the discipline or in U.S. society. At the time, Black History was an appendage of U.S. history, lacking recognition as an independent field of study. Moreover, white historians controlled the production of Black History. "White historians," Harris explained, "were still the gatekeepers in graduate training, research funding, and publication."[19] These "gatekeepers" were especially fearful of Black historiography suggesting that black Americans developed a coherent, separatist culture informed by African practices and committed to racial nationalism.

In the 1960s, however, black American historians began to reject the notion that their culture and community was a derivative of white society. A new racial consciousness emerged, which linked African cultural practices to racial identity and forged a new "Black Nationalism" that reverberated through the discipline. In Harris's view, then, Black History came of age after the 1960s. The civil rights campaigns, urban uprisings, and Black Consciousness Movement shaped how Black History was researched and written. Black American historians transitioned away from studies of black achievement and progressive race relations to studies about the African background, racial slavery in the United States, and the causes and consequences of U.S. Reconstruction. This new focus on the evolution of a distinct black American culture inspired historians to adopt revisionist and cyclical interpretations of the black past.

According to Harris, the roots of revisionism are found in the works of W.E.B. Du Bois. For Du Bois, Harris explained, "the race problem existed primarily because whites did not know the important contributions made by Afro-Americans." He thus tasked himself with correcting misperceptions about black Americans with well-researched studies of black achievement. To challenge the "myths, distortions, and omissions" that accompany racial oppression, Du Bois recharacterized black Americans as consistent contributors to American democracy. The problem with this interpretation was that the line of argument was predetermined; black American historians were reacting to white stereotypes and countering with stories of black achievement. It became increasingly difficult to capture the complexity of the black experience when the focus of historical analysis was disputing prejudicial claims. By the 1980s, then, the revisionist approach was losing its primacy in Black historiography.

Since the 1980s, the cyclical approach has supplanted both liberalism and contributionism as the dominant interpretation of Black History. According to Harris, the cyclical interpretation showed that the social, cultural, and political conditions black Americans experienced changed continuously but in predicable patterns that repeated one another over time. He believed that historians who adopted this approach abandoned the view that Black History marched forward in a straight line toward "progress" in U.S. society. Rather, the black American experience followed a "spiraling" course that moved in cycles but never returned to the same point. "The events [in Black History]," Harris explained, "have not been identical although the processes have been similar." For example, the modern Civil Rights Movement has been characterized as the "Second Reconstruction," closely resembling postwar Reconstruction between 1865 and 1877. Separated by nearly a century, the First and Second Reconstructions were aggressive political efforts to incorporate black Americans as full-fledged citizens of the United States. While some historians may view the First and Second Reconstructions as successive steps toward progress in Black America, others with a cyclical interpretation point to the declining status of black Americans following the first reconstruction. Indeed, the denial of constitutional rights granted by the Civil War amendments inspired black Americans to coordinate a second political movement to demand the civil, legal, and political equality promised to all citizens of the United States.[20]

Another way to view the cyclical interpretation of Black History, Harris explained, was that this approach "sought to explain successes and failures [in the Black experience] as similar to the rhythm of nature."[21] The long, cruel winter of slavery began to thaw in 1861 with the first salvos of the Civil War. Black Americans fought this war in the name of liberation, and what followed was a brief summer known as Reconstruction, when black Americans acquired equality before the law and the power of the vote. They also erected towns, schools, and churches, and they elected men from their own communities to lead them into a life of freedom. But reactionary forces in the South targeted Black communities and white citizens who supported them. Terrorist organizations attacked them and assassinated local leaders. Southern "redeemers" thus inaugurated the fall season in Black History, when the southern states reneged on their support of the Constitution and the rights it entitled black Americans. Soon another long winter emerged, the winter of Jim Crow, marked by its segregation, disfranchisement, and lynching of black Americans. Winter lasted more than half a century, until the brave southern activists of the World War II era ignited the fire of protest, bringing spring again. The modern Civil Rights Movement started in the 1950s, and this summer lasted a little longer than the last. But, alas, the season changed again.

Why did these seasons change when they did? For Harris, the first and second reconstructions ended because the coalitions that coordinated them splintered as new conditions in U.S. society emerged. "Each [period]," he wrote, "became fragmented as the nation turned to other issues such as the economy, women's rights, Indian claims, and foreign affairs to mention a few."[22] Black Americans had had their day in the sun, and now it was time for other people to have theirs.

The cyclical approach to Black History helps to explain why the social status of black Americans seems to stall at the bottom rung of U.S. society. The implication, of course, is that the United States only begrudgingly accepted black Americans as citizens during Reconstruction and that white Americans fought hard to create and enforce limits on Black citizenship. The spring and summer warmed up in the hope that equality would prevail, but the fall and winter devolved into an Orwellian cliché—that is, some citizens are more equal than others. The slave and the second-class citizen did not share the same legal and political standing, but the processes that created them were similar, and their social position remained at or near the bottom of the hierarchy. The cycles of Black History course through periods of gain and loss.[23]

Factors of Decline

The post–Reconstruction era has long been characterized as one of great loss. In fact, Rayford Logan's idea of the nadir reflects his conclusion that after Reconstruction the U.S. government and the national press turned against black Americans. The government traded protection of black American citizenship and voting rights for national reconciliation between the North and the South. While the South created laws that violated the fourteenth and fifteenth amendments and alienated black citizens, the U.S. government refused to intervene. The national press stereotyped black Americans as imbeciles and criminals to justify disfranchisement and second-class citizenship. Vilified and stripped of their rights, black Americans suffered as greatly as—perhaps more so than—they did during slavery.

The new nadir is sufficiently like the first nadir to warrant comparison. In important ways, federal and state governments have seemingly turned their backs against black Americans in the twenty-first century. The U.S. Congress, for example, has refused to create national policing policies to protect black communities from police brutality or anti-discrimination laws to stem the disproportionate imprisonment of black citizens. Many young black Americans charged with felony convictions have their voting rights abrogated. In states with large black American populations, mass incarceration is disfranchising black voters through purportedly colorblind laws that seemingly target specific racial groups. Moreover, the Supreme Court has struck down aspects of the Voting Rights Act of 1965 that required the federal government to review changes made to state voting laws. As a result, state legislatures across the nation have begun to create new restrictions on voting. State lawmakers cite the need to prevent voter fraud as the purpose of their electoral reforms, but the policies they implement have reduced the number of black American voters in state elections.

The national press has also exacerbated racial tensions in the United States by depicting black Americans as rebels and criminals. The #blacklivesmatter movement, which emerged in 2013 to protest the police killings of unarmed black Americans, has been stereotyped as rioters and criminals. National news outlets limit their coverage of the protesters' grievances and political platforms while amplifying coverage of violence and looting on the fringes of the movement. Some media outlets like Fox News have gone as far as to characterize them as domestic terrorists trying to stoke the flames of racial tension. They seemingly blamed black Americans for being targeted by police because of their criminal habits, and then blamed black Americans for civil unrest because they protested the killing of unarmed civilians in the hands of police.

While the federal government reneges on its protection of black Americans' civil rights, and the national press circulates anti-black stereotypes, economic inequality, police killings, and mass incarceration serve as three additional signs of decline for black Americans. A significant proportion of the black American population faces social and economic conditions not unlike those they faced during the nadir. To begin, racial inequality in income has remained a consistent feature of the U.S. labor market over the last forty years. As political scientists C. Matthew Stripp and Sin Yi Cheung have shown, black American men and women have increased their earned income since 1970, but these increases have only modestly closed the gap between their earnings and those of white American workers. In 1970, white American men's median earned income was $49,958; then $48,440 in 1990; and $47,670 in 2009. By contrast, black American men's median income was $30,676 in 1970; $32,005 in 1990; and $31,890 in 2009. The difference in median earned income between white and black American men decreased from an estimated $19,000 in 1970 to $16,000 in 2009, which still leaves a considerable gap in earnings across race. Among women, the difference in median earned income across race was never as great as among men, but racial inequality has persisted. In 1970, white American women's median earned income was $21,327; then $25,950 in 1990; and $31,050 in 2009. For black American women, the median earned income in 1970 was $16,653; $25,639 in 1990; and $27,240 in 2009. The difference in median earned income between white and black American women decreased from an estimated $5,000 in 1970 to $4,000 in 2009, which indicates a slower rate of change that that of men. These data show the persistence of racial inequality in income even as black American men and women see increases in their earnings over time.[24]

Furthermore, white American police officers patrol impoverished black neighborhoods aggressively as part of their broken windows policing strategy. James Q. Wilson and George L. Killing popularized the broken windows thesis in a 1982 article in *The Atlantic Monthly*. They argued that visible signs of disorder in neighborhoods, if left unaddressed, will inspire more disorder. "One unrepaired window," they wrote, "is a signal that no one cares, and so breaking more windows costs nothing." The analogy extended beyond deteriorating property. For Wilson and Kelling, people who live in neighborhoods with unrepaired windows will suffer "the breakdown of community controls" if police do not increase patrol of the area.[25] In other words, "signs of visible disorder" in a neighborhood—which include black Americans who loiter, especially with known gang members—can lead to the collapse of community and climbing crime rates. According to legal scholar D. Marvin Jones, black Americans are viewed as visibly lawless, whether they are committing a crime or not, and even before the police have arrived.[26] As a result, policing in black communities grew increasingly aggressive, best exemplified in the acceleration of "stop and frisk" policies in New York City, which disproportionately impacted black and Latino populations.[27] This type of racial profiling has also led to egregious killings. Beginning in 2009, unarmed black American males like Oscar Grant and Trayvon Martin were killed extrajudicially by police officers and vigilantes, and local governments failed to convict their killers. The acquittals have signaled to black Americans that the criminal justice system does not protect and serve their communities as it does others.

Moreover, the rise of the U.S. prison industrial complex has coincided with the imprisonment of a disproportionate number of black American men and women. States across the United States began to spend exorbitantly on the expansion of the prison system. California, for example, spent close to $8 billion to increase their prison capacity by 53,000 beds.[28] Aggressive policing in black American neighborhoods and draconian drug laws with high sentences for first offenses have resulted in a massive expansion of the black American prison population. African Americans constitute a disproportionate number of arrests in the United States. They are 30 percent of those arrested for property offenses and 39 percent of those arrested for violent offenses—both figures being exceedingly high given black Americans' 12 percent share of the population.[29] According to Department of Justice data from 2003, African American males are significantly more likely to go to prison than any other racial or ethnic group. One of every three African American males born in the twenty-first century can expect to go to prison in their lifetime; meanwhile one of six Latinos will be imprisoned, and one of seventeen white American males.[30] Moreover, the ex-felons who return from prison find various political and economic obstacles during their reintegration, including exclusion from public housing, discrimination in the labor market, and voting restrictions. These "collateral consequences" can lead to fractured families, destabilized neighborhoods with residents cycling in and out prison, and limited employment opportunities. Data suggest that black Americans' wage earnings decrease by 44 percent by the age of forty-eight because of incarceration.[31] Mass incarceration has thus wreaked havoc on black American communities nationwide.

The New Nadir

In 1954, Rayford Logan coined the term "nadir" to describe the treacherous descent of race relations between 1877 and 1921 in the United States (especially the South), where black Americans were forcibly segregated from white Americans, systematically denied their voting rights, and targeted by racial terrorists. Today, the absence of lynching and the rejection of overt displays of racism have reasonably convinced U.S. citizens that race relations have improved. But the persistence of racial inequality has produced several crises in black American communities that suggest the descent into a new nadir in race relations.

This new nadir began in 1968, following the assassination of civil rights leaders like Martin Luther King, and it has continued to the present. This period constitutes a new low point in race relations marked by racial divisions, social and economic inequalities, and state violence against black communities. The issue of race has become so divisive that black and white Americans cannot talk about race or racism without shouting at one another or shutting off the conversation altogether. The socioeconomic inequities between white and black Americans suggest a systematic exclusion of black Americans from opportunities that lead to social and economic stability. And criminal justice policies and practices negatively impact black communities at disproportionate rates given the size of their overall population. Because of these characteristics, the tension, distrust, and dissention across the color line seems to be as bad today as it was in the early twentieth century.

State Sanctioned Violence

There are three distinct characteristics of the new nadir. The first is the increased use of state-sanctioned violence to decimate black American communities. Consider fatal encounters between police and black Americans. Since the killings of Oscar Grant in 2009 and Trayvon Martin in 2012, citizens have begun to demand greater access to use-of-force data. "Controversial use-of-force incidents," sociologist Ben Brucato argues, "are often cause for various publics to declare expectations that investigations be handled transparently and for agencies to improve reporting."[32] Governments have been outperformed civilian organizations in reporting on investigations and discipline concerning deadly force incidents. *The Washington Post's* "Fatal Force," the *Guardian's* "The Counted," *Killed by Force*, and *Fatal Encounters* are online databases that document police killings. They compile their data using news reports, public records, internet databases, and original reporting. These databases share the beliefs that police "are too frequently using force without sufficient cause" and that compiling and publicizing data on the deadly use of force is the "necessary early step" to stemming and preventing police killings.[33]

Data compiled in the "Fatal Force" database hosted by the *Washington Post* offer a poignant illustration of the impact of state-sanctioned violence against black Americans. Between 2015 and 2017, 2,940 people were shot and killed by police officers. Of this total, 680 were black Americans, which constituted approximately 23 percent of all fatal interactions with police.[34] United States Census data for 2017 present the black American population as 13.4 percent of the U.S. population.[35] The percentage of black Americans killed by police officers nationwide thus proportionally exceeds the percentage of the population that black Americans comprise. When compared to white Americans, the racial inequality in extrajudicial killings committed by state institutions is starker. A total of 1,420 white Americans were killed by police, or 48 percent of the total.[36] United States Census data show that white Americans constitute 76.6 percent of the population, which suggests a proportionally low percentage is victim of fatal force by police officers.[37] Black Americans are statistically more likely to be killed in police interactions than white Americans.

Black American citizens have also been targeted by vigilantes, and state agencies have failed to convict these murderers, leading black families and communities to distrust white neighbors and U.S. legal institutions. For example, Trayvon Martin, a seventeen-year-old Florida boy who was walking through a gated community, was shot and killed by a neighborhood watchman, George Zimmerman, who provoked the confrontation because the young man allegedly looked suspicious. According to legal scholar D. Marvin Jones, George Zimmerman's extrajudicial killing of Trayvon Martin in 2012 shows the tacit acceptance of what he terms "reasonable racism." Zimmerman defended his action by claiming that Martin looked criminal and thus needed to be captured. This legal reasoning, Jones argues, "is saying [that] profiling is necessary, natural, and good." The problem with this reasoning was that Martin was denied due process before being labeled a criminal.[38]

D. Marvin Jones argues that racism is qualitatively different today than it was in the 1950s. Whereas hate fueled racism in the mid–twentieth century, since the turn of the millennium, racism has become "a claim of knowledge." In other words, the stereotype that black Americans are prone to criminality and predisposed to violence is considered true, if not common sense; therefore, the prejudicial actions that white Americans take in response to these stereotypes—like racial profiling by police or extrajudicial killing by vigilantes—are viewed as reasonable given the race traits ascribed to black people.[39]

The idea that racism is "reasonable" or "common sense" reflects a shift in perceptions of racial discrimination. Whereas social justice activists succeeded in representing racial hatred as irrational in the 1950s, the perpetrators of racial discrimination in the early twenty-first century appeal to science and rationality to justify it. "The reasonable racist denies that he is acting on emotion," Jones explains, "He claims to know something about the black people who he targets for violence or arrest based on who they are."[40]

Jones's observation is an astute one. The proponents of anti-black racism have adjusted their discourse so that a once irrational assumption about the nature of dark-skinned people is now couched in empirical rhetoric. In this case, the myth of the black criminal that fueled fear and reactionary violence in the early twentieth century is now accepted as fact because of crime statistics that purportedly prove the stereotype true.

The identification of race and criminality is the result of a century-long "racial data revolution that became the linchpin of an emerging white supremacist discourse on saving the nation through knowledge and acceptance of black death and self-destruction."[41] Historian Khalil Muhammad explains that between 1890 and the 1930s "ideas of racial inferiority and crime became fastened to African Americans."[42] By the end of World War II, the association of black Americans and criminality had deepened such that deviancy was considered a natural trait of dark-skinned people. One writer opined "it is not so much discrimination which distorts the Negro's criminal record, as it is certain characteristics of the Negro population."[43] In other words, disproportionate representation of black Americans in prisons and newspaper crime blotters was not a result of discriminatory law enforcement but, rather, a reflection of fixed race traits. More than half a century later, the notion that black Americans have "certain characteristics" that predispose them to criminal behavior has completed its journey from myth to fact to common sense.

It should be remembered, however, that anti-black racism has operated this way over centuries. It was not uncommon for white Americans to present racial stereotypes as observable "facts." One illustrative example is the stereotype of the jovial, docile slave. In the 1850s, both slaveholders and abolitionists believed that slaves were happy and obedient, albeit for different reasons. Slaveholders pointed to the singing and dancing they saw slaves perform in the quarters as evidence of their acquiescence to slave status. On the other hand, abolitionists sought to shame slaveholding by representing its black victims as docile and obedient; after all, they continued to be passive and productive workers even as their owners viciously exploited them. Therefore, both sides of the political divide concerning slavery in the mid–nineteenth century perceived black American slaves as content with their condition based on their observations.[44] It seemed like common sense: if a subordinate group endured dishonor and degradation without organized, violent resistance, then they must have been sufficiently inferior to the dominant group to deserve oppression or salvation from it.

The myth-turned-fact that black American slaves were jovial and docile was a self-serving logic. Both the proponents and opponents of slavery were perpetuating white supremacy and simultaneously obscuring structural racism with a focus on the emotional and psychological characteristics of the enslaved. The point is, even in the nineteenth century the hatred fueling anti-black racism was veiled by appeals to reason. White American racists attached behavioral traits to skin color and prejudged all black people according to those characteristics. At the time it would have seemed like common sense to view dark-skinned people through the lens of stereotypes. Nearly two hundred years later racism does the same ideological work.

It is in this context that broken windows policing has proven especially dangerous to black Americans. Black victims of extrajudicial killings by the state and vigilantes were deemed "visibly lawless" even before the police arrived.[45] According to Jones, visible lawlessness is a legal concept that arose in criminal proceedings from the late 1990s. In response to increased gang activity, the City of Chicago passed an ordinance to prohibit gang loitering. The ordinance stated that the:

> . . . presence of a large collection of obviously brazen, insistent, and lawless gang members and hangers-on on the public ways intimidates residents, who become afraid even to leave their homes and go about their business. . . . Loitering in public places by criminal street gang members creates a justifiable fear for the safety of persons and property in the area because of the violence, drug-dealing and vandalism often associated with such activity.[46]

In *The City of Chicago v. Morales* (1999), the U.S. Supreme Court struck down the city ordinance because its definition of loitering was not specific enough to enforce without violating the due process of city residents. The court claimed that it would be unconstitutional to criminalize "each instance a citizen stands in public with a gang member," thereby making it difficult to discern what kind of loitering to which the ordinance would apply.[47] Even as the U.S. Supreme Court struck down the ordinance, the identification of black American gang members in public with societal harm became part of U.S. criminal justice and jurisprudence.

Put another way, black Americans have been stereotyped as criminals such that simply standing or walking in public could be interpreted by (white) onlookers as criminal acts.[48] The direct association of black Americans with gang members—the visibly lawless—puts them in the crosshairs of law enforcers and vigilantes. Police officers have been trained to patrol neighborhoods where there are visible signs of disorder like broken windows, and gang members have been equated with such signs. Similarly, white American vigilantes have adopted a racial view that black Americans are predisposed to crime and violence, and thus feel compelled to protect themselves from the black Americans they prejudge as menaces. As a result, black Americans are viewed as visibly lawless, whether they are commissioning a crime or not. For many black communities, both types of fatal encounters—that is, with police and with vigilantes—are reminiscent of the racial terrorism their ancestors experienced during the old Nadir, another time when criminal justice was deadly for black Americans.

Colorblind Laws

The second reason for the new nadir is the triumph of colorblind ideology as an allegedly antiracist strategy. Between the 1960s and 2016 presidential campaign of Donald Trump, overt expressions of racial hatred have become taboo in the United States. Civil rights activists successfully redefined racism as un-American, and politicians, judges, and law enforcement officials no longer endorsed racist policies and practices and condemned racial discrimination. This shift marked a victory for U.S. colorblind ideology, as most white Americans, as early as the 1980s, "support[ed] the antidiscrimination principle."[49] Michelle Alexander has accurately depicted the last fifty years of race relations as the "era of colorblindness," when "it is no longer social permissible to use race, explicitly, as a justification for discrimination, exclusion, and social contempt."[50] U.S. citizens pushed racism below the surface in a valiant attempt to eradicate discrimination based on skin color.

Social justice activists cultivated the colorblind ideology during the Civil Rights Movement. To combat racism based on skin color, supporters of the movement—especially whites—began to argue that they could not see skin color, that when they interacted with nonwhites they saw people, not races. This rhetoric evolved into an antiracist ideology. Proponents claimed that by ignoring skin color one could better appreciate one another's common humanity. This philosophy found its most poignant expression in Dr. Martin Luther King's "I Have a Dream" speech at the March on Washington in

1963. "I have a dream," King exhorted, "that my four children will one day live in a nation where they will not be judged by the color of their skin, but by the content of their character."[51] To end the scourge of racism, then, it was deemed that one must stop judging a person's abilities by the skin color and start emphasizing shared values as human beings.

Colorblind ideology was soon codified in U.S. law. In Congress, supporters of colorblind ideology demanded that new legislation expressly prohibit discrimination based on race and color in public spaces, housing, employment, and voting. U.S. lawmakers thus passed the two most important pieces of legislation to combat racial discrimination since Reconstruction. The 1964 Civil Rights Act sought "to enforce the constitutional right to vote, to confer jurisdiction upon the district courts of the United States to provide injunctive relief against discrimination in public accommodations, to authorize the Attorney General to institute suits to protect constitutional rights in public facilities and public education, to extend the Commission on Civil Rights, to prevent discrimination in federally assisted programs, [and] to establish a Commission on Equal Employment Opportunity," among other initiatives.[52] The 1965 Voting Rights Act sought "to enforce the fifteenth amendment" by prohibiting qualifications as "prerequisites" for voting and empower federal attorneys to review the voting procedures of U.S. states to ensure that citizens were not being unfairly denied the right to vote.[53] These laws prohibited the use of race and color to deny citizens their equality before the law. They mark major political victories for the Civil Rights Movement and colorblind ideology.

While colorblind laws were being codified in law, U.S. lawmakers began to reimagine the meaning and application of colorblind ideology. Whereas its early intent was to combat racism by refusing to conflate skin color with personhood, in the 1970s lawmakers started to use colorblind ideology to dismantle the social safety net created to combat socioeconomic inequality. Sociologists Michael Omi and Howard Winant describe this process as rearticulation, "a practice of discursive . . . reinterpretation of ideological themes and interests . . . such that these elements obtain new meanings or coherence."[54] Opportunistic lawmakers in the Republican party employed "code words" to refashion colorblind ideology. This coded language indirectly referenced race in political appeals to reactionary citizens who viewed social justice activism in the 1960s and 1970s as disorder and lawlessness.[55] For examples, Republican candidates nationwide began to promise a restoration of "law and order" in U.S. society when elected to office. On its face, this rhetoric was an innocuous plank on a candidate's platform, but in context the candidate spoke in code words to voters who opposed social justice activism. This appeal to law and order was a not-so-veiled promise to suppress civil rights protest with aggressive policing.

Using code words and colorblind rhetoric, Republican lawmakers in the 1970s and 1980s launched a multipronged attack on the Civil Rights Movement and Democratic social safety.[56] First, southern governors in the 1950s evoked the "law and order" rhetoric that would accompany the rise of the conservative wing of the Republican Party. Most were reactionary white men threatening to suppress the activism of black American citizens who were demanding an end to segregation and disfranchisement. These governors condemned civil rights protesters as lawbreakers for violating Jim Crow statutes. They promised to restore law and order to the Jim Crow South, indelibly linking this rhetoric to the "massive resistance" opposing the Civil Rights Movement.[57]

By the mid-1960s, conservative ideologue and U.S. Congressman Barry Goldwater began to popularize law and order rhetoric. In 1964, he ran as the presidential candidate for the Republican Party against Democratic candidate Lyndon B. Johnson. That same year, race riots exploded in New York City and Rochester, New York. On the campaign trail, Goldwater decried civil rights activists for their violent protests, referring to them as "mobs in the street" and warning voters that Johnson and his civil rights agenda would only increase disorder nationwide.[58] Goldwater lost the election in an historic landslide, but his appeals to law and order and identification of civil rights activism with disorder would become pivotal planks in the Republican platform thereafter.

In the 1960s, the United States experienced an increase in crime rates, in part because there was a surge in the population among fifteen- to twenty-four-year-old men, a demographic historically linked to crime. At the same time, race relations in U.S. cities frayed, largely because white American police officers used excessive, sometimes fatal, force when policing black American neighborhoods. Riots exploded across the country, especially during the "long, hot summer of 1967," when there were more than 150 race riots, and again in 1968 following the assassination of Martin Luther King Jr. Elected officials sought to clamp down on crime with tougher laws. Republicans especially seized the opportunity to recruit new voters with their "law and order" campaign rhetoric.

In 1968, Republican presidential candidate Richard Nixon executed a successful "southern strategy" to expand the Republican voter base. His campaign's goal was to persuade white Democrats in the South and in northern cities who were angered by their party's civil rights agenda to vote Republican in the 1968 election. Kevin Phillips, the architect of this political strategy, believed that Republicans could achieve political supremacy by appealing to white American racism using coded anti-black rhetoric. One of Nixon's advisors consented: "You have to face the fact that the whole problem is really the blacks," he said. "The key is to devise a system that recognizes this while not appearing to."[59] Nixon employed this strategy effectively, winning office in 1968 and setting the stage for the "conservative revolution" that dominated U.S. politics through the end of the century.

Presidential candidate Richard Nixon thus appealed to disaffected southern Democrats who were infuriated by the federal government's civil rights legislation and court decisions. He wooed them with promises of slowing the progress of the Civil Rights Movement. Further he interpellated this voting block as the "silent majority" who rejected racism but refused to participate in social movements that threatened order and the rule of law. Nixon thus engineered a major shift in the two-party system, winning for Republicans millions of voters in the South who abandoned the Democratic Party to reject the Civil Rights Movement.

In addition to recruiting the "silent majority" to the Republican Party, Nixon promised to restore law and order in U.S. society. This party plank was a thinly veiled threat to black American civil rights activists, whom reactionary racists had long labeled as rogues and criminals. Nixon promised to quell the social revolution by expanding the police state, arresting and imprisoning social justice activists, demonizing working-class and underemployed black Americans, and developing a black elite class sympathetic to conservative politics and willing to condescend toward poor blacks.[60]

The use of colorblind laws to prevent freedom and equality for black Americans has a long history. In fact, one tactic used to secure white supremacy in the South after slavery was the ratification of colorblind disfranchisement laws. In 1898, after the U.S. Supreme Court ruled in *Plessy v. Ferguson* that segregated accommodations for white and black Americans were legal if there were equal accommodations, Southern states passed Jim Crow laws to segregate and disfranchise black Americans. Louisiana innovated legislation that restricted black American voters through what was called a "Grandfather Clause." According to Louisiana state law, voting was permitted only for state residents who could vote in 1867 themselves or whose father or grandfather voted in state elections before 1867. Since there were no black Americans in Louisiana who could vote in 1867, the Grandfather Clause effectively excluded them from elections.

In legal devices like Louisiana's Grandfather Clause, we find the origins of colorblind laws. Because the 15th Amendment prevented voting restrictions based on race, color, or previous condition of servitude, state officials could not expressly target black Americans by race. Instead, they restricted voting by targeting social conditions that would exclude black Americans without reference to race. In this case, the franchise was denied to residents who hadn't voted before 1867; there was no reference to a specific racial group. Still, black Americans were denied the right to vote en masse, ensuring that white Americans remained the political and economic decision-makers in Louisiana. Colorblind laws preserved white supremacy.

Today, ostensibly colorblind drug laws are enforced in racially discriminatory ways because of broken windows policing and the presumed "visible lawlessness" of black Americans. In turn, felony convictions operate much the same as grandfather clauses. Black community members are disproportionately represented in U.S. jails and prisons on felony drug convictions, making them more likely to be disfranchised because of their criminal record. Like grandfather clauses, voting restrictions based on criminal record do not violate the 15th Amendment, but they impact black Americans at a much higher rate than white Americans. Let's consider Mississippi. Mississippi has the second largest black American population in the United States; about 37 percent of state residents are black. There are approximately 22,000 people in Mississippi jails and prisons, and 57 percent of that population is black. That makes black Americans overrepresented in the state's criminal justice system. Now, Mississippi enforces voting laws that permanently restrict the voting rights of certain ex-felons. That means a significant portion of the black American population in Mississippi is locked in an inferior political position because of colorblind laws. Put another way, black Americans in Mississippi, where they have the demographic advantage to form a powerful voting bloc, nevertheless have their electoral power diluted just as it was during the old Nadir.

Crisis in Black Leadership

The third and final reason that we're experiencing a new nadir in U.S. race relations is related to black American leadership. Despite frayed race relations during the old Nadir, black and white Americans threw great support behind black American leaders who accommodated the status quo in U.S. political economy. Booker T. Washington, for example, enjoyed unprecedented popularity among Americans, especially white Southerners, in the

1890s and early 1900s. Washington advocated voluntary separation of the races and self-improvement in black communities. He was willing to compromise social and political equality in exchange for economic cooperation between white business leaders and black workers. This accommodationism worked well for him individually, as he became one of the wealthiest black entrepreneurs in the United States and even founded his own school to train skilled black workers in the fields of construction and manufacturing. But Black communities nationwide continued to suffer from Jim Crow policies and racial terrorism.

There are eerie parallels between Booker T. Washington and the great black leaders of our own time. According to Keeanga-Yamahtta Taylor, the rise of black economic and political elites has been the "most significant transformation in all of Black life over the last fifty years." The success of Black elites, however, has corresponded to increasing inequality, incarceration, and disfranchisement for black Americans. Therefore, the importance of this historical development is not that black leaders have helped improve the social and economic conditions of black communities nationwide but, rather, that they have exacerbated the problems plaguing black communities. In fact, many black economic leaders have advocated privatization and political leaders, austerity, and this combination has had a net negative effect on many of the black Americans who support these leaders.[61]

The "black electoral turn" offers an excellent example of the crisis in black leadership. One of the most promising outcomes of the Civil Rights Movement was the mobilization of black voting blocs in cities across the United States. Grassroots activism in the black freedom struggle evolved into electoral campaigns to advance black candidates who promised to affect change in black communities. Like most campaigners, however, black political candidates appealed to donors who could improve their chances of winning. They began to serve private rather than public interests. "As money and power exerted greater influence on the outcome of elections," Taylor writes, "the capacity to raise funds and attract lucrative suitors distorted the political objectives of infusing 'soul' into the political process."[62] Candidates who once promised to lift the community from the bottom up found themselves "administering cuts and managing meager budgets on the backs of Black constituents" who voted them into office.[63] Black American voters have had no good reason to believe that participation in U.S. politics can actually improve their lives.

Carl Stokes, former mayor of Cleveland, Ohio, and Barack Obama, former president of the United States, offer two concrete examples of how the electoral turn has led to a crisis in black leadership. No one will deny the historical significance of these men: Stokes was the first black man elected as mayor of a major U.S. city, and Obama the first black American U.S. president. Both appeared to usher in a new era of "Black power," when black American voters elected leaders from their own communities to lead the United States and cities toward equality. Yet Stokes and Obama passed policies that, and appointed functionaries who, stalled progress in black communities. Stokes, for example, administered an urban renewal program in Cleveland that paid lucrative development contracts to private corporations but did not prevent the displacement of low-income communities, many of which were comprised of black residents. Stokes also appointed a repressive police chief whom he supported even when black communities complained that he was unfairly targeting their neighborhoods and using force abusively.[64]

Obama has also received (justified) criticism for his reluctance to advance black American political interests. While Obama worked diligently to pass economic policies that saved the banking and automobile industries from bankruptcy, he did next to nothing to stem rising unemployment in black American communities. Worse yet, Obama recycled the "culture of poverty" rhetoric that conservatives have used historically to blame black Americans for their economic struggles. He cited what he perceived to be problems in parenting, diet, sexual practices, and leisure activities as the reason that unemployment rates remained high in black communities.[65] While economist and political scientists have shown that the structural disintegration of the economy in 2008 disproportionately impacted black Americans, Obama seemed to think better cultural practices would have protected them.[66]

Moreover, President Obama's economic policies did little to stave off racial inequalities in society. His administration subsidized a political economy that watched racial disparities in income spike. The median income of black households in the United States in 2016 was just $43,000, while that of white households was $71,300. The Obama administration also seemed to side with law enforcement as mass incarceration expanded and police interactions with black citizens grew increasingly fatal. Undoubtedly, President Obama inspired hope in the black community, but his administration may have also increased disillusionment with U.S. politics. Why promote interracial cooperation in electoral politics when black elected officials preserve institutions that disfranchise and decimate black communities? Why promote racial integration when it doesn't lead to social and political equality?

The electoral strategy has not been an effective catalyst for change in Black America. The republican model of government relies on the premise that one individual can represent the interests of many diverse constituents in a given geographical unit; the incapacity for one person to meet so many demands is why republicanism is fundamentally flawed. Democracy certainly has its problems, too; majority rule does not necessarily ensure that political and economic decisions will benefit the majority that makes them, nor will it necessarily obviate the oppression of minority groups. The communal vison of activists like Ella Baker was far more effective at putting community interests ahead of individual ones, even as it incorporated aspects of republicanism and democracy. Group-centered leadership was premised on the capacity of everyday people to lead their communities collaboratively rather than rely on one individual speak for the collective.[67] There wouldn't be one leader but several, each trained to secure the needs of their families and neighborhoods from local and national governments. The electoral strategy that grew out the Civil Rights Movement, however, betrayed this burgeoning communalism, using its political momentum to win office. New leaders have not been cultivated, nor have the needs of black voters been met.

Worse yet, black elected officials fomented further distrust of U.S. politics. After all, black leaders like Stokes and Obama won the highest offices in city and federal governments and were unable or unwilling to address the needs of the black constituents who played a vital role in putting them in charge. Not only have black American leaders failed to alleviate the poverty, unemployment, and housing and food crises in black communities, but they have also showed "complicity with and absorption into the worst, most corrupt aspects of American politics, including accepting donations from the most notorious corporations in the country."[68] They have seemed easily corrupted by the powerbrokers they met while on the campaign trail and in office. Black political elites have proven themselves every bit the same as the political class they replaced, except their success has further undermined the gains of the black liberation struggle that brought them into existence. A new generation of black American voters thus sees little reason to trust black leaders and, by extension, the U.S. political system.

Cycles of Ascension

The United States has sunken to a new low point in race relations. Black and white Americans live in separate societies, a white one where social mobility is possible and police protect and serve, and a black one where poverty is endemic and police shoot to kill. Making matters worse, black and white Americans no longer have the language or the strategy to bridge the racial divide. During the Civil Rights Movement, integration was the social vision to which racial justice advocates aspired. President Obama's election symbolized the pinnacle of this racial vision, yet his administration failed to narrow social and economic inequalities across race. Now integration seems ineffective as a goal, and racial justice advocates are scrambling to find a new strategy to effect racial equality.

When Rayford Logan first studied the nadir in U.S. race relations, he noted that "American Negroes have made notable progress toward first-class citizenship in recent years."[69] He likely alluded to groundbreaking legislation like President Truman's Executive Order 9981, which abolished racial discrimination in the U.S. armed forces in 1948, as well as litigation coursing its way through the United States Supreme Court, namely *Brown v. Board of Education of Topeka, Kansas*, which was decided in 1954, the same year Logan published his monograph. Social justice campaigns by black Americans and their allies have historically brought declining race relations to a halt, humanizing marginalized groups so that U.S. legal and political institutions begin to honor its values of freedom and equality for all. The Civil Rights Movement, burgeoning in the 1950s, both dismantled legal segregation and disfranchisement and inspired social justice campaigns among other marginalized groups, including women, Native Americans, and others. Cycles of decline are broken by recurring cycles of ascension, however brief and incomplete.

To rise from the new nadir, social justice activists may consider rehabilitating the philosophy of integration. Writing in 1963, Dr. Martin Luther King Jr. articulated a vision for a racially inclusive society that transcended integrated schools and lunch counters. King's philosophy of integration demanded that society respect all people *as* people (not things), protect individuals' right to make decisions freely, and honor the inherent identity of all human beings.[70] Herein was a philosophy that permitted people to be individuals while still promoting solidarity based on shared experience. The nuance of King's integrationist philosophy undergirds the contemporary activist ethos, even as his "dream" is equated with fantasy.

In the current moment of crisis, Dr. King's "dream" and philosophy of integration ring hollow in the hearts and minds of black thinkers and doers. One need only consider Ta-Nehisi Coates's lament to his son, warning that the American Dream, no matter how alluring, "has never been an option because the Dream rests on our backs, the bedding made from our bodies." The message from the previous generation to the present has been that racism persists and, with it, a society that deems black Americans exploitable and expendable. Whereas essayist James Baldwin in 1963 implored his nephew not to define himself by what white Americans perceived of him, Coates tells his son that "the question of how one should live within a black body, within a country lost in the Dream," may take a lifetime to understand and still be unanswerable.[71] This is not a society that meets the ethical demands of integration as King proposed them, nor is it one that expects these demands to be met.

In "A Letter to My Nephew," Baldwin took a bold stance on integration, defining it as the responsibility of black Americans to reveal the racism of white Americans and compel them to change it: "that we [black Americans], with love, shall force our [white American] brothers to see themselves as they are, to cease fleeing from reality and begin to change it, for this is your home, my friend."[72] More challenge than lament, Baldwin called on his nephew and black Americans to change the hearts and minds of white America, which fueled social justice activists during the Civil Rights Movement. In the twenty-first century, however, when state-sanctioned violence, racially enforced colorblind laws, and crisis in black political leadership have produced a new nadir in race relations, Baldwin's challenge seems misdirected. The black liberation struggle today quite reasonably focuses on self-preservation and self-defense. Indeed, the anger and despair felt by black Americans who suffer state violence and racial discrimination is not unlike the righteous rage that ignited riots in cities across the United States in the "long, hot summer of 1967."

In the current racial maelstrom, the Movement for Black Lives has led the charge for social justice. Historian Barbara Ransby views the Black Lives Matter movement as a response to vigilante and police violence that continues to evolve into an international movement seeking both racial justice and social transformation. Equally important, Ransby argues that the movement embraces the Black feminist tradition in the United States and women-centered leadership; supports issues related to sexual orientation and gender identity; and emphasizes "the needs of the most marginal and often-maligned sectors of the Black community: those who bear the brunt of state violence, from police bullets and batons to neoliberal policies of abandonment and incarceration."[73] The Movement for Black Lives comes closest to King's and Baldwin's radical views of integration today, demanding freedom, declaring the equal value of all human life, and challenging themselves and allies to educate and change the people who perpetuate racism.

The next step, one surmises, is the creation of a humane vision of cross-racial solidarity that demands social, economic, and political equality in the United States. Only a new vision—an ideology that can link the struggles for black liberation to others for social equality and human dignity—can fully permeate U.S. social and political institutions and eradicate the structures of white supremacy creating the present nadir. That vision must not be anchored in the idea of freedom, which has structured the liberalist interpretation of Black History and been manipulated by pundits and politicians, but, rather, it should be grounded in the notion of equality. The frontlines of this battle for racial equality are in schools, churches, and community centers as well as courthouses and capitol buildings. Ideological transformation must begin at the neighborhood level, with everyday people who empathize with one another and the community they represent. The challenge will be, first, having an honest, uncomfortable conversation that shakes up long-held prejudices and stirs emotions and, second, committing to a cross-racial solidarity based on human equality.

Chapter 3

Emotion, Race, and Cultural Trauma in #BlackLivesMatter

ERIN M. STEPHENS

> I can't get his voice out of my head. He said, "I can't breathe." As tears dripped from her face, she pointed at her own body and asked, "How can people just hate us, as a group, so much?"[1]
>
> —Louwanda Evans

Above, sociologist Louwanda Evans recounts her tearful outburst as she struggled to process the repeated deaths of Black people killed by White police officers. Though she did not personally know Eric Garner, his final words uttered through heaving breaths were seared into her mind. His death was a stark depiction of the disposability of Black life; his body trapped under the weight of White police officers represented her own. This alone caused her deep despair, but what compounded the pain was the response of her White coworkers when she turned toward them in pain and confusion. One responded with a shrug and another with silence. Reading her account, I was reminded of the moment I chose to do my dissertation research. I was in an evening class on November 24, as images of protestors being assaulted with tear gas in Ferguson, Missouri, started rapidly spreading across social media platforms. I sat quietly in class shaking with despair and fury, struggling to be present and to hold off tears. No longer able to restrain myself, I finally brought up the unfolding conflict between protestors and police. My non-Black professor and classmates agreed to the injustice of the situation, some emphatically, yet none expressed anything like the emotion that I felt. It caused me to wonder: how was it that this event provoked such a profound emotional response in me but apparently not in them?

This research is grounded by a question: why is it that certain instances of social suffering become significant to social groups, while others are forgotten? Cultural trauma theory posits that the answer lies in the mechanisms and symbols through which collectivities persuasively represent this suffering. As carrier agents (spokespeople skilled in using persuasive speech and institutional resources to make public claims) broadcast characterizations of events and make claims of fundamental injury on behalf of a collective group, they construct a story that defines the injury, articulates its causes, and identifies avenues for institutional repair.[2] In this trauma process, carrier agents engage in communicative action in various institutions to craft a master narrative through which social suffering becomes meaningful to collective identity. Cultural trauma theory has focused primarily on the cognitive dimensions of the trauma process, identifying narratives, identity, memory and claims as among its chief elements. While many scholars recognize that emotion is part of the cultural trauma process, beyond the deep emotions that instigate the trauma process or increase public sympathy, few explain its role.[3] In this chapter, I attend to this oversight by uncovering the various emotional dimensions of #BlackLivesMatter and surrounding discourse as expressed on Twitter, online narratives, and movement spaces. I ask, how does *emotion serve the spiral of signification and crafting of a master narrative of cultural trauma? Toward what ends do carrier agents engage emotion in the trauma process? What are the consequences and what is achieved?*

My answers to these questions are based on a social media ethnography of online #BlackLivesMatter discourse from 2015 to 2017.[4] During this period I engaged in routine and systematic participant observation of social media platforms such as Twitter and Facebook, collecting tweets and images, blogs, articles, and videos. Additionally, I conducted participant observation in movement activities related to the Movement for Black Lives in the Washington, DC, metropolitan area and Philadelphia. Through the examples from this research, I reveal here the work of Black intellectuals—writers, activists, experts, and journalists—as carrier agents and emotion workers engaged in the tasks of articulating and reworking emotion in terms of collective identity. I argue that the trauma process itself is more than representation, but also an *experience* of trauma when it involves marginalized groups making public claims about their suffering. I begin with a survey of the emotional landscapes produced through online #BlackLivesMatter discourse, showing how emotion serves as a precious resource for carrier groups engaged in contentious politics as they challenge systemic racism. This section is followed by an examination of the boundary work activists engaged in online to cultivate emotional resources to sustain movement discourse. I uncover the emotional labor activists perform to protect the trauma narrative, locating it in gendered emotional dynamics between Black and White women. Finally, though cultural trauma is a process of representing trauma rather than the actual collective experience of trauma, I point to the demands of this process by uncovering one more unattended emotional dimension of cultural trauma: how carrier groups engage in emotional repair in order to sustain public claims-making and organizing around a narrative of trauma.

Emotion as a Resource

In his book *Tweets and the Streets*, Paolo Gerbaudo examines how activists use social media to construct emotional spaces to facilitate the formation of solidarities and mobilize collective action. He argues that blogs and social networking sites constitute "crucial emotional conduits through which organizers have condensed individual sentiments of indignation, anger, pride and a sense of shared victimhood and transformed them into political passions driving the process of mobilization."[5] These online emotional spaces surround on-the-ground activism as activists utilize social media to generate emotional tensions that facilitate collective gathering around the issue. This emotional construction facilitates a feeling of togetherness, while also serving as an impetus for collective action by stirring emotions toward protest and other movement activities. When movement claims are captured by hashtags, what Gerbaudo calls "emotional condensation" occurs, as claims echo one another with similar expressions of emotion. The masterful phrasing of #BlackLivesMatter is an excellent example of how activists in this movement have been able to "exploit the emotional power of social media" by capturing the struggle of Black people to be afforded humanity and dignity in institutional interactions.[6]

In the proliferation of #BlackLivesMatter-connected discourse that emerged on Twitter, we see a condensation of anger and sadness as hashtags were deployed to harness emotionality toward elevating trauma claims. For example:

> In front of #TerenceCrutcher father no less. I'm sick. Disgusted. Stop asking us to remain calm when you both kill us and then lie about it. @LeslieMac
>
> This really hurts my heart #SandraBland #SayHerName #Black LivesMatters @melaninist
>
> #Ifidieinpolicecustody Do not make calls for peace or forgiveness. Do not speculate about my mental state. I'm Black and constantly enraged. @CharleneCac

In these cases, emotion functioned as a tool to collectivize trauma within the carrier groups. Amid the constellation of emotions expressed, online patterns emerged as hashtags of victims' names became representative of these claims. Blog posts were used for extended articulations of emotional states that foregrounded all sense-making. Damon Young of the popular blog Very Smart Brothers writes about breaking down in tears when he first viewed the newly released dashcam video from Sandra Bland's arrest.

> I'm sure the anger will come. And then the outrage. And then my mind will be clearer . . . But right now, at this moment, I just feel a sadness. An all-encompassing, panoramic, sadness that plateaus momentarily and then crescendos every time I write Sandra Bland or see Sandra Bland's name.[7]

The title of this piece denotes his shock: "They Killed Her. They Fucking Killed Sandra Bland." Here, Young emphasizes Bland's name, while leaving unnamed the officers involved in her arrest and even the name of the jail where she was found dead. We see in the discourse emerging from this movement, particularly as it relates to the names of folks killed by police, solidarities are formed as Black people collectively identify as victims of systemic racism.

This collectivization was not only evident in tweets and blogs, but also as Black journalists leveraged major news media websites to engage mental health experts as validators for the claims of racial trauma. In an article on the *New York Times* website, one journalist wrote, "All the rage and mourning and angst works to exhaust you; it eats you alive with its relentlessness . . . They force you to reconcile your own helplessness in the face of such brutal injustice, and the terrifying reality that it could happen to you, or someone you hold dear."[8]

In these cases, emotion serves as a critical resource for embedding the trauma in collective identity. Research on the deleterious effects of race-based stress demonstrates how tying emotions like anger and sadness to collective identity comes with risks. If these emotions are not tethered to empowering action, they can become debilitating and isolating. Consider the comments of an interviewed man who shared his reaction to the video of the dying Philando Castile with *The Huffington Post.*

> I was instantly angry. I just kind of get that—it's like a rage. The rage you really can't do anything about because you don't know what the outcome is going to be. You're just angry. You're mad at everyone and everything . . . You never know when the next incident is going to be . . . You never know if you're going to be that next case.[9]

Noting the connection between emotional stress and psychic trauma, clinical psychologist Monnica Williams asserted: "There's a heightened sense of fear and anxiety when you feel like you can't trust the people who've been put in charge to keep you safe. Instead, you see them killing people who look like you . . . Combined with the everyday instances of racism, like microaggressions and discrimination, that contributes to a sense of alienation and isolation. It's race-based trauma."[10] How then might experiencing race-based trauma affect the trauma process?

Over the course of the research, I frequently read Facebook posts and heard directly from people that they were taking breaks from social media because of the emotional stress they experienced every time another video was released of police brutality or a name trended. Illustrating this desire to escape the psychic trauma, during the summer of 2015 YouTube user "Evelyn from the Internets" posted a video called "Calling in Black," which was widely shared online among Black social networks. "Evelyn" recounts and acts out a typical morning for herself and presumably other millennials, which starts with waking up for work and scrolling through social media feeds on her phone:

> You slowly start to notice something: another unarmed Black person assaulted and/or murdered. Your emotions and thoughts

> could run the gamut from hopeless and confused, to infuriated and reckless. But the other day, when I was driving to work and I noticed water randomly pouring from my eyes, I realized something—I was grieving. The specifics might differ. Swap a grown man with a teenage girl in a bathing suit, switch the skittles for loud music or not using turning signal or praying in a church or walking; every reblog, retweet, repost of citizen video footage that ultimately will never see the light of a courtroom; every Vine you watch of someone you know from Twitter getting pepper sprayed; and every link to a racist GoFundMe page. Sure, the specifics might differ, but watching the same narrative play out over and over and over and over and over and over again, takes a toll. Sometimes I need a minute, ok? And that's where a calling in and Black would be so clutch.[11]

The phrase "call in Black" became a popular refrain that summer and the headline of several other articles by Black writers echoing her need for a break.[12] This desire to escape reveals that collectivizing psychic injury can pose a threat to the trauma process. Social networking sites make it possible to spread claims quickly and widely across dispersed populations, but often people engage with these sites in physical isolation. Collectivizing trauma over these sites thus runs the risk of alienation, as users may disconnect from the trauma process rather than engage in the public task of representation. For example, finding themselves increasingly cynical, exhausted, and obsessive over social media follows and likes, the Black activist group the Dream Defenders (formed in response to Trayvon Martin's death) took a several month break from social media. Carrier agents are thus posed with the challenge of creating emotional spaces that can serve the trauma process, even as they advance narratives that trigger psychological pain in order to elevate movement claims.

But this is not the only challenge. To issue claims of systemic injury as members of a minority group adds to the emotional demands of the trauma process, as emotions themselves are subject to power and control. For example, social research and accounts demonstrate how Black people engage in emotion work to manage racial stereotypes to be seen as credible in White spaces[13] and that even in interracial activist spaces where emotions are centered, Black emotions are exploited for White emotional gain.[14] There have been many cases where White women respond to Black women's expressions of anger at injustice with tears, derailing the conversation as White emotions become centered.[15]

In this structural imbalance, activists must also work to give Black emotions equal status. In a statement defending rage and resistance, BYP100 issued, "Black rage is justified rage. Let us stay steadfast in our mission and stand unapologetically with our people."[16] The co-founders of Black Lives Matter sent a statement to *The Huffington Post* in the wake of the protests in Baltimore. In it they expressed support for those who rallied, concluding with, "Black people, we are fully deserving of the room and space to fully express our humanity. This is what Black Lives Matter is truly about. We support all of our emotions, from our bliss to our anger to our grief. All of it is welcome, as this is what it means to be human, to love and to lose those that we love so much."[17] In both statements the organizations validate Black emotional expression as justified and evidence of humanity, rejecting any condemnation or social control of emotions. We also see here that emotion is articulated as a cultural resource for movement work—and like other resources, to be useful it must be cultivated, harnessed and managed. To make visible emotion as a cultural resource, in the following section I discuss the ways Black activists, in full recognition of uneven power dynamics, attempt to mitigate the ability of "White emotion" to undermine claims of social injury.

Cultivating Emotional Resources for Movement Work

> Sometimes I wish I had been born a Black woman. You all seem so strong.
>
> —Anon Facebook Post, November 2016, White woman

Thus began a Facebook conversation that would later be tagged with: #thisdragwillgodowninhistory. At first, the Black women in the original poster's network responded with measure. "Im gon have to find some strength to properly respond to this," and then the short response: "We don't have a choice." But then the original author, seemingly unaware of (or more likely unconcerned about) the rocky waters she was treading, wrote: "Can I get some?" And the storm was unleashed.

The long string of comments began with a new writer, a Black woman, calling the original poster's comments "microaggressive as fuck bullshit." Continuing with ample fucks and abounding pejorative colorful references to White women like Becky, MethAnne, and Hermoine, she proceeded to lay out the oppression and suffering that Black folks had and continued to endure under White supremacy.

> First let me burst this fucking bubble . . . this shit is not fucking endless . . . it comes with an incredible, constant strain and pressure on the mental health . . . but when we're fucking sick and angry, you pathologize us . . . but you want our fucking STRENGTH, Hermione?"

She continued, Black woman's strength, born in pain and struggle, was not magical, nor was it endless. Black women's emotions were not a commodity to be consumed at will.

> You don't want this strength because you're too much of a coward to endure and survive what it takes to develop it . . . you don't want to bleed and fight and cry and die for this strength . . . be tortured, physically and psychologically, for centuries, until we see ourselves as LESS THAN YOU!!

When this Facebook exchange came across my screen in November 2016 it had 1.1K thumbs up, hearts, and laughing reactions, with Black women dominating the comments, giving thanks, cheering, and wholeheartedly agreeing. In this performance of anger involving cursing, censure, and pejorative labeling, and substantiated with historical interpretation, the responder produced a moment of vindication where Black women's emotions were centered, effectively shifting power in this interaction with a supporting chorus. This anger was not only hers but belonged to all Black women.

This Facebook exchange represents one among many wherein emotion was characterized in terms of race and used as a tool for resisting White supremacy. Another example is the following tweet, written as part of a yearly writing of haiku poems led by Spirit House, a Black woman healing collective in North Carolina. The poems tweeted in 2016 were firmly situated in the constellation of emotions constructed through this movement.

> i am Black as fuck
> i don't give a fuck about
> your White ass feelings
> #BlackAugust575
> *@Hatzigut*

In this tweet, emotion is bound with racial identity as a racialized boundary is set regarding the validity of emotions. "White feelings" is used to capture emotion-laden responses that were issued in contestation, invalidation, or competition with "Black feelings." I would argue that neither this case, nor the other, are about essentializing emotions as Black or White. Rather, they situate emotional response to social trauma within a matrix of domination[18] as anger is wielded as an oppositional tool within intersecting power relations of race and gender. Research has shown that, for women, anger has unique potential power for disrupting and upsetting power relations by challenging social control.[19] Black lesbian feminist Audre Lorde identifies anger as strategy for women responding to racism in her essay "The Uses of Anger":

> Anger expressed and translated into action in the service of our vision and our future is a liberating and strengthening act of clarification, for it is in the painful process of this translation that we identify who are our allies with whom we have grave differences, and who are our genuine enemies. Anger is loaded with information and energy.[20]

Anthropologist and Black Lives Matter activist Bianca Williams referenced Lorde's essay as she reflected on how her own anger informed her work.

> There are moments when I can feel anger raging inside of me. I feel it now as the District Attorney in my city pushes forward with his case against Clarence MosesEL, a man that has served 28 years in prison for a crime he did not commit. And if I'm honest, it didn't start with the killing of Michael Brown. It didn't start with Sandra Bland or Michael Marshall or Korryn Gaines or Trayvon Martin. If I think back to identify the moment when the simmering anger spilled over into my belly, and I wanted to pull my hair out with frustration, cry deep pools of tears, scream at the top of my lungs, and run into the streets to ask people "What the heck is going on?!? Are you paying attention?!?!," it was in 2011 with the execution of Troy Davis. It was then that I slowly gave myself over to the anger, day by day trying to figure out how this well-stocked arsenal could help me do something productive, while recognizing that it also had the potential to eat me alive.[21]

Anger functions within the trauma process as a tool for mobilizing and attributing responsibility for the social injury. Anger can also be a critical tool for Black women working through ongoing collective trauma.[22] However, as is illustrated by Williams. anger may be productive and empowering, but it also can be painful and exhausting. And often on the other side of anger responding to racism, is pain.

Consider the following sets of tweets. The first tweet was written by the poet Saeed Jones in response to the protesting in Baltimore because of Freddie Gray's death while in police custody. The second is an excerpt from a series of tweets written by activist Johnetta Elzie, who became widely known through her activism following Michael Brown's shooting near her childhood home.

> Part of myself is going numb. Like, I can't feel as intensely about Baltimore as I did/do about Ferguson. I don't have it in me.
>
> I never thought—in my lifetime—I'd risk PTSD simply by being a young Black man who loves following current events. And yet.
>
> *@theferocity*

> Today is so much.
>
> Literally just had back to back police killings with Philando and Alton. Now again. Tyre, Terence, and Keith.
>
> Today I feel really fragile. TBH. On the verge of tears, or snapping, or both.
>
> Being Black in a White space is the last place I want to be today. I'm not going to pretend
>
> I'm okay. I'm not going to smile for you. Nothin
>
> It's fair if you're not okay today. And it's okay to make them uncomfortable.
>
> Can't even begin to unpack the trauma of the last one before the next one even happens. Can't even mourn.

> In the last 30 mins I've gotten texts from a range of different kinds of Black folks saying
>
> "I'm not okay" :(
>
> Artists, protesters, lawyers, doctors, actors, students, professors & even a. Nurse.
>
> 14 Black folk check in to name they're not okay & don't want to cope.
>
> "Don't want to cope" is a theme. A shift. We've been taught how to cope, put on the mask and pretend we're okay. Not anymore.
>
> *@Nettaaaaaaaa*

Both cases capture the real danger of trauma to activists' ability to sustain resistance through continued articulation and mobilization around collective trauma. There is already a degree of emotional stress produced through direct and sustained engagement in thinking, working and confronting the power-brokers and systems they aim to displace. But Elzie's mention of White spaces points to an emotional vulnerability as Black people struggle to handle an articulated pain that is not only the fault of the police or state but can even be connected to daily interactions with coworkers or classmates. Smith, Allen, and Danley suggest that such interactions can cause an accumulation of negative psychosocial and physical effects that they call "racial battle fatigue,"[23] as African Americans cope with racial microaggressions and racism. Here is the importance of attending to the emotional dimensions of articulated trauma. It is not only a sense of being wronged by a nation, but of an offense that is part of the fabric of the social relations that permeate one's life. The mourning over a boy shot, a boy who looks similar to your cousin, is compounded the next day when one attends a church under White leadership and the pastor says nothing about it. A non-Black coworker shrugging off the failure to indict another police officer becomes another reference to the erasure of Black life and contributes to the feeling of systemic and sustained psychic assault. We might consider the ultimate example of racial battle fatigue in the death of Erica Garner, the daughter of Eric Garner. Following her father's death, she dedicated herself to police reform. After suffering her second heart attack (her first during a pregnancy a few months prior), the twenty-seven-year-old died from massive brain injury in December 2017. Many interpreted her death as the consequence of systemic racism and the toxic stress she endured in her activist work.[24]

#NotYourMule: Protecting Black Emotional Labor

Because resistance work requires sustained engagement within the very dynamics that perpetuate injury, various strategies were engaged off and online to mitigate the harm. Online, hashtags like #carefreeBlackgirl or #carefreeBlackboy and #Blackgirlmagic served as emotional spaces where depictions of Black people excelling or experiencing joy were used to counter the effects of traumatic images and discourse. A key strategy employed by organizations like BLM and BYP100 was the use of Black-only spaces to create spaces absent of White oppression. As Nigerian writer and cultural critic Luvvie Ajayi asserted, "Black trauma is never given space to heal because we have to make sure the White people who hurt us don't feel too bad about it. Even as victims, we're told to care about the feelings of those who harm us."[25] To create this space, activists constructed boundaries on who could participate and produced spaces where emotion could be reworked and harnessed toward movement ends. To this point, activist and writer Michal "MJ" Jones listed five reasons Black-only spaces were needed:

1. Non-Black People Actively Oppose Us Having This Space
2. We Need an Escape from Everyday Racial Oppression [safer space]
3. We Need Our Own Space—Yes, Even From Other People of Color and White Allies [to be able to process lived experience]
4. We Need to Address Issues Within Our Communities [transphobia, violence, sexism/heterosexism, classism, ableism]
5. We need to Heal, Uplift, and Love

BLM DC led a weekly Black-only space called #BlackJoySunday where Black folks would gather together in a park or in someone's home for fellowship and engage various affirmation of Black cultural identity like jumping rope, dancing, and playing cards. During my first attendance of the event, one of the leaders shared being invited by a college to participate on a panel discussing the movement to say #AllLivesMatter rather than #BlackLives Matter. They were going to pay her a couple hundred dollars, but her answer was firm: "You aren't paying me enough to defend my Blackness." Everyone responded with emphatic agreement. The refusal of #AllLivesMatter advocates to acknowledge the claims of specific injury embedded in #BlackLivesMatter felt like an erasure of the particularities of the Black experience in the United States. Sharing the story among other Black activists, she experienced validation and understanding without having to explain herself.

Of course, this strategy of crafting safer emotional spaces was not without challenge from White people. BLM Philly was inundated with angry tweets for three days after one of their Black-only events was publicly advertised.[26] Indeed, for activists involved in online claims-making about police violence, different strategies had to be used to assert emotional boundaries. One common strategy was to simply block people who launched vitriolic attacks on their social media accounts. However, as key to the work of intellectuals is elevating trauma narratives beyond carrier groups, they had to use a different strategy to navigate communication with White allies.

Figure 3.1 is a snapshot of exchanges following a tweet from feminist author Roxane Gay. In it she expresses resistance to White entitlement to her labor, calling it "an epidemic." Black intellectuals and activists were quite clear that managing the emotions of White allies was at their expense. There were

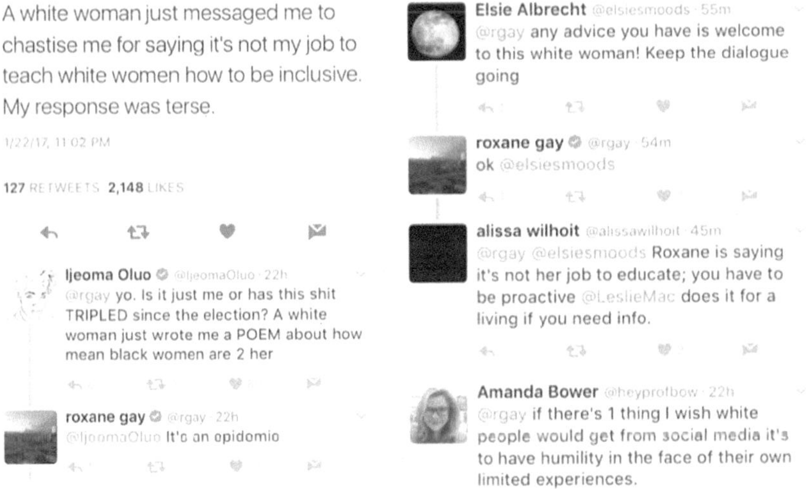

Figure 3.1. "It's an Epidemic." Twitter exchanges, Roxane Gay. Photograph courtesy of Erin M. Stephens.

of course White allies who attempted to hold White folks accountable, as is evident in replies to her tweet. Yet, the emotions were brought to the feet of Black activists working to confront and heal their own trauma. Consider activist Brittany Packnett's comments on the pressure she felt to consume videos of police violence: "We're supposed to be able to provide language for people's grief that is informed. And in order for it to be informed, there's this unspoken obligation to consume the images, to watch the videos. It's easy to forget that activists are affected too."[27] This exemplifies Hochschild's concept of emotional labor, which involves performing and managing emotions related to a job, often at one's expense.[28] In an attempt to ameliorate the burden of this work, intellectuals assert feeling rules but still become entangled in the work of managing these emotions.

Slate reporters Aisha Harris and Jamelle Bouie joined sociology professor Tressie McMillan Cottom and the co-host of a prominent NPR podcast on race and identity, Gene Demby, in a discussion of a pattern of White progressives going to people of color to be educated on racial issues and the ensuing emotional burden this put on Black people.[29] As prominent voices on mass and social media outlets, they were particularly interested in the expectation that White allies placed on them in virtual spaces. The conversation emerged from an encounter Demby had with a White woman Twitter follower who asked his opinion on a comic that she perceived as racially problematic. His response: "A request for a break from being y'alls racial confessor and being the Black person you've race-inflated into "friend" bc Twitter. Thx." Commenting on the situation, Demby shared, "That lady said, explicitly, that she wanted to talk about race, but she said she, as a White woman—her words—had to make sure she was safe." Each of the public figures recounted multiple incidents of self-identified White people contacting them through private message to get confirmation that they weren't racist. "Oh yes," agreed Cottom, "Black people have one primary job: to manage White people's emotions. Their emotions are high right now and we're being overtaxed with it." In the discussant's view, the major problem is that many White allies lacked consistent relationships with Black people, instead turning toward Black public figures who publicly speak and write about race to get answers. Cottom had commented just a few months earlier on her blog how she was navigating her emotional response to seeing protests for Keith Lamont Scott in her North Carolina hometown: "I am only giving myself permission to *think* about Charlotte in public, not feel. Feeling is for private."[30] In attempts to manage the emotional demands cast upon her as a public intellectual, specifically by White people, Cottom set boundaries and crafted a personal Black-only space where she could feel and heal.

Echoing their frustration, the editor-in-chief of the website "Good Black News" wrote an editorial titled "What I said When My White Friend Asked for My Black Opinion on White Privilege."[31] In it she shares her recent response to being tagged in a Facebook post by an old high school friend—a White man. The classmate asked his Black and mixed-race Facebook friends to provide examples of institutional racism so he could better understand White privilege. In her response she expresses appreciation for his interests in learning and proceeds to list ten examples of institutional racism and how they illustrate White privilege (or the absence of it). While her lengthy response suggests her willingness to educate despite their distant relationship, she ends her list with "there's more but I'm exhausted. And my kids need dinner. Remembering and reliving many of these moments has been a strain and a drain (and again, this ain't even the half or the worst of it)."

Their stories illustrate how Black intellectuals' articulation and interpretation of news and culture becomes an educational and instructive resource for White people defining allyship and even figuring out how to think and feel. Black intellectuals in effect become sense-makers, frame-setters and create the feeling rules for White allies. Twitter became a surrogate for a personal relationship such that followers, with no other social connection, initiated intimate communication with these figures. The examples shared by the *Slate*-led panel included receiving personal emails about biracial children, relationships to Black people and former Black nannies. Black intellectuals are thus burdened with navigating this assumed access and entitlement to emotional validation and providing additional labor beyond the writing and other knowledge production they were already doing. In particular, writers and journalists who have chosen to take up the task of representation as agents of carrier groups become tasked with an emotional labor that is distinct from the emotional labor that activists intentionally engage in to further solidarities. Here, emotion work falls not along the needs of the movement for mobilizing participants but is the work of cultural trauma. This labor is tied to delineating and protecting the narrative of the social injury, particularly in the defining of the nature of pain and identifying whose pain it is. When Black intellectuals publicly choose not to engage with White allies, they are invalidating and shutting down White access to the emotional resources they need to continue their activist work.

An alternative approach to managing White emotions was taken by Safety Pin Box, a business started by Black women activists Marissa Johnson and Leslie Mac. The business was launched after Trump's election when, people in the United States—inspired by a similar movement following Brexit—began adorning themselves with safety pins to identify themselves as allies with the racial groups the president elect had maligned.[32] However, Black women, among others, expressed public critique of this idea, claiming that the symbolism felt appallingly short of any sort of productive action that posed a challenge to Trump or advanced social change. The business was a box subscription service with tools for White allies to move from guilt to actionable steps toward Black liberation. On its origin Johnson said, "We want Black women to be paid for their labor and have ways to educate and do justice work that are less traumatic than what we are often subjected to."[33] On their website, Safety Pin Box asserted, "Ally work is a privilege and not a right. No White people are entitled to Black revolutionary efforts of Black spaces. Ever." A quarter of proceeds from the business were represented as reparations and used to sustain Black women engaged in activist work. As an answer to the frequently posed question of why the organization only supported Black women, they wrote on their website: "Often Black people, and especially Black women/femmes are expected to labor for everyone but themselves. Safety Pin Box is an act of radical collective self-preservation and we openly declare we are #NotYourMule."

By commodifying their emotional labor, Johnson and Mac render visible the emotional labor demanded of Black activists by White allies. They challenge White emotional entitlement by articulating and utilizing emotion as a resource for Black liberation. In this way, White guilt is moved from performance to productivity by Black movement actors, as is Black women's emotional labor for allies. Emotions are expressed as part of identity work and are further solidified within a social structure of racial hierarchy. By labeling this work as emotional labor, intellectuals also validate their position and value to the movement, as emotions are publicly managed toward protecting narratives of social pain. However, this symbolic boundary work is demanding. How then are the emotional demands of cultural trauma sustainable?

Emotional Repair

MJ could not sleep as they struggled to process the community response to Freddie Gray's death. "I was frozen in hopelessness, despair, rage, and numbness. Like many other Black folks, I'd felt these emotions a hundred times before . . ." After describing finding comfort in their lover's arms, MJ continues,

> I felt such an overwhelming warmth of love and presence that I felt like crying all over again. I knew this feeling before, too, as many Black folks have: validation, openness, love, care. I have felt it when my auntie lifts up my chin and tells me to be proud, stand up straight; when I dream of my ancestors who prayed for their children and grandchildren; when I see our people creating new ways to survive and thrive; when we create our own families and open our homes to folks in need. . . . we mustn't overlook is that we know what ails us, and when we come together, we create tools that heal us. We are some of our most powerful reminders that our lives do matter, do hold value and worth and complexity and beauty. We have incredible power to heal and love ourselves even when society refuses to.[34]

MJ's narrative points to how movement actors were affected by the demands of the trauma process. Throughout my research I observed and experienced Black people working to create tools for healing, rather than waiting on criminal justice reform.

There was a recognition across Movement for Black Lives groups that organizing around anti-Blackness had deleterious emotional impacts on its members. Alongside spiritual healers and professional mental health workers, lay healers emerged as a key resource in the movement as leaders engaged healing practices as part of sustaining the movement. Wellness spaces were created around the country for Black people to process their emotions amidst the proliferating images of Black death by police. In the summer of 2015 I participated in one of these spaces organized by BLM DC called "Emotional Emancipation Wednesdays." It was a Black-only space guided by a curriculum developed by the Association of Black Psychologists. The curriculum, rooted in the legacy of Harriet Tubman as a freedom fighter, was designed to enable Black folks to find freedom through emotional healing. The facilitator created a supportive space that enabled participants to build emotional solidarities and create strategies to experience "emotional freedom" within and beyond the space. An opening prompt was based on a poem by Lucille Clifton, "everyday something tried to kill me and has failed." She would ask the group, *What tried to take you out this week but didn't?* At the close of the evening, attendees were offered cleansing sprays of water mixed with essential oils.

Healing was engaged not only for internal activities, but also woven into public movement activities through rituals. At a People's Assembly in Baltimore, a woman poured out libations as we collectively repeated names of the slain in remembrance. In the basement of the MLK Library in downtown Washington, DC, we sang of Black women freedom fighters to uplift spirits and encourage continual movement forward. In a DC park, as we chanted names of the dead, balloons were released in mourning. A collective healing event led by a coalition of racial justice groups started off with collective breathwork exercises and centering movements; massages were offered to attendees as well. I participated in a nationwide altar building for Black women and girls who died as a consequence of police/state violence. The Washington, DC, Event was advertised on Facebook and attendees were invited to bring items to build the altar such as lavender oil, cloth, and candles. Once the altar was built, we stood in a circle and space was given for attendees to mourn, reflect, and vent their emotions. There was a range of emotions, from rage to sadness to admonishment: we've been here before and we'll make it through. Following the event, the national coordinator provided an online resource for altar-building so attendees could make altars in their own homes.

While MJ speaks to emotional resilience and healing repair techniques rooted in ancestral struggle, Terrion L. Williamson identifies another resource in Black social life: "Black social life is, fundamentally, the register of Black experience that is not reducible to the terror that calls it into existence but is the rich remainder, the multifaceted artifact of Black communal resistance and resilience that is expressed in Black idioms, cultural forms, traditions, and ways of being."[35] Cultivating joy through Black sociality for emotional repair was another key strategy for sustaining movement activism. BYP100 published a love letter to Black people released the week after Trump's inauguration, writing, "Cultivating Black joy will be instrumental to developing the resilience needed to fight another day."[36] In the advertisement for the weekly #BlackJoySunday gatherings, BLM DC wrote:

> Black Joy is a transformative force. It is a visceral, deeply embodied reminder of the precious euphoria of our humanity. It is the source of Black resilience which is itself the wellspring of Black Liberation. #BlackJoySundays are a supportive place we can be

> affirmed in our Blackness, fellowship with other gorgeous Black people and discuss some of the racial stress we experience. Please bring your love, and your pain and, yes, your anger.

Rooted in the history of Black prison resistance, Black August events were organized for Black people to gather around food, culture, and political education and to support Black businesses. Often these spaces were Black-only or preferential, such as a holiday party where only non-Black attendees were charged an entrance fee. Crafting emotional spaces based in Black sociality created opportunities to process emotions, build emotional resiliency, and solidify collective identity.

Both BLM and BYP100 created healing arms within their organization. In a toolkit released by the Healing Justice Working Group of Black Lives Matter, the authors write (original emphasis):

> *Organizing against violence and for Black liberation can consciously or unconsciously trigger us to relive unhealed experiences in which we, our ancestors and our communities have been oppressed and violated.* That revisited pain becomes the anger that motivates us into action. Yet, sourcing our wounds and trauma in this way takes a hefty toll.[37]

In the kit they offer a definition of *healing justice* as analysis of resilience and trauma, posing two foundational questions: "How do we scaffold and support our well-being through direct action and confrontation?" and "How do we begin to draw energy from naming and sourcing our visions more often than our wounds?" They argue that healing justice is critical to their work, asserting "Black Healing and Wellness are essential to our Liberation" and "Black Wellness is Self-Determination."

If the direction of cultural trauma is toward social repair and restitution within a context where power lies in oppressive and ambivalent institutions, then emotional repair becomes a way for carrier groups to sustain the emotion work and emotional labor involved in the difficult work of claims-making. The focus on healing as part of movement strategy widens the conceptualization of the social repair of cultural trauma as one based in the victim-oppressor relationship to one located in the carrier group. The tear in social fabric is conceived here of having traumatic effects that go beyond claims to the State. There is a recognition that the psychic harm caused by the social injury cannot be healed by those responsible, and even a rejection of their involvement. Rather than building adaptive coping strategies, the emotion work here is aimed at cultivating resiliency and emotional healing that is situated in collective identity as participants are freed to process their emotions away from White interpretations and contestations. Still, these emotional repair spaces afford limited protection from the demands of White allies, particularly given their role in extending trauma claims to the broader public. It is unclear if the repair work can keep up with the emotional demands of cultural trauma when the trauma narrative is in jeopardy.

Conclusion

After Donald Trump's election, the country seemed to reel. While in the car the day after the election, I heard a speaker on an NPR radio show suggest that Trump's election was the most traumatic thing the nation had experienced since 9/11. This was particularly acute among longtime Hillary Clinton–supporting White women, which some called the "Pant Suit Nation," who had expected to see Clinton elected. On social media they posted videos of them crying, expressed their disbelief, and some even claimed being traumatized by the unexpected outcome. Many liberals began work to shift from emotional response to organizing. Facebook pages popped up with plans to appeal to the electoral college or try other ways to prevent Trump's inauguration. Indeed, what would follow in the coming weeks and month demonstrated that his election was an arresting moment for the nation. White nationalists and sympathizers were energized by his election, tagging property with symbols, claiming their nation was back in their hands. Hate crimes were reported in the news. This was a victory in their eyes. But for the rest of this nation, was this really trauma?

While certainly people of color on social media expressed dismay and frustration, there was less surprise that this could happen in America—this was not a social injury that tore at their collective identity. "Saturday Night Live" captured the disbelief in a sketch featuring the Black comedians Chris Rock and Dave Chapelle at an election watch party with White members of the comedy show acting as the other attendees. While the latter exclaimed shock and had mental breakdowns after Clinton's loss is announced, Rock and Chapelle trade mirthful insider looks, not surprised at all by Trump's win. As is captured in the SNL skit, for White liberals, some of whom had been sympathetic toward Black claims of police violence, the election of Trump came to represent their own sort of assault and trauma. Black people looked on askance, troubled but not surprised. Meanwhile, sympathetic White allies attention shifted from what it meant to support Black folks and people of color to what to do about their nation.

Within days after Trump's election, a White woman in Hawaii decided to organize a Million Women's March in Washington, DC, to protest his presidency and the misogyny that characterized his campaign. She was initially joined by another White woman, but then women of color launched critiques of the lack of diversity on the planning committee and that the pair were co-opting the work of Black women in the 1990s who organized a march with the same name. The organizers thus decided to diversify the planning committee and change the name. With the new name of "The Women's March," three women of color emerged as key organizers: Linda Lasour, Tamika Gregory, and Carmen Mendoza. In solidarity, sister marches were organized in cities around the nation and around the world, from Iceland to Iran.

Still, many women remained critical of the march, particularly Black women. This critique was launched with reminders that the majority of White women had voted for Trump, as opposed to the vast majority of Black women who voted for Clinton. Black women expressed exhaustion and disinterest, if not dismissal of the march. Some Facebook discussions emerged as arenas for conversations about privilege, with women of color telling White women to "check their privilege." Despite the fact that, as a colleague put it, "Not all pussies are pink and not all women have pussies," the pink pussy hat became the emblem of the march adorning the heads of thousands of women during the march. While excitement grew as the march approached, so did critique from women of color and anger from White women who felt unfairly judged.

The rising tension was not only about representation, but about also the contesting narratives of social injury. Below is a series of tweets by the writer Ijeoma Oluo, capturing the expressed feelings of many Black women I observed during my research.

> I'm really, really tired. But for all you Black and brown women out there who are also tired.
>
> For all my Black and brown women who can't help but look at crowds of millions of women and wonder, "Where were you when our babies were being shot in the streets, locked away

> in prison, deported away from the only home they've known?"
>
> For all my Black and brown women who can't help but imagine how many of their brothers and sisters and sons and daughters and husbands and partners could have been saved if our oppression and our murder could have inspired 1/10th this level of action and care.
>
> For all of my Black and brown women who cried today for all the opportunity lost, for all the people we lost waiting, fighting, crying, screaming begging for somebody to help.
>
> I hear you. And I am with you. And this isn't okay. What has been allowed to happen to us. It has never been okay. And what you are feeling right now is valid and true.
>
> @IjeomaOluo, 1/21/17

For Black activist women engaged and invested in the Movement for Black Lives there was deep frustration to see this immediate mass mobilization of women, many of whom claimed to be allies. Many chose not to go to the march for this reason. A picture from the march that captured the raced emotion division would soon be widely shared on social network sites to the satisfaction of its critics. In it, a Black woman clad in a white cap reading "Stop Killing Black People" holds up a sign that reads "White Women Voted for Trump."

Following the march, I saw continued criticism by Black women online, along with comments about the ways police treat White women bodies differently than Black bodies evidenced by the lack of arrests. As if to prove their point, I saw several pictures on The Women's March mobile app of women posed with police officers captioned with "Thank you!" In an effort to redirect expressions of exhaustion and frustration, BLM founding activist Alicia Garza and scholar activist Keeanga-Yamahtta Taylor each published op-eds urging that such critique was better directed to building solidarities and productive action to continue mobilization. But the threat was not just a new narrative of trauma, it was also that the new president was hostile toward #BlackLivesMatter discourse. Despite the criticism of President Obama not doing enough for the movement, he acknowledged a relationship between Blackness and police violence; President Trump ran on a platform of more law and order.

It is evident across this chapter that the emotional tension manifested most in between White and Black women. This is particularly clear in the interactions of the Women's March. These are not new tensions; since the Suffrage Movement, Black and white women activists have experienced conflict along different analyses of oppression and commitments to equality and liberation. This is also not surprising given the emotional work that women contribute to social movements and progressive causes. The repeated emotional entanglement of Black and white women points to the role of allies' cognitive and emotional validation of trauma claims in the spiral of signification from event to representation as cultural trauma. Black activists describe this entanglement as exhausting and laborious, which points us to an overlooked aspect of cultural trauma: the emotional demands on marginalized groups engaged in claims-making regarding dominant institutions and culture. As has been illustrated thus far, the process of representing an injury as traumatic is accompanied by extensive collective emotion work that serves to validate trauma claims, but also comes with emotional demands. Emotional condensation is achieved through the construction of a meaningful and resonate narrative around the trauma being experienced by Black people. In the emotional tension produced through the trauma claims of activists multiplied through retweets, users engage in emotional management to assert and protect the narratives, setting rules about what the emotional response should be, the form and function of emerging solidarities, and what sort of action it should ignite. Through this management, activists seek to draw boundaries—Whose trauma is this? Whose and which emotions are valid?

An analysis based on cultural trauma points to the issues of social tearing and social repair, but the emotional content of trauma claims points to other dimensions of the collectivization of trauma. Collective memory and identity are experienced through emotion. Trauma is defined through claims made to the state as emotional identities are formed through narratives of trauma that assert "this is happening to us, we have a right to be upset and sad, and here are those who are at fault for our physical and psychic struggle." Material and symbolic boundaries are issued to cultivate emotional resources for activist work. Maintaining symbolic boundaries require its own sort of emotional labor. Even as social media allows an opening for individuals to express their emotions, the use of it to achieve movement ends poses difficulty for movement intellectuals engaged in emotion-laded claim-making in contentious virtual spaces. Yet it remains that this emotional labor is integral to the work of crafting persuasive narratives of social injury—of defining discrete events as part of something larger and resisting the systemic oppression that perpetuates the trauma.

Chapter 4

Hoodrat Praxis in a Time of Love and Fury

YOMAIRA C. FIGUEROA-VÁSQUEZ AND
JESSICA MARIE JOHNSON

Vanessa

> Tell them that even though she called the police a few times when he hit her, she would [later] drop the charges. [We] could not use [that evidence] in court. He got away with murder.
>
> —Carmen Otero

Vanessa Otero, twenty-one, oldest daughter, second of four children, generous, brilliant, beautiful, funny, serious, diligent, shy, cariñosa. Vanessa was a first-generation college student majoring in psychology at Jersey City State University and working part time. She was mourning the recent loss of her father and was newlywed and living with her husband of two years above the laundromat owned by his parents in our tiny square-mile town right outside of lower Manhattan. Vanessa was just twenty-one when she was killed in October of 1997. In the early hours of the morning, a bullet from a sawed-off shotgun wielded by her husband Jose Mendoza pierced the right side of her forehead. At her wake, Vanessa's casket was positioned so that the left side of her body faced the mourners because the stitching on the fatal wound could not be hidden. There, in an ivory casket with gold accents, lay beloved Vanessa. Her warmth eviscerated, her waist-length cascade of black curls shorn to the neck—a necessary cut, we were told, in the failed efforts to save her life.

The night of her murder, Vanessa's husband Jose had returned to the couple's apartment intoxicated from a DJ gig ready to fight. Knocky, his best friend, would tell us later that Jose had planned the murder in one of his drunken rages. "I'm going to kill her tonight," he'd said while they unloaded his equipment from the car and brought it up the long two flights of stairs to the apartment where Vanessa had been sleeping. Knocky, the only one to hear these words, precursors to the events minutes later, lied on the witness stand and denied the confession he had made to the family just hours after the murder. "Jose loved her," he said with tears in his eyes on the stand. This is a refusal to bear witness. Knocky, who most likely greeted Vanessa on the stairs when she awoke to help bring up crates of records and equipment, didn't even glance up to the left side of the courtroom during his testimony. I imagine those moments, the sleepy greeting at the stairs, the crates of house music passing hands, the farewell with no warning, and the bullet that severed the lives of our family for generations to come. Jose was not found guilty of first- or second-degree murder but, rather, involuntary manslaughter. He served six years. This is a refusal to bear witness.

Vanessa's death is a haunting that follows the family. In every home, she is present, held static in photos from her high school graduation, from her wedding, and looking longingly from amid her siblings and cousins. Every few years I search online for Vanessa, committed to finding proof of her life beyond our photos and memories. I look for news stories, scour the obituaries placed in the local papers, and search for articles reporting the murder and trial. Each time I come up empty-handed. The internet refuses to bear witness. There are nights that I obsessively click page after page, but the internet it seems, has scrubbed clean what I remember very clearly: being woken up by Mami incredulously whispering, "mataron a Vanessa" and then walking the seven blocks by moon-and-street light to the laundromat. There, in the building where she had been killed, we waited for answers, unable to walk the next two blocks to the hospital. I remember, too, my father, unmoored by the loss of his niece, his suffering only an echo of her mother's and siblings' pain. I most vividly remember the line for Vanessa's wake, a serpent of mourners wrapping around the block on Washington Street. I can still see our family, tangled in every aisle and corner of the funeral home, inconsolable for all the accompaniment in grief. I remember the reporters and cameras and lights, and the newspapers with photos and the stories about the girl who was so loved that people stood for hours in the rain waiting to pay their respects or waiting to peer dolefully into the floating about-face casket.

Vanessa was buried on a bright and beautiful morning in October. It was my middle-school picture day, and my only proof of this fact is a rueful eighth-grade graduation photo taken after returning from the cemetery. In it, I sport red swollen eyes and a grief I still carry in my heart. I can recall that my cousin Taina, Vanessa's only sister, wore brown earth tones she told me quietly; and know now that Taina would never be the same. Later that afternoon, my best friend Dana took me to get a slice of pizza. There at the pizza shop directly across the street from the funeral home from which we had processioned that morning, two men joked about how the girl who got killed "probably deserved it"—maybe she "cheated," they chuckled as they tossed our slices into the metal ovens. Without skipping a beat, we—two thirteen-year-old hoodrats—let loose wild tongues in defense of the dead. At thirteen years old we recognized that the murder of a woman could be justified because masculinity is sacred. Not even dead women were spared dismissal, but we would not submit to those who refuse to bear witness.

I asked my aunt Carmen for permission to write about Vanessa. She wants you to know that Vanessa called the police on multiple occasions. Jose had a history of physical and emotional abuse, and of threatening whomever she would confide in about her terror. The National Coalition Against Domestic Violence reports that one in four women experience severe intimate partner violence in the United States, and that the presence of firearms in situations of domestic violence increase the potential for homicide by 500 percent.[1] Black women, girls, transwomen, and nonbinary people are made especially vulnerable to intimate partner violence and are killed at higher rates than any other group.[2] My aunt Carmen wants me to tell you that her daughter Vanessa dropped the charges against Jose every single time, and that those reports couldn't be used in court as evidence of his pattern of abuse. We know that her in-laws, the Mendoza's, knew more than anyone else because they heard the fighting, saw the bruises, negotiated with the police, and pleaded for Jose to stop. Jose's parents and sister advised Vanessa to leave him, to move back with her mother, to flee, but when the time came, they too lied on the stand. This is a refusal to bear witness.

There were so many possible witnesses to this violence against Vanessa. We know that there is more to Vanessa's life than what the official transcripts and court documents could ever tell us. The lack of documents, footage, and the void of the archive bears no indictment on her value. We who hold the memory of her were not there on the night of October 25, but we are faithful witnesses to Vanessa's life. She was a Black Puerto Rican woman caught in the matrices of domestic violence, the sociopolitical structures that uphold and protect perpetrators of abuse and the institutions that disproportionally harm women and femmes.

It has been twenty years since Vanessa. I search and cannot find her except here, in my love and fury.

Witness

> "The avoidable tragedies of Baton Rouge, Louisiana, and Falcon Heights, Minnesota—and other places we don't happen to have camera phone footage of."
>
> —*New York* magazine, July 10, 2016.
> Approval matrix: Highbrow/Despicable

When I heard the news of the murders of Alton Sterling and Philando Castile I was thousands of miles away from Baton Rouge and Falcon Heights.[3] The distance afforded by my work in Europe in the summer of 2016 removed me from the immediacy of the mourning, the vigils, protests, the reeling punctuated by love and fear and fury. I witnessed this tumult of feeling from afar, trying to come to terms with how digital technology provided an ability to witness these deaths on social media sites in the form of automatic rolling videos and still photos. Horror on loop. A choral outpour. Perhaps a sigh of relief ("they can't deny it now"), for these images show what our communities have known to be true: Black lives are routinely and systematically snuffed out by state-sanctioned violence. And even as this footage showed so explicitly the violation of human life, many viewers engaged in acts of refusal. Instead of a technology that allowed for all viewers to bear witness to these murders, on too many occasions the video evidence was wielded against the dead over and again in op-eds, comments sections, and conservative media. And while I regularly dive into the chasm of the comments section, I never feed the trolls. I tell myself that this will steel my psyche against dehumanizing rhetoric, but instead it sends me into a furious panic, into inconsolable outrage.

Then on August 1: Korryn Gaines, a twenty-three-year-old mother, is murdered by police as she cradled her five-year-old son in her arms. Her child, the sole witness, was also shot by police. He survived.

Then on August 2: news outlets report the murder of twenty-three-year-old Joyce Quaweay, beaten to death by her husband and his best friend (now former police officers) in front of her two daughters, ages two years and ten months.

Then in September 2017: Jeannine Skinner, a thirty-five-year-old professor, is murdered in her home by her partner.

There is no footage for Korryn or Joyce or Jeannine or Vanessa. We stand alongside these strangers made sisters through an unthinkable kinship. We believe, like our elders of the Combahee River Collective, that "Black women are inherently valuable." For them we must make the choice to faithfully witness that which can never be seen. And we are well versed in this labor.

We stand at an intersection of state-sponsored and intimate violence.

Do we survive?

How do we witness faithfully at this intersection?[4] How do we witness beyond the snare of widely circulated footage? How do we bear witness to Black lives in the face of refusal and in instances where there is no evidence? How can our labor of witnessing faithfully leave evidence of the love and lives that have been stolen?

This Bridge

They practice on us first.

Yomaira is telling me about her book. She's writing something new, something we aren't likely to get tenure for. It is her story, her history of growing up with Puerto Rican parents, dark brown skin, and nappy hair in Jersey. She's telling me about dating black men who desire white mestiza women with olive complexions and straight dark hair. About dumping them or being dumped by them because when those men looked at her, kinky and black, white "Italian" women with straight dark hair and stick figures walked behind their eyelids.

"They practice on us, you see?" And as she says it I'm thinking about serial killers and desire. "Their best moves. They practice on us and then they move on."

"I've never heard practice used that way outside of sexual assault and rape contexts. You know? Like how activists talk about men practicing sexual violence on black women, women of color, because we are expendable. Because they can get away with it. Then move on to white women."

And she nods. "Exactly." There is no shrinking from me in her gaze—her face is tight. "Exactly." And somewhere under her skin is the trait we all share as women whose skin color gets described by flavor and taste—chocolate, caramel, almond, mocha—that tense trembling that is our fear that we won't be believed. When we say it. When we tell. When we explain. When we accuse.

Mentirosa. Lying bitch. Bitter. Busted. Bust down. Jealous. Negrita.

Wench

I am sitting across from my homegirl and we are discussing street harassment. We are out. We are celebrating the tenure and birthday of one of our own, we are eating fatty, delectable things for brunch, drinking wine and gin and coffee, black. We are live and lit and young and free.

"In Jamaica," she is saying, "they used to strip black women and whip them."

We are wearing our finest and flyest breakfast wear. Some of us have dangly earrings on. Some of us still have makeup on from last night when we danced into the evening and then laughed so loud in the hotel rooms that security was called on us. Too much black, black joy.

"This was a thing the abolitionists were fighting against. Because they used to strip black women naked and whip them." She speaks with her hands. "The problem was, slaveowners would go to court to defend themselves and they would say that the courts just didn't understand." I chew warm waffles and listen to her describe how slaveowners feared enslaved women's scathing retorts, how they would complain about the thoroughness with which black women would curse them out. How humiliating and emasculating they felt to be verbally exposed and accosted in the street. How cruel these black wenches were! So slaveowners had to whip black women. To force them to submit. As she explained, she laughed out loud at the legacy we inherited—the resistance practices of black diasporic women who talked back, whose verbal acrobatics were so acidic it pushed slaveholders to abject, physical, naked terrorizing just to keep the words from coming from their mouths.[5]

And also, what a vicious cycle. Enslaved women lacked shame, Earl Bathurst, the British colonial secretary, wrote after an 1824 rule banned flogging enslaved women in the colonies passed, because of how they are punished. As a result of slavery, black women had no shame, had lost their sex, their womanhood, were degraded. Men like Brathurst supported new laws against corporeal punishment because "making a distinction of treatment between the male and female slaves, cannot fail to raise this unfortunate class" and "restore to the female slaves that sense of shame which is at once the ornament and the protection of their sex." For Bathurst, and allies of the law, changing enslaved women's mode of punishment would return to enslaved women their shame and, thus, their womanhood to them.

What a thing! To be female and to be free and white is to be shamed, is to be like an open sore, uncovered, exposed, inviting irritation, violation, and pain.

But to be female and to be a slave, and to be a slave and therefore also black, is to be an open sore infected with willfulness, to be womanish with sharp tongues that require naked beatings.

> *"The first object" says our author "which attracted my compassion during a visit to a neighboring estate, was a beautiful Samboe girl of about eighteen, tied up by both arms to a tree, as naked as she came into the world, and lacerated in such a shocking manner by the whips of two negro-drivers, that she was from her neck to her ancles [*sic*] literally dyed over with blood."*

To restore black women's shame, abolitionists rang a bell that could not be unrung—black female pain and subjection, nude and exposed, filled eighteenth-century travelogues, sold well and often, and enslaved women engaged in a labor of pain, sex, and violence they could and did not consent to, could not and did not profit from. To emphasize the brutality of the whip, abolitionists fixated on corporeal punishment of enslaved women, on the terror and violation of being stripped naked, on the impact of the whip and the tearing of skin, on where the weight of the whip fell and the lacerations left behind. Their strategic condemnation mapped the stripes across the backs of enslaved women, but they didn't hear their screams. This is a refusal to bear witness.

> *It was after she had received two hundred lashes that I perceived her, with her head hanging downwards, a most affecting spectacle . . . Upon investigating the cause of this matchless brutality, I was credibly informed, that her only crime consisted in firmly refusing to submit to the loathsome embraces of her detestable executioner. Prompted by his jealousy and revenge, he called this the punishment of disobedience, and she was thus flead [flayed] alive . . .*

Abolitionists tied slavery to levels of unconscionable physical violence and subjection so complete there could be no moral recourse except abolition, but even they perceived nothing beyond "a most affecting spectacle." Even they understood punishment to be a result of jealousy and revenge, the twisted and decrepit love bred by colonialism's embraces, so they did nothing, said nothing on the stand, witnessed no womanhood beyond the gristle and meat of ungendered flesh. And, in the end, even they refused to stop the terror.

> *I endeavored to stop him, but in vain, he declaring the delay would not alter his determination, but make him take vengeance with double interest. Thus I had no other remedy but to return to my boat, and leave the detestable monster, like a beast of prey, to enjoy his bloody feast, till he was glutted.*

Witness

What do we call this labor of witnessing? A labor of love and fury. An ethics beyond the intimacies of coloniality. We call it a hoodrat praxis. It is a knowing of the value of Black femmes and Black lives. It is a working-class, working-poor, lived experience that teaches us to cut our eyes behind and above, to seek safe passage for our kin, our sisters, and our community, and the kind of furious loyalty that puts us in harm's way.[6] In 2015, Jessica reached out to Yomaira concerned about Simone, a friend who had all but disappeared since entering into a relationship with a documented abuser.[7] Simone was Yomaira's neighbor, and when Jessica, who lived hundreds of miles away, called at about 11 pm to share her concern for Simone, Yomaira marched down the hall to check on Simone. Faced with an abusive partner who would not let Simone speak to her friends, Yomaira put herself in danger and demanded to speak to Simone, to put eyes on her, to bear witness to her living, to look for evidence of abuse, isolation, or domination. After this event, Jessica and Yomaira discussed the actions of that night as a hoodrat praxis: a reckless and purposeful quest to secure the welfare of kin and community. This is not unlike the practices undertaken in the streets of cities and neighborhoods across the world. Femmes cutting across lines, time, space, and possibility to seek out the safety, justice, and liberation of their own. Hoodrat praxis is a politics fueled by diasporic and classed lived experiences, by misogyny and matrilineal consciousness, by fear and love.

Recently, we have been writing about Afro-Latinx and Caribbean decolonial feminist thought, histories of slavery from the perspective of

Black diasporic women, and Black feminist and women of color feminisms. Figueroa argues that what can fuel us toward radical relational decolonial praxis is "love and fury."[8] That is, a love of one another across difference, a decolonial love steeped in differential consciousness that strives toward myriad forms of liberation, and a fury ignited by the living realities of coloniality (gender, power, being, knowledge).[9] Johnson argues that Black diasporic women have spent centuries cultivating an insurgent, femme-loving, audacious practice of freedom whose roots lie in creative and defiant resistance to their own enslavement. In the end, across time and space, what unites our praxis, and the praxis of our forefemmes, is a refusal to submit, our determination to see the parts for the whole, and our belligerent fight for our kin. This is a hoodrat praxis.

In the face of state and intimate violence we are told that the "smoking gun" evidence of brutality, of surrender met with mercilessness, can induce sympathy from the viewing and purportedly believing public. That in some imaginations these acts of savagery caught on tape will lead to more "reasonable" uses of force, and if we are lucky more body cameras to roll footage. But we have been this before; we have been told this since the eighteenth century. We have been told this since 1566, when the *Santiago* carried seventy-seven captive African women and children to Puerto Rico. We have been told this since 1444, when the first cargo of 235 enslaved African women, children, and men landed in Portugal.[10] So we know that even seeing is not believing when privilege and power (re)write and refuse the scripts, when we depend on affect numbed by coloniality for our own freedom.

We are she on the corner or in the cabins or on the ship who already believed. We believed before the ubiquitous video. We remember the evidence that never made it to trial, we read against the attempts to shame us into silence (or womanhood), the violations large and small that rendered us expendable to the state. We have been "faithful witnesses" without having to see.[11]

We know the value of our lives and theirs over and against the faulty litmus tests of doubted digital footage, refusals to bear witness, and incomplete archives. We ride our love and fury and refuse silence, obscurity, denial, and death. We choose to see.

Delete

Vanessa's life and death are scrubbed from the internet—there is no trace of her there. Most of these women will become footnotes, echoes, ghosts in the endless archive of the web. We won't know who they would be now, but alive. But we can imagine that they'd be more radiant and loving versions themselves.

Joyce

> [Joyce] Quaweay's boyfriend, and the father of her two children, beat her to death with his fists and baton after stripping her naked and handcuffing her to a bench. Marquis Robinson, 41, Wright's best friend, restrained Quaweay and moved her body so that Wright could beat her . . . while Quaweay's two daughters with Wright, aged two years and ten months, watched nearby.
>
> —Philly.com News Report, August 2, 2016[12]

I lay in bed with my lover and wonder about a woman named Joyce Quaweay. A woman in love. Who may have thought it to herself that evening—as he beat her with his fists and a police baton, as he let his best friend lay his hands on her body, twist her to make her more accessible to his blows—"I thought he loved me." This man she shared domestic and intimate space with. Who may have felt sad or guilty or tired, under the fear. Who, as she slipped away, may have felt heavy with what should have been.

She should have been happy ever after.

She had two daughters. They will never grow up and not see their mother naked and beaten to death and beaten in death by two men who were supposed to love her (these men who murdered her will be charged with, among other things, abuse of a corpse because they would not stop), who she *thought* loved her. Her partner and his best friend—she didn't know they were part of the secret fraternity of men who kill together, of black men who beat women who will not submit. They did not stop beating her naked body until after she was dead.

I want to unleash an archive of punishment, pain, terror, and grief on the page and in the world that will make her murder make sense, bring justice to her story, shake the rage out of black men who look away, and black women who, in our mutual terror, lay blame at her feet. If I could, I would do it. I would open a Pandora's box of fury and fire that would rip this world to shreds, build us anew, bring her back, wrench these memories from the minds of her daughters, break the curse.

But there is no way to write it. If only visualizing our pain worked that way. If only the archive held us and our stories that way. If only our deaths weren't so tasty, so easy and *important* for the empire to consume. Abolitionists knew. They knew and they stoked an appetite for black female flesh and death and they did so in the name of moral outrage, but I remain unconvinced that this strategy worked, that this is how we ended slave trades and slavery and got free. Something is broken because we remain a bloody feast for others to consume—we continue to be created out of the same recipe. And I find I am completely tired regardless of what I do.

. . . 2 parts dark and illicit beauty . . . 3 parts whipped naked . . .

Witness

If there was a recipe for black womanhood, according to abolitionists, if we read them between the lines, we might read it as such:

Black Womanhood: An Abolitionist Recipe

2 parts dark and illicit beauty
3 parts whipped naked
2 parts sexual use and labor on demand
1 part a thing to labor
1 part a thing to be saved
1 part a thing of disobedience that would not submit

Directions:

Shake, stir, burn, boil, pickle, beat, slice, or fry as the occasion demands. Good for state dinners or small families or building nations or reproducing empires.

When I try to write my way into the sound and words that will make a mother like Joyce live again, all I hear is, "This is what they did to slaves."

Joyce was not a symbol, and she was not theoretical. She was . . .

> *. . . a beautiful Samboe girl of about eighteen, tied up by both arms to a tree, as naked as she came into the world . . .*

. . . real. She was here with us. She was the same age as my youngest sister.

> *. . . and lacerated in such a shocking manner by the whips of two negro-drivers . . .*

I closed my laptop and thought I left the world of slaves behind. You left the archive and thought you left the world of slaves behind. I climbed into bed and lay my head on a warm shoulder; I woke up and made breakfast. You woke up and planned your syllabus, listened to a podcast, maybe went for a walk. We thought we left the world of slaves behind. We were wrong. Our curse is confounding the link between slavery and the ability of a man you love (a black man) to strip you naked and beat you to death because you would not submit. We have our histories of bondage ungendered and unsexed, and thus we have refused to bear witness to a history of gendered violence that we must be accountable to if we are to dismantle the New World. In the wake of this terror, the names of our dead become prophecy and result.

I am a wreck. There are no words for this, where we live. There is no time travel to explain this.

Femme

When we disappear, we mark time, we wait, hold vigil, sit at wakes. Partus sequitur ventrem begat black and feminine, then severed it from the body, reworked it as flesh, presence, and performance. Abolitionists couldn't advocate for, forgot there are infinite forms of woman, instead bound themselves to a false archetype of Woman. Slaveowners couldn't bear to imagine black womanhoods that exceeded productive reproductive acts. But invisible within an impossibility, impossible within invisibility, there have always been women whose glittering being shone like stars.

In the face of mass destruction, the black femme and the black and feminine—women all—cry out from the dark heart of themselves, claim love and kin. Skye Mockabee said "yes baby" when her lover texted her to make sure she was alright. She texted her mother from the future and told her "how much she loved her and appreciated her." She texted that the "two would always be together." Did she speak from the concrete? Did she text because there was blood in her mouth? Why are we always saying goodbye to stars?

Witchcraft

> She a hood witch bitch like ha ha ha ha haaaaa.
>
> —Nitty Scott, "Creature!"

We need new words for what we do, for how and why we stay, for the labor of making black love and black joy and black pleasure in a world of this. For laughing over coffee as the world burns down. For wrestling with these stories and words through a haze of grief that is witchcraft, that is a constellation of hope. We need hoodrat, ratchet, rutting, dutty, raunchy, raucous words that sound like sweat and spit and moans and sighs and transform these bodies from flesh to be tied and whipped naked (in front of our daughters) to things beloved.

#SayHerName Vanessa Otero
#SayHerName Korryn Gaines
#SayHerName Joyce Quaweay
#SayHerName Jeannine Skinner
#SayHerName Skye Mockabee

PART II

SHAPING COLLECTIVE PROTEST AND SPEECH THROUGH AFFECT AND EMOTION

Chapter 5

The Hoodie Stands Witness[1]

& Other Poems

LAUREN K. ALLEYNE

The Hoodie Stands Witness

for Trayvon Martin

I was built for bodies
like his, between boy and man,
sauntering in angles he couldn't hold
but swung his limbs from, careful
cool in every step.

I can tell you the story of him,
unexceptional—
he put change and candy
into my pockets, the necessary
jangle of keys and cellphone
hushed in the sock of me.

I watched him from the soft pile
he made of me on the floor
of his messy adolescent room

where I lay beside his sneakers
and backpack.
He did his homework
with chat windows open;
white headphones hooked
him into some steady beat.

That day, he was thinking
of nothing in particular.
He was quiet in his skin;
tucked into the shade of me,
he was an easy embrace
until an old ancestral fear
lay its white shadow
across us like an omen.

I can tell you his many hairs
raised in warning beneath me;
his armpits funked me up
with terror. His saunter slipped
into a child's unsteady totter
under the weight of a history
staggering behind him
mad with its own power.

He clung to me then, wholly
unmanned, a baby clutching
his blankey. He pulled me close
and I stroked his head, caressed
the napps he had brushed to waves
that morning. I felt him brace
his bones beneath me, his heart
a thousand beating drums.

The bullet ripped through us
like a bolt of metal lightning.
His blood, losing its purpose,
ran into me and I wished
we were truly a single body,
that I could have held

its rush and flow like a second,
sweaty skin. I can tell you
how his spirit slipped out—
like steam from cooling water
—slowly, fading by degrees,
until he stilled.

Poetry Workshop after the Verdict[2]

for the Trayvons

Morning lights your four windows,
and you wake. It is, already, another day.
You stumble, befuddled, into the bathroom,
so white it's like you're inside the moon.
You look in the mirror, then turn away;
better to just leave. Get your body out the door
and into the blue day. You follow the brown—
sparrow, maybe?—perched outside on the rail
like a guide. Bring everything already packed
inside your skin—a dead brown boy and his free killer,
his judge and jury of women, the six *not guilty* bells
clanging again and again in your weary ear.
No, that's your alarm; it's time to be a poet.
You bring your pen and notebook, your poet's eye.
You try to follow instructions: *Write what you see.*
It's simple. You walk down the road,
safe in your pack of poets—women, white.
(You do not write this in your notebook.)
Instead, your eyes find and follow the lines
that run everywhere—across the street,
up the railings, across windows and shutters,
siding, shingled rooftops—parsing the landscape
into cells. Your white journal pages, ruled.
You write down all the signs: *Closed;*
Peter's Property Management; Not for public use;
These dunes aren't made for walking; stop.
But you cannot stop. You follow the wind,
ripe with salt and already-sweaty bodies.

You see a pile of beached boats lumped
like bodies in a mass grave; a stone wall drowning
while sleepy dories drift by; sun-bleached
stumps, slowly going to rot; You see
the sun marking time as it slips higher
and higher, the day stretching overhead,
last night's dark already memory. You see
an American flag, and below it, the reddening back
of a white boy lying face down on the sand,
his body the opposite of a chalk outline. You write:
the light skitters brilliantly atop the bay's piercing
blue. You write: *A boy, his light hair lightening to gold,*
his body, so still, still breathing. You write: *Not guilty,*
Not guilty, Not guilty, Not guilty, Not guilty, Not guilty.

Elegy[3]

for Tamir Rice

This was going to be a curse poem—
me hexing the man who ghosted you,
slivering his days into two-second
increments of agony. I began writing
the playground you could make of his body,
surfing his blood, making monkey bars
of his ribs, dancing his heart's rhythm
on his neck—an inexhaustible mischief,
an incorrigible spirit of boy let loose
in the white country of the murderer's
unshielded body. I would wish him dead,
but I want him nowhere near the realm
he exiled you to, so instead I composed
a soundtrack for his nightmares, a mixtape
of your laugh/the gurgle of your blood
exiting the wound he gave you/a festival
of sirens/your sister's scream/bang/repeat.
This, I understand, is the grief talking.
This is the unchained melody of rage.
But to write his haunting is to name you

hell and you have been misnamed enough,
sweet boy. I make of these words an altar,
instead. I breathe this poem into a prayer,
each syllable a taper burning in memory
of you. Sweet boy, let me build you here
a new body, radiantly black, limber, poised
to become its most beautiful becoming.
Let it be spirited with starsong and rich
with tomorrows. Let me make you a lifetime of days honeyed with love: feast.
You are safe here. Let me write you
again into your name, Tamir, baptize
you with tongue and tears. Tamir. Tamir.
Let me write you a black boy's heaven,
where freedom is a verb conjugated
by your being, where your only synonym
is beloved, blessed, child of the universe.
Instead, I imagine you there, beginning.

Post-Verdict Renga[4]

for Trayvon

Provincetown, MA

Heat. Bodies gleaming with sweat and sun. Day pressing itself against everything: unforgiving. I am walking down this street thinking of another walk in another city, of a boy who never makes it home. I, too, am armed with thirst and a craving for sweetness; I, too, wear his brown skin and do not belong here, to this city of leisure and narrow streets. Fear passes through me, a phantom, and is gone. Overhead, flags flutter in the thick, salty air. *Not guilty*, they say. *Not guilty. Not guilty. Not guilty. Not guilty. Not guilty.*

Beginning is red—
a door, a car, the bowed lips,
a nameless flower.

*

I have so few names for things
here, I fall into silence.

Two men, black as God,
their shirts golden as morning.
No words between us.
*
So much passes in the glance
that the throat cannot muster.

Three headless torsos
in a store window. A light
trick makes men of them.
*
In this city of flesh, you
can almost forget the ghosts.

Fat daylilies crown
long green stalks, their orange heads
the color of grief.
*
No candlelight vigils here:
only the living, living.

He walks, oak brown, bald,
belly like a commandment—
I am here: make way
*
Nothing I say will save you,
but how can I say nothing?

Thick black curls cut close,
buttoned black shirt. Caramel face
diamonded with sweat.
*
a dark, ageless face
wise and innocent as earth—
how have you survived?

I can't stop counting
the bodies that look like yours:
five this whole morning.
*
I can't say if this matters,
just that I saw, I did see.

Heaven?[5]

for Sandra Annette Bland

Where does a black girl go
when her body is emptied
of her? And her wild voice,
where does it sing its story
when the knots of history
make a grave of her throat?
What of her future, blue-
broken, unmade? Her name,
—say it!—Sandra, unhoused;
her dreams and memories
lost to their source. Where
does a black girl's love go
when her heart is snapped
shut like a cell door, the key
out of reach as any justice?
And what gift is lost when
a black girl is made a body,
her light dimmed into shadow,
gone? How many angels weep
when a black girl is torn
into wings?

Chapter 6

I can't breathe

Visual Economies of Resistance

SIONA WILSON

Almost immediately after the cell phone video showing the death by illegal police chokehold of Eric Garner went viral, people began to walk around New York City (and elsewhere) with handwritten signs inscribed with his final words: "I can't breathe." Not just at protest marches but going about their business—on the way to and from work, out for an evening—black women and men wore this statement of ultimate bodily crisis against their bodies. It served as both a living memorial to the life, and a protest against the tragic, brutal death of Mr. Garner. While this phrase referenced his inhuman treatment on the video footage, it also served to overwrite this disturbing visual record with language, his words. This substitution of the images of state violence with the victim's words was also accompanied by another, bodily substitution. Living activists stood in place of the dead victim. With the deceased's final cry held against the bodies of the living, they served as an embodied form of witness to the injustice of his death. Mr. Garner's final words soon after traveled elsewhere and became a rallying cry in protests against other police shootings. For example, on August 9, 2014, when an unarmed eighteen-year-old African American teenager, Michael Brown, was shot in Fergusson, a suburb of St. Louis, Missouri, Mr. Garner's words appeared as part of the widely reported series of public protests that followed. Later in the year, "I can't breathe" became more than a reference to Mr. Garner's death, it served as a broader metaphor for the feelings of exasperation at the inability of the justice system to adequately respond to blatantly illegal police killings. The substitution of the visual footage with Mr. Garner's words became all the more significant when the cell phone footage showing his death failed to function as visual evidence. This reinforced a long-established pattern in the U.S. justice system in which visual evidence of violence against black men and women was routinely disregarded.[1]

I can't breathe was also the title of an exhibition that I curated at the gallery of the College of Staten, the City University of New York, in spring 2016. In re-performing this phrase as part of an exhibition, I sought to emphasize bodily vulnerability as a site for political agency. Although only one of the artist's works, Patricia Silva's *Mass Swell* (2016), directly referenced recent political events—it was a short film about the Fergusson protests—the exhibition also included a visual timeline of activism by Staten Islanders Against Racism and Police Brutality (SIARAPB). This group of students, faculty, and local Staten Island residents formed after the failure to indict Officer Daniel Panteleo in the death of Eric Garner in December 2014. The timeline was designed by a photography student, Charlie Tagel, and included a range of vernacular photographs from demonstrations and events donated by the group (see figure 6.1). The other works in the exhibition, by Nona

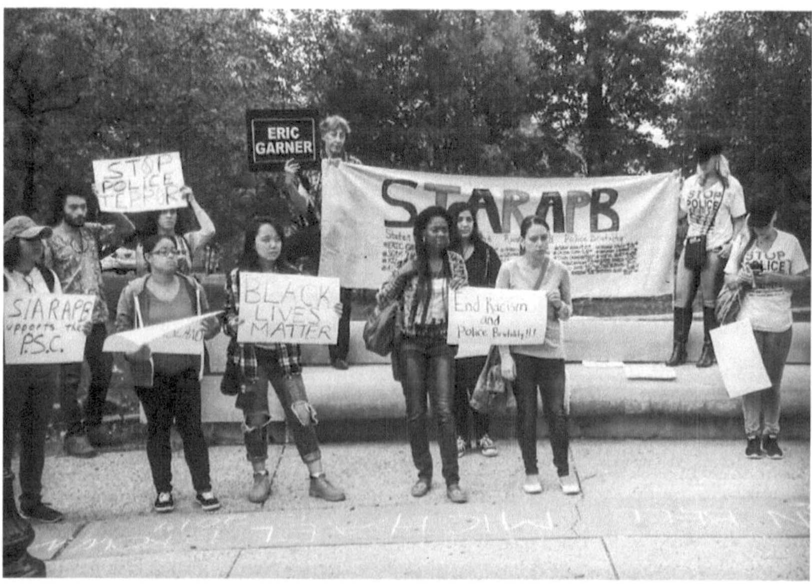

Figure 6.1. College of Staten Island. Detail of SIRAPB activist timeline from *I can't breathe*. Photo courtesy of Jay Arena and Danielle Yhap.

Faustine, Kara Walker, and Emma Wolukau-Wanambwa, focused on the black female body in states of public vulnerability and evoked longer histories of violence, but the whole exhibition was prefaced by this contemporary visual timeline of local activism. Together with the phrasal title, these affectively charged vernacular images reframed and offered a political anchor for the issues of gender, race, embodiment, visibility, and the circulation of images that were thematized in the exhibition as a whole.

My use of this exhibition title was partly a memorial to Eric Garner in the borough that he lived and died, and, like other uses of the phrase it was a metaphor for ongoing struggles. At the same time, my decision to emphasize the female body and the work of women artists was indebted to the movement #SayHerName, which began in 2015. While the majority of media attention had been focused on police violence against black men and boys, #SayHerName sought to highlight less widely known women victims and in doing so to draw attention to the particular issues that black women faced. Furthermore, the exhibition responded indirectly, in its gendered theme, to the powerful role women have played in positions of (often unacknowledged) leadership in the Black Lives Matter movement. For example, it was three women, who identify as queer, Alicia Garza, Opal Tometi, and Patrisse Cullors, who invented the widely disseminated hashtag in response to the acquittal of Trayvon Martin's killer, George Zimmerman, in 2013 in Florida.[2] Again, two queer women, Alexis Templeton and Brittany Ferrell, played a powerful role in the Fergusson protests and in the course fell in love and were married. These two women figure centrally in Silva's video *Mass Swell*. And finally, women leaders were also central to SIARAPB and took up a place of visual prominence in the timeline of images on display.

The exhibition activated different temporalities, different forms of embodiment, and very different affective states without providing a clearly drawn chart for how to bridge the links.[3] Images showing the furious energy of contemporary protest and its visual dissemination coexisted alongside quieter reflections on the legacy and visual history of America's formation as a slave-based capitalist democracy. Like the students shown in numerous contemporary protests, the historically-charged art works also emphasized embodied experience.[4] While this open-ended structure was intended to invite viewers to build their own connections, it also had unforeseen effects. As we drew close to going public, the conservative politics of the borough, its official political culture, began to play a more active—if invisible—influence. *I can't breathe* became subject to attempted censorship at many different levels of the College administration, and even via Facebook's algorithm. This was focused on Faustine's work in particular, or rather, the image by her—in conjunction with the phrasal title—that circulated to advertise the exhibition. My argument, necessarily speculative and anecdotal, will address these responses in light of the visual history of gendered racial violence in America. Although this will involve a close visual analysis of the particular image by Faustine, I am more interested in how this and other related images are understood as part of a "visual economy." Theorizing the workings of a visual economy means emphasizing images as mobile and shifting according to how they circulate within society and between differently embodied social actors, rather than the idea of images as fixed by an unchanging power differential between viewer and viewed.[5] I am thus interested in how images can be *active*, not simply at the point of their production, but also through their circulation, appraisal, interpretation, and re-evaluation.

Wall Street

A nude black woman with close cropped hair and a full figure stands precariously in white heels on a small wooden box in the middle of New York's Wall Street (see figure 6.2). This contemporary symbol of U.S. capital was

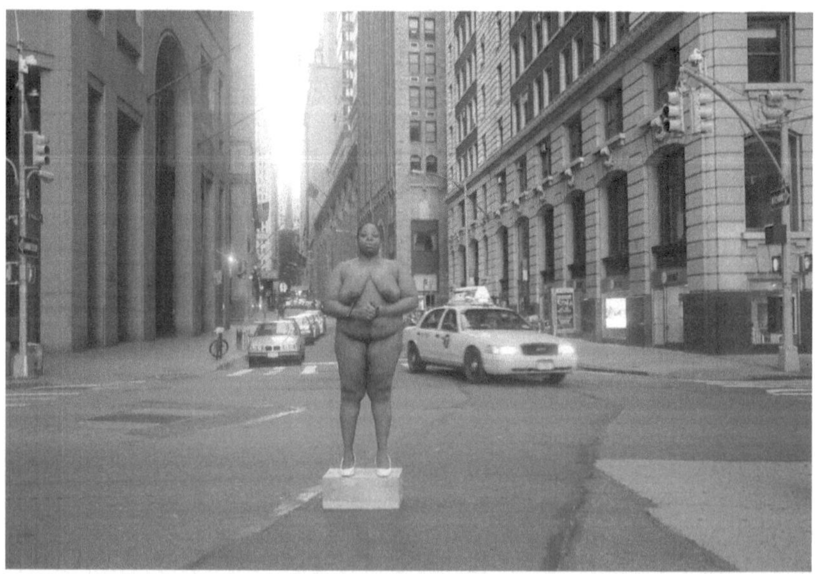

Figure 6.2. Nona Faustine, *From Her Body Sprang Their Greatest Wealth, Site of the Colonial Slave Market, Wall Street*, 2013. From *The White Shoes* series. C-print.

also the site of New York's colonial slave auction, the source of America's founding wealth. In the postcard I'm holding in my hand the figure looks small and fragile in the empty street. The manacles on her wrists are not immediately visible, and with the iconic yellow taxi cab rounding the corner, many viewers might take it for a surreal digital montage. But it isn't. This is not simply an image juxtaposition, but a performance for the camera. Traveling from her Brooklyn apartment in the early dawn with a friend to press the shutter and her sister for moral support, the artist's socially inscribed body is filled with historical ghosts.

When faced with the photograph in the space of the exhibition, its large-scale format changes our encounter. Statuesque and imposing, rather than small and vulnerable, our bodies meet her body. Ours protected by clothing, hers exposed. Our shape may echo hers, or it may not. But our encounter is now a different kind of embodied one than the casual handling of a postcard. We do not only read it semiotically, as a layering of signs to be understood in terms of historical and cultural codes, but also we meet her image, her exposure, walking in our own bodies. Before this encounter with Faustine's image we have scrutinized a series of small photographs showing collective groups of bodies protesting in public spaces. These approximately two-by-three inch photographs show a range of affective states: bodies animated by excitement and anger, bodies inanimate as they play dead in "die-in" protests, and bodies adopting gestures of happy camaraderie, posing with handmade signs. The small scale of these images demands that we come in close to see the faces and read the identifying information about time, place, and protest. The shift in scale and image quality on encountering Faustine's image means we step back and stand upright. The often animated, collective bodies of the activist timeline is replaced with a quiet, still, and solitary figure. If the memory of the protest images carries over into our engagement with Faustine's, this is further highlighted by an aural bleed from Silva's video *Mass Swell.*

The repetitive sound of a familiar call and response chant echoes around the gallery. An exhausted woman cries out, "who are we?" and receives the faithful response, "Mike Brown!" The call changes from the expected message of identification to a statement of love. Now more subdued and even more tired, the caller's declaration, "we love y'all," is met with the crowd's response, "we love you!" On reaching Silva's video *Mass Swell,* playing on a small handheld tablet mounted on the wall, we do not see the typical news footage that magnifies and isolates rare moments of violent skirmish. Instead it shows a coalition of black and white faith leaders together with a broad spectrum of protesters—male and female, black and white, gay and straight, old and young—aligned in nonviolent solidarity. The chants of love are addressed as much at the lines of armed police as they are to each other and the camera's point of view from amidst the protesters is intimate. Yet Silva did not shoot the footage in Missouri—she sourced it from her computer screen in New York City. *Mass Swell* shows us handheld footage made by protesters themselves that she filmed from materials live streamed directly over the internet. It thus draws on the very circuits of distribution that enable the dissemination of these activist images. And, at the same time, Silva's film was also a project of archiving lost footage, since the sites that the protesters were using to host these materials did not save or store the imagery. *Mass Swell* brings this visual material into another circuit of distribution—it takes the necessarily ephemeral footage and makes an activist film. At the same time, it is also a kind of fan film for the two women activists, Alexis Templeton and Brittany Ferrell, who, as their social media followers know all too well, fell in love during their involvement in the protests against the shooting of Michael Brown. While the film stages the coexistence of anger, love, and exhaustion in a complex way, the gaze from behind Silva's camera lens is also affectively charged.

Turning back toward Faustine's Wall Street scene it now seems to echo with the sounds of another recent protest. Occupy Wall Street was only blocks away in Zuccotti Park in 2011. Faustine's image mines Wall Street as a symbol of economic inequality for America's founding history as a slave-based economy. Likewise, the political mobilization of Black Lives Matter has surely taken part of its energy and important lessons in communication from the Occupy Movement.

Delia

The Wall Street photograph is part of Nona Faustine's series *The White Shoes*. In each image she is the model; her plus-size body performing a historical palimpsest of sex, race, and money. *The White Shoes* offers a map of New York's hidden history: from the Atlantic Coast in Brooklyn, where slave ships once landed, to a historic slave burial site in Chinatown, now a playground; she appears at another African burial site in Tribeca that has long ago been overbuilt, its history erased, to make way for the U.S. justice system. All of these locations are unmarked historic sites of New York's slave past. Faustine brings these places into historical visibility and animates them through her own socially inscribed body. The artist's nudity is an act of historical imagination and visual repetition. Her physical and emotional vulnerability is the source of the work's political strength. The nude figure occupies places where history has been reduced, as Katherine McKittrick has put it, to mathematics. "Historic blackness," McKittrick argues, "comes from: the list, the breathless numbers, the absolutely economic, the mathematics of the unliving."[6] Where race and gender meet, this work of cold reckoning becomes even louder. There are no existing autobiographical accounts of women who survived the middle passage, only bare statistics of the dead that makes for a potentially dangerous form of necromancy. The visual history is equally troubling. The illustrations of Sara (Saartjie) Baartman, the so-called Hottentot Venus, are surely echoed in Faustine's work, contained by her body, as a whisper that is lived by, embodied in Faustine's generous build.

The earliest photographic images of American slaves are of particular interest to Faustine. Delia (her dates are unknown) was photographed by a portrait photographer, J.T. Zealy, in 1850 at the instruction of the Swiss naturalist Louis Agassiz (see figure 6.3). We know a lot about Agassiz,

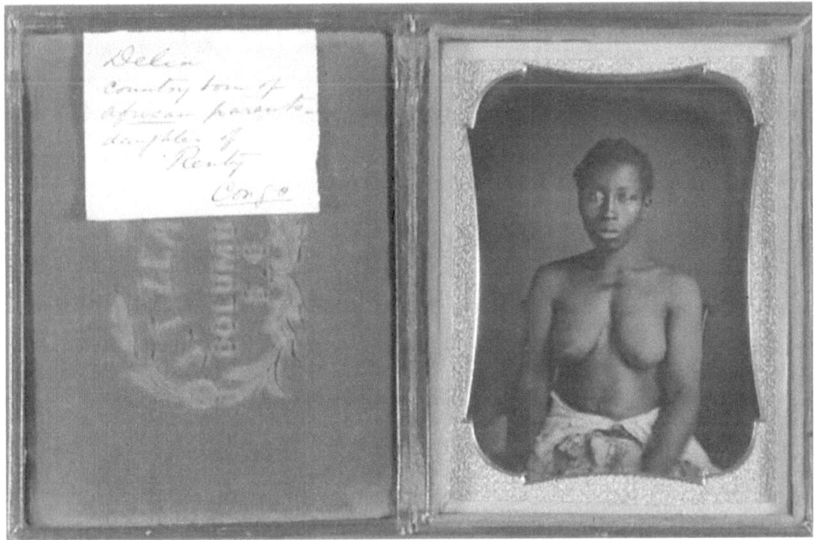

Figure 6.3. J. T. Zealy, *Delia* (c. 1850). Daguerreotype, leatherette, $4\frac{11}{16}$ in. × $3\frac{13}{16}$ in. × $\frac{13}{16}$ in. Commissioned by Louis Agassiz. Collection of the Peabody Museum, Harvard University.

the minutiae of his personal history, personality, scientific resume, fear of free American blacks, and the separate origins ideology that provoked the commission of this and the six other images.[7] All we know about Delia is her first name, her occupation (blacksmith's assistant), and the slightest of details of her defined solely as the property of a South Carolinian plantation owner, and then, as part of a legacy he passed on to his wife. This, and the other images taken by Zealy for Agassiz—two women, including Drana, five men, all identified by first name—were discovered at the Peabody collection at Harvard University, ironically, in 1976, the year of the bicentennial of American Independence. All the photographs are in pairs, showing front and side view shots from the waist up. Clothing has been removed or pulled down to reveal nude torsos, for men and women alike. In the photograph of Delia the top of her disrobed dress is still visible in the frame. It is an especially disturbing image because it so casually seems to evoke sexual violation.

To Agassiz, Delia was a scientific specimen and, even now, looking at this photograph is indelibly marked by this point of view. She appears as an object on display, but despite this the image speaks back, her presence emanates from the photograph. This image, like all photographs, contains more than the photographer or commissioner was able to control. Photography's excess, or "abundance," as Elizabeth Edwards has put it, is the source of its historical power. This abundance allows for "the recuperation of alternative historical narratives and voices embedded within."[8] In her attempt to see from a historical position, defined by a racist and sexist vision, and also to see differently, to read the photograph's excess, Molly Rogers has described her encounter with this image in the following terms:

> She was both "there" and "not there." Physically, she was fully exposed, every detail of her upper body on display and minutely recorded by the camera, but at the same time there was a complete lack of emotional presence in the picture, as if the woman had put on a mask to conceal her identity. Most unsettling were her eyes, which gazed out from the picture unflinchingly but were blurred in an otherwise sharp image, as if filled with tears. It was this combination of precision and ambiguity, presence and absence, that made the image utterly fascinating.[9]

Delia's Tears is the title of Rogers's book, part historical account of these images, part fictional imagining. She responds to the biographical gaps by drawing on slave narratives and other source materials. The failure of the historical record is both explicitly addressed and at the same time this absence is filled with the work of the literary imagination. She weaves new stories drawn from other slave narratives that reveal the violence of history's erasure. It is possible that Rogers may be seeing her own tears, rather than Delia's, when she looks at this daguerreotype, but this kind of affective looking, even if it risks sentimentality, is part of her redemptive, or reparative history of the images.

Carrie Mae Weems in the series *From here I saw what happened and I cried* (1995), was the first to offer, in artistic form, a strategy of affective address toward the Zealy images. These early daguerreotypes constitute four of the thirty-four found photographs of historic blackness that make up her image/text series. Weems's "appropriation" of this image, to use the artistic terminology of the time, is a pointed political act. The significance of her intervention might become clearer if we use a different term, now current in visual anthropology. *From here I saw* is a work of "visual repatriation," which involves both a political act of reclaiming these images and a form of historical work on them.[10] The artist repositions them in the present, in the mid-1990s America, in order, as Edwards has put it for another context, to "make sense of that past and make it fulfill the needs of the present."[11] How do viewers, differently embodied, both black and white, encounter such images that seem so blatantly to declare that black lives do not matter at all? And further, how do these historical images relate to contemporary events and the contemporary image world that so frequently reiterates this view?

From here I saw was produced and exhibited just three years after the Los Angeles uprisings in 1992 that responded to the acquittal of the police officers in the beating of Rodney King. This was a particularly significant case of failed visual evidence, since King's beating was caught on video by a local resident. Yet the defense successfully reframed the video, breaking it into individual stills in order to argue that the officers' were shown to be rightfully defending themselves. The fate of the cell phone footage showing Eric Garner's death by illegal police chokehold was understood by many to echo and repeat these West coast events from two decades earlier.

The timing is crucial to the decisions Weems made. All but two of the images from the series are cast in red, as if temporally suspended in the red light of a darkroom for all time. Weems's critical challenge to this visual history takes place through written statements and rhythmic poetry that is etched into the glass that covers the enlarged images. Her text rereads, contests, and addresses the images, their imagined viewers, and the subjects depicted, in language filled with emotion. Across the image of Delia she writes, "You became a scientific profile," across another from the Zealy series showing Renty, "A negroid type."

As Jennifer Doyle has described, Weems's work was the first in a series of commissions of contemporary artists' work by the J. Paul Getty Museum. Weems was invited to respond to an historical exhibition of American photographs drawn mainly from the private collection of Jackie Napoleon Wilson that spanned the invention of photography up until the end of slavery. A significant number of these images show African American subjects, both as background figures in plantation scenes as well as in other conventional (humanizing) everyday views such as suited up for respectable portrait photographs. According to Weems, the Peabody would not grant permission for her to use the Zealy images in her work. The institution in fact threatened to sue the artist if she went ahead with the project. Instead of pursuing legal action, they successfully reasserted their propriety and avoided the public debate that Weems was hoping would ensue by purchasing her series as well.[12] The ironies of this conflict over the rightful ownership of these images of slaves is of course precisely the critical intervention that Weems's work was making. And the additional irony involved in the institution buying *From here I saw* was not lost on the artist.

Doyle has suggested that we read Weems's work as a kind of exhaustive act of mourning. She links the contemporary context of the ineffectuality of the King tape with the historical violence of the Zealy images. Doyle concludes that "*From here I saw* might be read as indexing anger, frustration, and exhaustion, a depression by dint of routine: theft, exploitation, appropriation, resistance, grief, mourning, and recovery—followed by the requirement that the artist produce the cycle within her work."[13] While Doyle's description is apt, I would suggest that this response could be understood in light of Ranjana Khana's idea of "critical melancholia."[14] Melancholia is often asserted as the negative of mourning. It might follow the rituals of mourning, but it fails because the melancholic cannot let go. Khana suggests that if the lost object is not known, it cannot be assimilated. Critical melancholia is necessary under the hopelessly violent conditions of necropolitics. It registers political disenchantment and functions as a politics of resistance rather than one of reparation.

Faustine's echo of Delia and of Drana is more indirect than Weems's use of these images. Moreover, with the hope and passion of a new era of black political activism, it might be able to suggest the reparative possibility that Weems could not. In Faustine's work, these historical images—fraught with anxiety—are most vividly present in the bodily stillness and the frontality of the Wall Street photograph. The blankness of the facial expression and the poseless pose of ethnographic objectivity evoke a powerful visual history. This audacious act of historical imagination, like Weems's poetic language and Rogers's descriptive projection, acts as an imperfect counterpoint to the mathematics of the archive. Since, as Saidiya Hartman has put it, "The promiscuity of the archive begets a wide array of reading, but none that are capable of resuscitating the girl."[15] In assembling Delia, Drana, and even Sara Baartman to her own specifications, bringing them into her body, into relation with her body, she must surely be all too keenly aware that the new whole she has made from these fragmentary historical parts, is "*not necessarily like any pre-existing whole.*"[16]

Visual Interruptions

Faustine's Wall Street image was used on the postcard, poster, exhibition brochure, and other advertising materials for *I can't breathe*. When the image and title were ready to enter public circulation, I experienced a persistent, yet largely concealed attempt to censor the work by various offices in the college. Unanswered emails, unexplained delays, brick walls, rumor mills, pass the buck. Phone calls and no more written communication. Nothing in writing, please. The problems began in the college mailroom—with the resistance to circulating the image—and went to the highest office, with little consistency or clarity in the reasoning (when any was given). We got approval to actually advertise the exhibition on the college website only the day before the opening reception, after my department chair threatened that he would go to the *New York Times*. This has happened before; everyone knew he wasn't bluffing.[17] The contemporary reference in the title to racialized police violence only heightened the fear and anxiety Faustine's work produced. As one upper administrator informed me, by phone of course, in a classic instance of mansplaining, you know, with the exhibition title and her African American nudity, people—less educated people—might think this is a reference to slavery. Well they'd be right, began my exasperated response. He did end up apologizing, but others remained defensive, equivocal, and vague (and this is a generous reading).[18]

This smoke screen of elusive resistance even registered in social media in mathematical terms. After posting the invitation card along with the exhibition title on her Facebook page, Faustine was censored by Facebook's algorithm, her posting removed, and she was locked out from the site for twenty-four hours. Since she had posted the image several times before without any problem, we could only surmise it was because it occurred in conjunction with the phrasal title that the censorship arose. But why this happened remains unclear. The other New York–based artist, who was white, didn't have the same problem with her Facebook invitation.

Although the conflict was about the public circulation of the image, our situation at the college was never openly debated or widely known. But a very public debate about censorship and an image of historic U.S. Blackness emerged the following year in relation to a painting by a white artist, Dana Schutz, presented at the Whitney Biennial in spring 2017. It makes for an illuminating comparison on many levels. *Open Casket* (2016) by Schutz is based upon a published photograph of the brutalized body of Emmett Till, a Black teenager killed by southern white men in 1955. The photograph was taken at his open casket wake and appeared in Chicago's *Jet* magazine, self-described at the time as "a weekly negro news magazine." Like almost all cases of racist lynching in the United States, the perpetrators—if the case even went to trial—were acquitted, and in common with the vast majority of other cases, the alibi for this brutal crime was a sexual overture toward a white woman. The accuser in the Till case, Carolyn Bryant, much later, in fact only in 2017, recanted. Till's mother, Mamie Till Mobley, after fighting to bring her son's body home to Chicago for burial, made the controversial decision to have an open casket wake. Thousands of mourners from the black community attended and the event was covered by three black publications, including images of the lines of mourners, and *Jet*'s now infamous close-up of the horrifically disfigured face of the dead boy.[19]

Schutz's painting received intense media scrutiny following an open letter from another artist, Hannah Black, calling for its removal and destruction. Black's letter was co-signed by forty-seven other artists and writers, and although several commentators in the media storm that followed suggested that Schutz's appropriation of the image was distasteful and ill-conceived, the call for its removal and destruction was widely viewed as an extreme and potentially dangerous response. It was soon branded as censorship and wildly compared to other historic instances, such as Nazi book-burning in the 1930s. But is censorship really the right term when the weight of institutional power is in fact reversed? Black surely had no illusions that the museum would actually comply with her request for its destruction, however cogently argued her critique of the work was. Isn't hers the work of *censuring*, of opposition, of protest, not *censoring*, an official act of suppression? Isn't it, as Malik Gaines has argued, a classically avant-garde call for the destruction of art and a critique of the institutional structure that profits from it?[20] Having experienced first-hand—more than one time in my career—the actual power and machinations of institutional censorship, it's very much a behind-closed-doors affair, not a signed open letter with positions clearly stated and names attached.

Faustine's mediation of the images of historical Blackness is very different from Schutz's. Of course, photography and painting do not have the same visual history or formal structure. But Faustine uses her own body as a vehicle for this historical work. It operates as a container for the visual history, or content, she animates. Whereas one of the strongest points of opposition to Schutz's painting rested on her *formalist* treatment of the subject. The disfigured features of the murdered child were rendered as a deep palette knife gash in the lush wall of impasto paint. It read more like a beautiful surface texture than anything close to the violent mutilation seen in the photograph. The source material—or content—seemed to be indifferently treated, rendered irrelevant in the face of these painterly marks. But the problem is not simply that Schutz failed to address the charged emotional, historical, and political significance of the image *content*, tending instead only to her work's painterly *form*, rather she failed to understand the complicated *form* of her source image.[21] In a certain sense Schutz treats form and content as an opposition whereas Faustine does not.

In revealing her son's shattered face for "the world to see," Till's mother animated the darkest of image genres, the U.S. lynching photograph. But in doing so she changed its mode of circulation and created a new audience that operated under a completely different affective economy. Lynchings were frequently public affairs organized by and for groups of white people. Sometimes the lynching was announced ahead of time in the newspaper.[22] As visual records show, attendees brought along dates, children even, and photographs were taken that later were sold as postcards and mailed to family and friends elsewhere. Alongside these visual mementoes, white attendees also collected grisly souvenirs from the body, including hair, nails, and even body parts such as fingers and genitals. This nexus of gendered racial power is visualized in the display of the lifeless black male body in juxtaposition with the live, excited bodies of white viewers looking on. The visual economy of lynching consolidated white racial power within communities through the intimacy of the shared, circulated image of looking at the abject black male body.

Placing my own hand over the image of the brutalized victims, Thomas Shipp and Abram Smith, and re-photographing the scene is an attempt to change our relation to this spectacle of racial violence (figure 6.4). It is a gesture of protection and an acknowledgment of structural complicity with its visual economy. Doctoring the image in this way recognizes, without counter-signing, the role played—whether enthusiastically or reluctantly—by white femininity. It is also an attempt to acknowledge myself looking at the scene, to mark this contemporary scene of looking, and to interrupt the circuit of gazes that it continues to offer. A hand held up in refusal—to guard, to shield, to defend against the violence that continues to adhere in the image. My hand becomes a kind of shroud for covering the victims, and in doing so it draws our attention to the crush of onlookers below. The pointing man in the center foreground now seems to gesture toward my fingers. Without the victims there on display we now focus on the faces of the audience, on their act of looking, which is also a series of exchanges outward to the

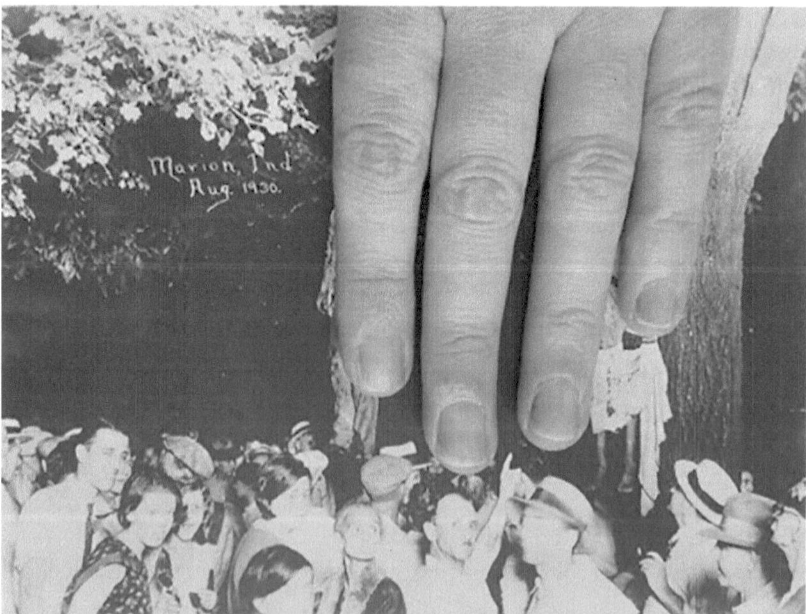

Figure 6.4. Author photograph of a reproduced postcard image of the lynching of Thomas Shipp and Abram Smith, August 7, 1930, Marion, Indiana. From James Allen, ed., *Without Sanctuary: Lynching Photography in America* (Santa Fe, NM: Twin Palms, 2000).

viewers of the image. This is a confusing scene of looking. Eyes are either hard, beady, like the pointing man who anchors our gaze, or vacant and empty, floating above slack jaws, as with the two women on the left. Some faces are bleached out by the flash or dissolved into tonal whiteness by a movement blur: unreadable. Only one face, the man to the far left, shows pleasure or amusement. But the overall arrangement of heads turned this way and that speaks most clearly of agitation—the excitement of looking.

While my gesture here is to look more closely at those looking, Mobley's intervention is much more profound. She changed the audience from aggressors to witnesses and mourners. Although the image of Till also interrupted the flow of this visual economy, it is nonetheless unable to fully disarm its in-built threat.[23] This is something that the artist Parker Bright vividly highlights in his performance protest in front of the Schutz painting on the first day that the biennial opened to the public. Wearing a t-shirt inscribed with the handwritten phrase, "Black death spectacle," when photographed and circulated, Bright's body became a black male Rückenfigur adopting the pose of aesthetic contemplation—but as a work of political aesthetics—standing witness in front of this abstracted image. He both guards the image of Till and stands as Schutz's accuser.

The visual economy of lynching prescribes an aggressor in the white male: he is perpetrator, on-looker, and empowered viewer for the subsequent images. He protects white female virtue, both as a fictive alibi and as an index of another dimension of his gendered power, but the white woman is nonetheless in an ambivalent position of privilege, a position that Schutz didn't seem to recognize. If the black man is rendered as an abject spectacle for coin and visual exchange, then the missing player, the absent figure, is the black woman and girl. She doesn't appear. The violence she knows happens off-stage, in the shadows, between the lines of the lists and statistics in the archive. This is a casual sexual violence that is the inverted mirror image of the endangered virtue of her white sisters.

These are abstract categories, dynamics of visibility and invisibility that operate through a U.S.-specific race-sex nexus. As the intensity of feeling generated by the Schutz painting demonstrates, these categories remain charged with emotion. The Whitney Museum debacle was defined by anger, a "strong emotion," as Sianne Ngai has put it, whereas the evasiveness of the institutional response to Faustine's image suggests a different emotional category altogether, something that might be closer to shame.[24] The desire was to cover—to cover her body—it was to hide, to make her invisible. It was as if her image was being erased, forced back into its invisible place within the visual economy of lynching. I could send out an email notice to the college community advertising the exhibition, but I wasn't permitted to include the image. A nonillustrated notice had to be specifically produced.

In preparing this chapter for publication I have presented it in an abbreviated form at public lectures. When I show images of lynching it is always with my own hand obscuring the victim. At a feminist conference at the University of Leeds (one of my Alma Mater institutions) I received two interesting responses. One from a white woman with a question focused on the Schutz incident. This is perhaps understandable because of its newsworthiness. The other, from a black woman, who wanted to know why I didn't talk more about the horrific violence against black men. The effect of these two questions, as two other participants thoughtfully reflected in an informal conversation later in the day, was to render Faustine's body invisible once again.[25]

Focusing on the black female body and its public vulnerability is not meant to overwrite or erase the many instances of lethal state violence experienced by black men in America. Movements such as #SayHerName do not participate in a zero sum competition for victimhood. But there is a connection between the visualization of violence against black men and the forgetting or rendered invisible of black women's experiences. We can look at this from two different perspectives. On the one hand, following Michael Rothberg's theory of "multidirectional memory," the public discourse about police violence against black men has enabled or prepared the ground for another conversation about the particular experience of black women in America.[26] Violence against women is less visible in part because it is more structurally complex. Sexual violence, for example, is often behind closed doors and subject to shame. Whereas on the other hand, the spectacle of violence against black men has its own (emasculating) sexual economy. Here we must see a line of connection between contemporary instances of police violence and the visual economy of lynching in the United States. The alibi for the latter was to protect the virtue of white womanhood against the fantasy of a violently virulent black masculinity. Surely the repeated overkill response in contemporary police shootings of black men and boys is inextricably linked to this vicious history. Many activists see these police killings as contemporary state-sanctioned lynchings, and the repeated failure of the visual evidence in the courts is another historical repetition.

The history in Faustine's *White Shoes* series is layered by other types of black femininity. The white shoes she wears are more modest than sexy. Together with the comportment of her body, the closed pose, they evoke the respectability of a church lady more than anything else. I can't help but see the fierce Christian matriarch alongside the historical bodies animated by her photographs. Faustine's strategy is less about representing this visual history and more a kind of embodied re-imagining of it. Christina Sharpe's concept of "wake work" is a particularly rich way of understanding the distinction. She is referring to the multiple meanings carried by the word. "Wake: a watch or vigil held beside the body of someone who has died"; "wake: the track of the water's surface; the disturbance caused by a body swimming or moved, in water" "wake: the state of wakefulness, consciousness."[27] For Sharpe, the display of Till's body by his mother was not about representation—which it has since become because of the famous photograph—rather, it was about embodied witness. Sharpe emphasizes the physical presence of the thousands of mourners from the community putting their own bodies into traumatic proximity to Till's.[28] This is even more so the case with Faustine. She brought these various historical bodies *into* her own. Her physical vulnerability and voluntary self-exposure bears witness to, and animates, a traumatic history, but without repeating its visual violence.

Chapter 7

"Stranger Fruit"

JON HENRY IN CONVERSATION WITH BETH HINDERLITER

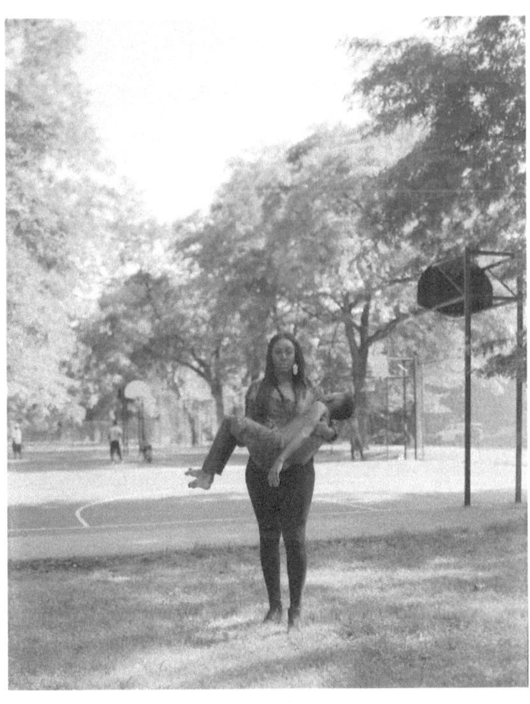

Figure 7.1. *Untitled #15*, South Side Chicago, Illinois. © Jon Henry.

Beth Hinderliter: In a *New York Times* article from 2015 poet Claudia Rankine elaborated on the condition of black life being one of mourning. Americans, she argued, are forced "to assimilate corpses in their daily comings and goings." Your work confronts this dailyness of grief—its immensity and its particularity—that Rankine invokes. Can you talk a little about how you process grief and mourning?

Jon Henry: Processing grief and mourning is difficult. The concept for this project began in 2008 as I heard the verdict of the Sean Bell murder. Sean was murdered (and his friends shot) at his bachelor party in Jamaica Queens, the night before he was to wed. As an African American, it is difficult for me, even while working on this project, to fully control my emotions when these tragedies happen. Maybe not that they happen, but that there is a lack of outrage on all sides. Young men, children, grown men are dying. They were not criminals. Why was death the final outcome for these events? Why can't people realize that this is a larger issue than what is seems on the surface? I feel for the families that have lost. No mother

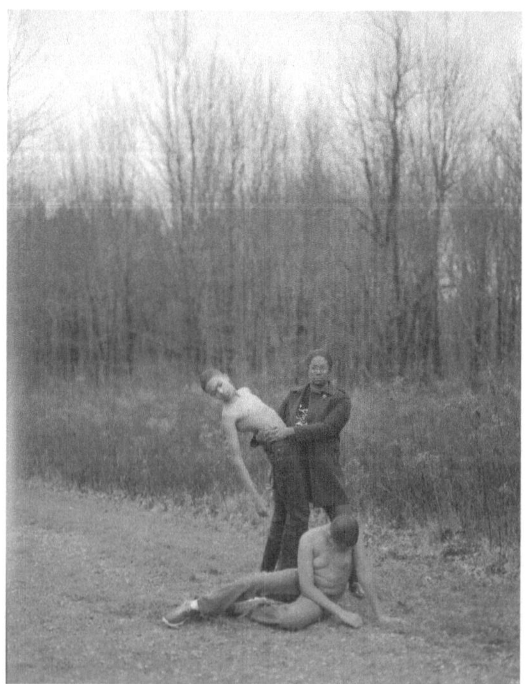

Figure 7.2. *Untitled #11*, Buffalo, New York. © Jon Henry.

should have to endure this type of suffering, from those sworn to protect and serve. The families in this project have not lost their sons, but they understand the reality, that this could easily happen to them.

Beth Hinderliter: Your series "Stranger Fruit" is performative on several levels—invoking Christian pietà images as well as the Mothers of the Movement for Black Lives. How have the people who appear in these works responded to the process of their creation? What emotions were raised?

Jon Henry: The responses have been overwhelmingly positive. I give all the credit to the mothers in the project. It is not easy to pose with your son as if they were dead, knowing that this could become a reality for them. I ask them about the emotions that come to mind after the shoot, and they all respond similarly—they speak of the range of emotion they feel. From fear to love, maternal instincts of protection, anger (that these issues still exist). I use a large-format camera for the project, so I work one image at a time. Sometimes we only make two images. It takes a few minutes to set everything, from the pose, to the frame so that duration, where the mother is holding her son, for a few minutes, really heightens these emotions.

Beth Hinderliter: Your work pairs seemingly opposed attributes like strength and fragility in often fluid ways. In the process of working on these series, how have you had to navigate mass media images and stereotypes of the black American community?

Jon Henry: One theme I am always cognizant of is trauma. While the bodies of the men in the series are shown lifeless, it was important that they weren't grotesque. I did not want to glamorize or fetishize these events. The images of Sean Bell and his friends, shot and bleeding (with Sean killed) while handcuffed, face first on the street remain etched in my brain. "Stranger Fruit" was created in response to this event directly. I feel that the community has endured so much, especially recently with the advancements of smart phones and other recording devices, that the trauma of witnessing these murders over and over can be too much to bear.

Beth Hinderliter: In some images of the series, women appear alone instead of holding the body of their child. Some are surrounded with children's toys or sit at the dinner table where an extra place has been set for an empty chair. How did you approach crafting these voids in the images—where we know people have been but are absent to our gaze now?

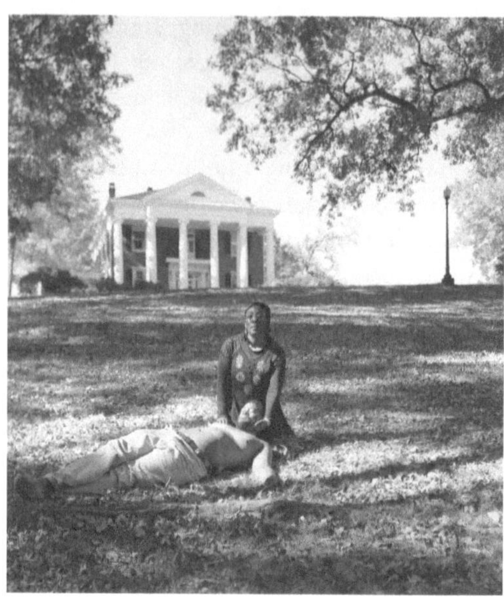

Figure 7.3. *Untitled #24*, Birmingham, Alabama. © Jon Henry.

Jon Henry: My thoughts were of the families who have lost their sons. What does day-to-day life look like, after these tragedies? I created these "portraits" with the mother turned away from the camera, so the viewer can place themselves in their mind. Sometimes there is an obvious presence missing, sometimes they are just alone with their thoughts, but again, when the trials are over and the media coverage stopped, my thoughts are with these mothers in particular.

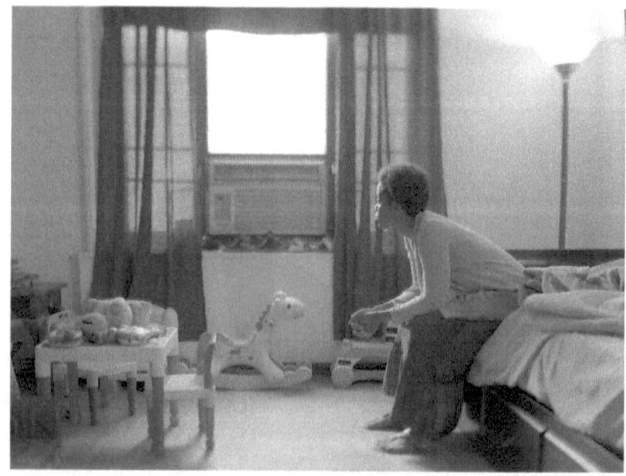

Figure 7.4. *Untitled #6*, Parkchester, New York. © Jon Henry.

Chapter 8

The Uses of Anger

Wanda Coleman's Poetry of Black Rage and #blacklivesmatter

SHANNA GREENE BENJAMIN

In late 2014, black people in the United States took to the streets in protest.* Spurred on by the failure of grand juries to indict neither Officer Darren Wilson for shooting and killing Michael Brown, nor Officer Daniel Pantaleo for choking Eric Gardner to death, black people gathered en masse—marching, chanting, and hoisting placards—to declare that #blacklivesmatter.[1] Public responses to the grand jury decisions, and then to the resulting protests, say much about how respectability politics, a term coined by Harvard historian Evelyn Brooks Higginbotham, circumscribe expressions of black rage. Following the grand jury decision in Ferguson, Missouri, Michael Brown's parents asked protestors to "channel [their] frustration in ways that will make a positive change."[2] President Obama concurred: "We are a nation built on the rule of law," he said. "We need to accept that this decision was the grand jury's to make. There are Americans who agree with it, and there are Americans who are disappointed, even angry. . . . I join Michael's parents in asking that anyone who protests this decision, do so peacefully."[3]

---

*This chapter previously appeared with a slightly different title in *Hecate* 40, no. 1 (2014): 58–79.

The call for black people to engage in peaceful responses to state-sanctioned violence against black bodies is part of a broader narrative that requires black people to respond respectably to their degradation, to rise above the fray and assuage the fears of white people intimidated by, or fearful of, congregating black bodies with the collective potential for mass vengeance. The life and work of Wanda Coleman, a black writer who expressed her anger with white supremacy and black elitism in equal measure, reflect the social risks and creative possibilities bound up in being a black woman poet who breaches African American social etiquette around anger.

"Since Black Sparrow Press released [Coleman's] first chapbook, *Art in the Court of the Blue Fag* (1977)," Jennifer Ryan explains, "Coleman has published thirteen books of poetry, two collections of short stories, two collections of essays, a novel, a memoir, and many uncollected pieces.[4] The dearth of Coleman scholarship is stark considering just how productive Coleman was before her passing on November 22, 2013. There were, when this chapter was originally published in 2014, approximately six published interviews, seven book chapters or journal articles, and five bio-bibliographic book entries about Coleman. In 1989, Tony Magistrale opened the door for Coleman scholars with "Doing Battle with the Wolf: A Critical Introduction to Wanda Coleman's Poetry," an essay that provided precisely what scholars needed at the time: an exciting context for understanding Coleman's work that encouraged scholars to take up Coleman as the subject of their scholarship. Followed by a paltry trickle of interviews and bio-bibliographic entries, it wasn't until a decade later, in 1999, that Krista Comer published the first peer-reviewed essay on Coleman. Comer's "Revising Western Criticism through Wanda Coleman" presents Coleman as a western "regionalist" who challenges narrow conceptions of "spatial perspective[s] circulating in contemporary western spaces."[5] By the turn of the century, Tyler T. Schmidt's essay " 'Womanish and Wily: The Poetry of Wanda Coleman" (2005), Malin Pereira's essay "Sister Seer and Scribe: Teaching Wanda Coleman's and Elizabeth Alexander's Conversations with Sylvia Plath," and Jennifer Ryan's book chapter "Shape-Shifting: The Urban Geographies of Wanda Coleman's Jazz Poetry" (2010) discuss how Coleman troubles "essentialist rhetoric"[6] of what it means to be black, what it means to be a black woman, or what it means to be a sexual being; how Coleman's work interacts with a broad range of literary "ancestors";[7] and how Coleman's "jazz and blues references" contextualize Coleman's "multivolume American Sonnets and her other poetry,"[8] respectively. Unfortunately, even as a prolific sonneteer with a 100-sonnet sequence to her name, Coleman lacks the critical attention afforded to other openly angry black poets, namely Amiri Baraka, who boasts scores of peer-reviewed essays, book chapters, and interviews dedicated to the study of his life and work. As the first to analyze the broad sweep of Coleman's sonnets, this chapter complements Ryan's 2015 *MELUS* interview by making legible the inventive ways Coleman's sonnets push back against cultural, poetic, and literary hegemony to imagine a literary space that centralizes the perspectives of individuals who live their lives on the margins.

The Ratchet, the Respectable, and the Price of Black Rage

The call to respond with restraint, not rage, to open acts of violence against black people is part of a longstanding tradition of black respectability politics where honest assessments of racist injustice must be presented in an honorable fashion. In the nineteenth century, Anna Julia Cooper wrapped her advocacy of black female advancement in Christian ideals. When Cooper asserts that "Only the BLACK WOMAN can say 'when and where I enter, in the *quiet, undisputed dignity of my womanhood, without violence* and without suing or special patronage, then and there the whole Negro race enters with me,"[9] she characterizes the political work of the black woman as a "quiet" endeavor enacted "without violence." In the twentieth century, between 1900 and 1920, the Woman's Convention of the black Baptist church developed a system of practices to govern the modes of self-presentation of black women. By engaging in what Higginbotham calls a "discourse of respectability,"[10] black Baptist women encouraged their sisters to adopt patterns of "manners and morals" when engaging in the "traditional forms of protest, such as petitions, boycotts, and verbal appeals" that were part and parcel of their social justice work.[11]

These well-intentioned women reasoned that in order to subvert stereotypical representations that portrayed black women as immoral and unclean, they needed to present themselves in a manner that placed them above reproach. Regardless of social standing or economic status, according to respectability politics, black women need only adhere to the values of "temperance, cleanliness of person and property, thrift, polite manners, and sexual purity" to rise above "their social subordination."[12] For black Baptist women, the road to uplift was paved with a dark and disheartening irony: while promoting respectability as the pathway to social and political uplift, they upheld "hegemonic values" without interrogation, subjecting poor blacks to intense scrutiny for even minor violations of social etiquette.[13]

On its face, respectability is built on noble ideals. Its enactment, however, disenfranchises black Americans because it encourages the sublimation of black anger in the interest of keeping up appearances with the hope that one day white people will acknowledge black humanity and treat African Americans as equals. Respectability politics hinges the dismantling of white supremacy on the manners and etiquette of black people and absolves racists from the responsibility they have to interrogate their complicity in the ongoing oppression of black people.

The pressure to perform politeness endures into the twenty-first century and carries with it specific assumptions about acceptable expressions of black rage. The focus on polite protest encoded in the comments offered by President Obama and Michael Brown's parents reflect the pressure placed upon black people, and the pressure black people are willing to place on themselves, to respond respectably even in the face of outright injustice.[14] In the vernacular, President Obama and the Brown family advocate for a "bougie" brand of anger that is respectable, not ratchet[15]—a modern-day distinction between categories once defined by "the black bourgeoisie and the poor."[16] Respectable anger calls lawyers; ratchet anger calls goons. Respectable anger throws barbs; ratchet anger throws bottles. Imbedded within calls for respectable expressions of black anger is an implicit belief that anger that performs itself in tank tops or athletic wear, through animated gestures or loud speech, with misplaced modifiers or without subject/verb agreement, is low-class. That is, if black folk are to be taken seriously by whites, then their responses should be cool and calculated—since, as bell hooks explains in "Killing Rage," "most folks associate black rage with the *underclass*, with desperate and despairing black youth who in their hopelessness feel no need to silence unwanted passions."[17]

Of course such distinctions between the respectable and the ratchet are not the totality of black life—all experience exists along a spectrum—but if African Americans as a whole are pressured to perform anger respectably, if at all, then black women find themselves burdened by race, class, *and* gender politics when striving to have themselves heard beyond the "angry black woman" stereotype. Wanda Coleman, as a woman and as a poet, rejected respectability politics and wrote sonnets that allowed her to organize and order her sometimes surreal and seemingly ineffable experiences with racism, sexism, police brutality, and academic elitism in ways that made legible the experiences of a black underclass. Studying Coleman's poetry prompts scholars of African American literature to wrestle with the role that respectability politics plays in the anthologizing and canonization of black literature.

When the first edition of the *Norton Anthology of African American Literature* was published in 1996, Wanda Coleman boasted seven entries; by the second and third editions, published in 2003 and 2014, respectively, Coleman was nowhere to be found. Did backlash from her scathing 2002 review of Maya Angelou's *A Song Flung up to Heaven* impact the deliberations to her detriment? Were there problems with permissions? Did the "north/south inclination of black geographical imaginations . . . rende[r] a [West Coast] poet like Wanda Coleman out of place" and, therefore, of little interest to black literary scholars?[18] While it is nearly impossible to know for sure why Coleman was cut, the new additions in "The Contemporary Period" (what was once "Literature Since 1975") are well-known and amply studied voices in contemporary African American poetry: Harryette Mullen, Elizabeth Alexander, Natasha Trethewey, Kevin Young, and Tracy K. Smith. While in this chapter I do not explicitly compare Coleman's absence with the anthologized presence of other writers, the implicit comparison illustrates one reason why certain black writers are visible and others are not. Coleman's angry approach to demanding democracy in poetic and political spheres may help scholars of African American literature interested in issues of class and respectability to unpack the role that middle-class standards of propriety play in how African American literature is anthologized and, by extension, canonized.

Coleman lived and worked "without a formal education beyond high school, without an academic position, often without a job or any money to live on, and with few of the institutional and professional support systems, networks, or awards most contemporary poets rely upon for career development and recognition."[19] Until her passing she expressed time and time again that she felt excluded from a coterie of black poets who were gainfully employed, adequately insured, and heavily praised. Whether this marginalization is real or imagined, Coleman yearned to be acknowledged by those who anthologize, teach, and study African American literature even as she pushed back against the professional network of which she desired to become a part. Easy as it may be to categorize Coleman as simply angry—her poem, "Wanda Why Aren't You Dead" asks, "wanda why are you so angry . . . wanda *what* makes you so angry . . . *wanda why are you so angry*" before wondering how Wanda lives on despite her personal pain—revisiting her sonnets in light of scholarship on black women and anger reveals that the rage embedded within her work masquerades an anguish that holds the potential for clarity and change.

Scholarship on black women's anger refutes stereotypical portrayals of black women while revealing how myths of the angry or even strong black woman make it difficult for black women to express vulnerability. In "The Myth of the Angry Black Woman," the first chapter in her book *Iconic: Decoding Images of the Revolutionary Black Woman*, Lakesia Johnson recounts the moment when Larry King, in an interview with Michelle Obama, showed a clip of Sarah Palin accusing Barack Obama of "palling around with terrorists"[20] to set up his questions regarding whether Mrs. Obama was "upset about the way that others treated her husband."[21] Despite King's attempts to goad the now-first lady into acknowledging her and her husband's anger, "Mrs. Obama's responses," Gina Athena Ulysse explains, "remained cool, collected, and focused"—in absolute defiance of the "angry black woman stereotype."[22] But at what cost does coolness come? Empirical studies, while documenting that African Americans "neither feel nor express more anger than whites,"[23] also show that black women report "a greater tendency to experience and suppress intense angry feelings rather than expressing them either physically or verbally."[24] There is no debating that "racial discrimination [is] a stressor" for black Americans;[25] there is, however, a debate over the true cost of suppressing the anger that results from racial discrimination. One outcome is that black women turn their "rage and hostility . . . inward on themselves and outward towards those who care about them."[26] Black women's persistent engagements with racism and sexism produce "frequent spells of impotent, self-consuming rage"[27] that prevent them from developing, in the words of Elizabeth Alexander, a "black interior" capable of providing a safe space for them to cultivate a subjectivity beyond their public engagements with oppression.[28]

Instead of suppressing her anger, Coleman expressed it to affirm her presence in the world, to assert her subjectivity despite its erasure, and to express her vulnerability even though it remained misunderstood by most. Like Baraka, Coleman "challenged the belief that art and social engagement are mutually exclusive" ("Why Study?"); unlike Baraka, however, when Coleman expressed anger—in her poetry or in public spheres—she was denigrated for it. Appreciating both the roots of Coleman's anger and its function in her poetry helps scholars of black literature interrogate the gendered double standard that affords men the right to be angry yet denies women the right to express the same. Coleman's anger, as Audre Lorde elucidates in "The Uses of Anger," is "loaded with information and energy"; this is information that "is a liberating and strengthening act of clarification, for it is in the painful process of this translation that we identify who are our allies with whom we have grave differences, and who are our genuine enemies."[29] David Orr complements this definition in his *New York Times* tribute "Adrienne Rich, Beyond the Anger," when he describes anger as "a complex, fluctuating power that encompasses the roots of the word 'anger' in the Old Norse term for 'anguish.' "[30] Together, Lorde's and Orr's definitions establish how anger functions as a tool for clarifying difference and as a device for exposing anguish. By reading Coleman through the definitions offered by Lorde and Orr, it becomes clear that there was more to Coleman than just her anger: understanding her anger is a gateway to understanding the anguish of a woman who felt deeply for her people. By expressing her particular brand of "killing rage," Coleman's poetry creates opportunities for the "transformative revolutionary action"[31] that precedes the dismantling of white supremacy and the enactment of democracy. In the same way that Phillis Wheatley's poetry pressed for the fulfillment of America's founding ideals, where freedom for the self would necessarily precede freedom for the nation, Wanda Coleman's sonnets with their anger critique the hypocrisy that forestalls the democratization of American verse and American life. Coleman, in sum, demands fulfillment of the democratic ideals Wheatley initiated centuries before. Wanda Coleman's anger, her impatience with racism, sexism, violence, and ignorance, lights the wick of dreams deferred, her sonnets proliferating from the explosion.

Flipping the Bird to American Exclusivity[32]

Angered by an encounter with a California State University Los Angeles professor who proclaimed, during otherwise "benign" dinner conversation, that "Wordsworth was the last great poet and that there was nothing written worth reading after World War II," Coleman penned "Dinosaur Sonnet" to "skewe[r] a dated academic patriarchy with its own language," and pinpoint the barriers that have forestalled the democratization of verse.[33] By critiquing a sonnet form often portrayed as inviolate despite a tradition to the contrary, "Dinosaur Sonnet" makes way for participation from a cacophony of voices as rich as America itself. "Dinosaur Sonnet," which may be read as Coleman's thesis on the sonnet tradition, opens with an epigraph that encapsulates future trajectories for a twenty-first century sonnet tradition: *care critique custody & control*. In this epigraph, Coleman alludes to a common exclusion existing in certain forms of liability coverage where the insurer is not responsible for damage done to items under the "care, custody, or control" (CCC) of the insured. If the sonnet, as a traditional form, has been in the CCC of an elitist "academic patriarchy," Coleman aims to expand access by engaging in a singular enterprise: *critique*. Coleman's critique clarifies, assesses, and evaluates whether the sonnet has been properly cared for while in the custody and under the control of a group the speaker feels excluded from because of her race, gender, and class. "Dinosaur Sonnet" reads:

> *care critique custody & control*
> the very academic versifier takes his time
> has a millennium in which to choose his rhyme
> the airiest well-financed contemplation has to offer—
> his! the rest are undeserving of attention
> are worth no mention. no praise. what do
> those savages know of poetry in its Elizabethan prime
> what could an underclass know of permutations of the line
> of discourse on the modern or an imagist divine
> to be born last poet—
> 'tis a curse. but to serve common tongue as
> pâté—(gasp) purely worse
> to allow havenotismistics to obviate the sublime 'tis
> beauty's most beastly most abhorrent crime.[34]

Visually, "Dinosaur Sonnet" looks like a traditional sonnet: a tightly compressed poem of thirteen lines where the elision of a fourteenth line denotes, like the extinction of dinosaurs, the extinction of tradition. Thematically, it challenges the mechanisms that have afforded mostly white and male sonneteers the time and financial resources to create while questioning what, if anything, a savage "underclass" can contribute to an Elizabethan tradition. As convenient as it may be to limit Coleman's critique to the white man she cites as the inspiration for this sonnet, "Dinosaur Sonnet" also speaks to the alienation felt by a self-taught black woman poet among her university-educated peers.

In a letter to E. Ethelbert Miller (E.E.), Coleman explores her feelings of alienation as she reflects on her participation in events celebrating the release of the *Norton Anthology of African American Literature* in 1998: the ground-breaking compilation edited by Henry Louis Gates Jr. and Nellie Y. McKay that canonized African American literature and bound together previously disparate texts to facilitate the teaching of the black literary tradition. In the passage that follows, Coleman explains how she feels at odds with a professoriate she deems elitist. At the same time, she concludes that her marginalization is particularly painful because it comes from those with whom she feels, even remotely, connected to because of her race:

> Now I return from Madison, Wisconsin, quite clear on why my fellow so-called Black intellectuals have never embraced me. At this point, I have seen them all—the best America's top ten universities could nurture. And this po' chile me—this niggah woman off the streets of Watts—simply IS the best; she eclipses them in her light.[35]

At the very moment Coleman acknowledges "the strength in [her] own gift," she rationalizes the rift between herself and a larger body of "Black intellectuals" by emphasizing the blinding power of her "light."[36] Subsequently, Coleman's anger gives way to anguish as she speaks to the economic and emotional cost of the alienation: "E.E.—*it wasn't the prizes.* Although they would've certainly helped my children. It was *the being left out,* the being rejected (that supercilious silence—or was it fear?) by those *I considered my own.* Stupid of me, wasn't it?"[37] In this passage, Coleman's anger shines a light on the contradictory feelings of attraction and repulsion she feels toward her peers. Coleman wants what they have but resents them for having it. Coleman's discontent is about more than money—after all, "*it wasn't the prizes,*" she explains. Coleman's anguish involves an unrequited love from her people, black people, with whom she feels a sense of racial solidarity regardless of her tendency to push them away.

This contradictory tension, Coleman's desire to be accepted by a coterie of black writers and her rejection of this very same group because of their status, is also a structural feature of "Dinosaur Sonnet." Despite Coleman's loathing of the "very academic versifier"[38] and association with "an underclass,"[39] the sonnet first adheres to standard conventions of meter and rhyme, standards presumably upheld by the "academic versifier," before rejecting them. The poem's meter, which begins with conformity and ends with variation, demonstrates Coleman's ambivalence with intellectual elites and practitioners of traditional forms. Coleman's reliance on tradition also engages in a curious enactment of respectability politics, since her adherence, in the beginning of the sonnet, to prescribed rules of meter and rhyme, allows her to wrap an otherwise scathing indictment of tradition in a veneer of respect for the tradition she critiques. The iambs in the first two lines become more difficult to find in the lines that immediately follow. The end rhymes in lines 1 and 2 ("time" and "rhyme," respectively) spiral into a rhyme scheme that appears to follow no discernible pattern (*aabcdaaaefgh/a(?)a*). The thirteen lines of the sonnet (not including the opening epigraph) have as few as six syllables and as many as seventeen.

What appears to be an outright disregard for the sonnet's traditional structure and thematic development is actually a curious play on the speaker's ironic desire to be included in a tradition that doubts the ability of have-nots to understand the structure, the "permutations of the line,"[40] or the history, a "discourse on the modern or an imagist divine,"[41] that informs poetry in general and the sonnet in particular. By writing mostly in iambs, offering a structured but not regular rhyme scheme, and ending with a tongue-in-cheek play on the sonnet's title, Coleman offers an alternative take on the sonnet as a form that permits mastery from the margins to condemn the notion that poetry is purely the purview of elitist academics. Coleman critiques this exclusive coterie of poets by writing in iambic pentameter, a move that suggests that any alienation of her race, gender, or class is the result of prejudice, not because she lacks technical ability. The first two lines of "Dinosaur Sonnet" mock the time-consuming, methodical process that the "academic versifier" follows "to choose his rhyme," and set up the rhyme scheme that will be improvised upon throughout the sonnet.[42] Even though Coleman rejects the pentameter of the traditional sonnet, she avoids an outright dismissal of form by following, at least in part, the conventions of the classical sonnet.

The speaker's play with duality continues with her reference to the "academic versifier"—since, lofty as the term sounds, versifiers do not just write poetry, they write inferior poetry. This double meaning—introduced in the sonnet's very first line—replicates the poem's contradictory impulses. On the one hand, the speaker desires to expose poetry's pretensions. On the other hand, the poet proves her technical skill in spite of her exclusion from the traditional canon of sonneteers. "Dinosaur Sonnet," like many of Coleman's other sonnets, blurs the line between speaker and poet, to effectively make the race, class and gender of the poet, of the speaker, constitutive to the meaning of the poem. This self-consciousness highlights the subjectivity of the poet to acknowledge the importance of the person at the same time as readers revel in the work of the sonnet. The extra syllables in lines 1 and 2—which exceed the typical ten-syllable line of traditional sonnets—not only nod to the inflated egos of "academic versifier[s]" but also push the limits of the sonnet by utilizing an uncommon meter. Coleman writes line 1 in iambic heptameter. And, except for the opening trochee, she writes line

2 in iambic hexameter. The metrical complexities that follow demonstrate the poet's technical virtuosity and make a mockery of her exclusion from the socioeconomic and gender hierarchies that alienate an "underclass" from the creative process.

As if compelling readers to contemplate line 3 in the same way that having patrons or independent wealth affords privileged poets contemplative space, Coleman disrupts the iambic heptameter of line 3 with a final foot that simply does not fit. Because of the unstressed syllable at the end of the line, the concluding foot is neither anapest (unstressed-unstressed-stressed) nor dactylic (stressed-unstressed-unstressed). In a line that posits "contemplation" as the birthright of certain poets, it seems ironic that no amount of thinking will reconcile what is irreconcilable. In other words, the existence of the extra syllable makes it impossible to categorize the final foot of line 3 according to the existing rules of the sonnet. In this technical move, Coleman proves that she knows the rules of the sonnet so well that she can take liberties to break them and, as a result, create alternative metrical configurations that exist beyond current sonnet nomenclature.

Through a deceptively technical sonnet, Coleman gains authority as she challenges the terms that have supported the haves in their exclusion of the have-nots. Coleman symbolically inserts those "undeserving of attention" who "are worth no mention. no praise"[43] into the conversation. Even though they, like the extra syllable, may not "fit" into the sonnet tradition, this "underclass" is still worthy of inclusion even if the existing discourse—a discourse they had no hand in forming—cannot accommodate their "savage" perspectives and alternate literary forms. The periods demarcating this line's feet lead readers into a uniquely gendered space where there are "no *men*":[44] no dinosaurs, no elitist intellectuals, no members of a dated academic patriarchy to confront. There is only the world where Coleman transforms her anger into art, where her virtuosity with the sonnet stands in as a careful critique that demonstrates a larger democratic vision beyond the extinction of those entitled to democracy.

In the concluding two lines, a couplet with a twist, Coleman flips the proverbial bird to the sonnet tradition and to those who would seek to alienate her from it. In these lines, Coleman's commentary on the speaker's relationship to the sonnet tradition comes when she returns full circle to her original dinosaur theme with the inclusion of two dactyls at the start of the final line. A foot of stressed-unstressed-unstressed syllables, the presence of *two* dactyls in line 13 suggests that Coleman wants to ensure that her purposeful inclusion of the metrical foot with the prehistoric name does not go overlooked. Pterodactyls, or flying dinosaurs, are also known as "winged fingers" from the Greek "pterodaktulos." In the final lines, Coleman flips a structural bird—in this case, a winged finger—to a poetic establishment blinded by its own privilege. "Dinosaur Sonnet" excavates a sonnet landscape riddled with the "dry bones of the past"[45] to reclaim its remnants and restructure the fossils according to the will of a black woman poet of the people. Hence, as Coleman considers the sonnet as a tradition to excavate, as dry bones to unearth, she takes the fossils of tradition and recreates a sonnet based upon a form she imagines in a way comparable to how palaeontologists recreate dinosaur skeletons from the fossils they exhume. In "Dinosaur Sonnet," Coleman dances with the historic, distinguishes it from the pre-historic, and re-orders the sonnet kingdom with a new species in place to wedge herself into tradition and take aim at racism, sexism and class inequality. Coleman's anger may be the impetus, but the insightful and incisive sonnet that results reveals how anger, controlled and manipulated through careful attention to form, provides an opportunity for catharsis while critiquing the structural inequalities that ignite her rage. In essence, form structures Coleman's anger and modulates her rage to offer critique and conformity at the same time. In spite of the irony interlaced throughout "Dinosaur Sonnet," Coleman pushes for the fulfillment of an American democratic ideal, where marginalized voices can find space to flourish by occupying the space she's carved out for their inclusion. Coleman's interest in democracy is aspirational and hopeful since, clearly, she is writing to an ideal she only wishes applied to her. Refusing to be defined or limited by her anger, Coleman finds a way to imagine possibilities beyond her experience at the same time she expresses vulnerability, her desire to be accepted and appreciated, through her rage.

Unrequited Love × Alienation = the Rage Equation

Sandwiched between excess and violence, the mathematical equation embedded within Coleman's "Sonnet #1" imagines a range of outcomes when "white greed" and "socio-eco dominance" come into conflict with "black anger" and "socio-eco disparity."[46] Published in *American Sonnets*, "Sonnet #1" sets the tone for the ninety-nine that follow. Unlike most sonnet sequences that compile related sonnets in a singular volume, Coleman's American Sonnets are dispersed across three volumes: sonnets 1–24 in *American Sonnets*; "More American Sonnets," numbered 26–86, in *Bathwater Wine*;

and sonnets 25, 87–100 in *Mercurochrome.* Like the series itself, "Sonnet #1" is a visually intriguing, canon-busting poem that reflects the musical, artistic and linguistic impulses that mark Coleman's American Sonnets as some of the most important contributions to the sonnet tradition. Even with anger as an organizing principle, the sonnet's technical turns toy with the algebra of race relations:

> the lurid confessions of an ex-cake junky: "i blew it
> all. blimped. i was really stupid. i waited
> until i was forty to get hooked on white flour
> and powdered sugar"

$$\frac{\text{white greed}}{\text{socio-eco dominance}} \times \frac{\text{black anger}}{\text{socio-eco disparity}} =$$

> a) increased racial tension/polarization
> b) increased criminal activity
> c) sporadic eruptions manifest as mass killings
> d) collapses of longstanding social institutions
> e) the niggerization of the middle class

> the blow to his head cracks his skull
> he bleeds eighth notes & treble clefs
> (sometimes i feel like i'm almost going)
> to Chicago. baby, you want to go?[47]

Embedded within a sonnet that appears visually improvisational and perhaps a bit random are three distinct sections—an opening quatrain, a middle sestet, and a concluding quatrain—that offer discretely takes on the oppressive nature of whiteness. Much like Craig Werner's articulation of the jazz impulse, where the jazz artist reworks her identity as "an individual," "as a member of a community," and "as a link in the chain of tradition,"[48] "Sonnet #1" reworks the "melody" of oppression from these three vantage points. The organizing idea, the overarching "problem" that constitutes the melody or theme reworked in "Sonnet #1," is whiteness. Whiteness here is more than an abstraction. Whiteness here is about more than "the man." "Sonnet #1" presents whiteness as a physical, economic, and social hand that is as violent and destructive as it is systematic and ingrained. The fourteen lines of "Sonnet #1," where the mathematical *cum* linguistic equation equates to a single line, reimagine the privileged landscape of the sonnet at the same time as it evaluates a variety of outcomes when white greed and black anger collide.

In the opening quatrain, refined carbohydrates and sugar symbolize the tangible ways whiteness is commodified and ingested only to destroy the persona from the inside out. Bloated through an addiction to sugary, floury substances that taste good but cause harm, the narrator is complicit in this compulsion, since the hand that leads the sweets to her mouth is, after all, her own. But instead of a compulsion that invites condescension, it is one that elicits sympathy since this is whiteness that tastes good, a whiteness that presumably brings pleasure even though it is simultaneously symbolic of the trans-Atlantic slave trade, the harvesting of sugar, and commodification of black bodies. The quotation marks that enfold the speaker's reflection on her addiction to "white flour / and powdered sugar"[49] enclose her thoughts in a way similar to how her body consumes the refined carbohydrates that become detrimental to her weight and waistline. Despite the physically damaging effects of white flour and powdered sugar, the narrator's tone is playful and self-deprecating, a tone that stands in stark contrast to the sestet that follows. The easy-going nature of the opening lines creates a camaraderie between speaker and reader regardless of race since not that many people would deny the pleasures of white flour and powdered sugar. But this is a set-up. In the next six lines (a sestet comprised of the one-line equation and five multiple-choice answers) the tone becomes more severe as the consequences of being seduced by the fleeting "goodness" of refined whiteness are laid bare. From the very beginning, Coleman challenges the privileging of whiteness in American culture by arguing against its presence in excess. She moves from anger pointed inward, at the speaker, for eventually succumbing to the lure of "white flour and powdered sugar," to anger pointed outward against systems of American dominance, namely, disparities that disenfranchise black people, as the sonnet progresses.

Black anger is an indispensable part of an equation that aims to calculate the inequality of race relations. Instead of solving for unknown variables like "X" or "Y," the equation in line five includes specific components: white greed over socio-eco dominance, multiplied by black anger over socio-eco disparity, equals one of five outcomes: "a) increased racial tension/polarization; b) increased criminal activity; c) sporadic eruptions manifesting as mass killings; d) collapses of longstanding social institutions; e) the niggerization of the middle class." There is an equals sign in this equation, but no equality. There is an equation, but it remains unsolved. Black anger finds neither release nor resolution in Coleman's algebra. But the clarity anger produces allows for a clear enunciation of the possible outcomes of this equation. Such truth-telling is, of course, a prerequisite for transformation and evidence of Coleman's interest in "condemning social problems and pointing her readers toward the possibility of change."[50]

At no point, however, does "Sonnet #1" suggest that the equation affects blacks only. In fact, quite the opposite is true. The multiple-choice answers to the equation implicate white and black, rich and poor. By pitting white greed against black anger, the sonnet works through the problematics of equality by means of a linguistic equation. The equation and multiple-choice answers inscribe the reader in a system proscribed by the narrator. There is no "all of the above." There is no fill-in-the blank. The choices, "a) / b) / c) / d) / [or] e)"[51] have been provided for us. Instead of offering a solution, the poem presents a series of options. These "options" merely provide the illusion of choice. In turn, these "choices" merely mask the extent to which those interested in solving the equation are ultimately contained within a racialized discourse that assigns socioeconomic dominance or subservience to distinct racial categories. The multiple-choice options embedded within "Sonnet #1" signify the failed ideals of American democracy—the lack of equal protection under the law, the lack of equal support for the pursuit of health and happiness, for example—and effectively name the systems of inequality that prevent democracy from becoming actualized.

The sense of hopelessness introduced in the middle sestet becomes the lived reality of inequality in the final quatrain, where violence against, presumably, black men creates a desire to flee and find an expressive outlet for anger in the blues. The speaker troubles the sense of resolution typically provided by the final couplet of Shakespearean sonnets by proposing running away from the problem instead of solving the problem itself. Having moved from an exploration of the dominance of white greed and the disparities that incite black anger, the poem introduces the musical violence of a cracked skull bleeding "eighth notes & treble clefs"[52] to move the equation from theory to practice. The tensions that erupt when race and socioeconomic disparities collide look less like choice and more like consequence, a fact supported by the shift from equation in the middle sestet to inequality in the concluding quatrain. By "fingering the jagged grain of [a] brutal experience," by revisiting the legacy of racial and socioeconomic disenfranchisement, Coleman "reaffirms [her] existence" both as poet and as black woman.[53] In so doing, she conjures the blues impulse's drive to create a "near-tragic, near-comic" lyricism to describe the brutality of black life.[54] The blues impulse of the middle sestet foreshadows the musical allusions of the final quatrain to move from an individual to a collective experience with oppression and to tap into the expressive possibilities imbedded within black musical expression.

The mix of violence and music conjures sounds of Louis Armstrong's "What Did I Do to Be So Black and Blue" while the parenthetical phrase, a line taken from the spiritual "Sometimes I Feel Like a Motherless Child" (which actually reads "sometimes I feel like I'm almost gone" and was once covered[55] by Louis Armstrong), couples the abuse of lines 11 and 12 with the feelings of abandonment in line 13, so that the only possible alternative is, going to Chicago.[56] The final lines offer physical brutality, "the blow to his head" that "cracks his skull"[57] as a source for the "black anger" referenced in line 5. Instead of bleeding blood, however, "he bleeds eighth notes & treble clefs,"[58] seeping music instead of draining life. The music, it seems, despite possessing the sweeping elegance of the treble clef and the gentle curve of the eighth note or quaver, is nonetheless borne of violence. The poet's desire to find some creative response to violence erupts in the final lines, but it does not absolve "white greed" for its involvement in the violence that results from the inequality it engenders. In "Sonnet #1," jazz and the blues translate anger into useable art even if the material realities of American inequality and injustice are inescapable components of America's racial equation.

The Poetics of Righteous Discontent

Just as Evelyn Brooks Higginbotham's work assigns women their rightful place in the story of political and social activism in the black church, Wanda Coleman's sonnets position her as a rightful heir to American democracy. "American Sonnet #100" exemplifies how Coleman uses anger to clarify, to name really, the labor required to democratize American poetry across the lines of race, gender, and class. At the same time, Sonnet #100 offers a surfeit of admiration for the little lyric through the poem's use of enjambment. As the outpouring of sentiment spills over from one line in the next, these lines mirror the overflow of Coleman's ample skill and the sonnet's inability to restrain it. Coleman, as speaker, boldly asserts that her work is a classic—or, at least, it should be:

when thou does find no joy in all famed Erato's
honeyed breast, wordsport a gangster poet's jest
how black and luscious comes each double-barrelled
phrase, like poisoned roses or a maddened potter's
glaze. words abundant dance their meanings on
a thrilling floor, the stolen song of ravens and
purloined harps galore. this is the gentle game of
maniacs & queens, translations of the highly-souled
into a dreamer's sputterings where dark gives voice
into gazer's light and writerly praise is blessed
incontinence, the spillage of delight. sing to me
thy anthem of untasted fruit. slay in me the
wretchedness that names me brute. liberate my
half-dead kill. come. glory in my rebirth.
come. glory in my wonder's will[59]

At the same time Coleman's initial reference to Erato evokes Homer's invocation of the muses at the beginning of the *Iliad* and *Odyssey*, she offers herself as a fulfilling alternative to dissatisfying encounters with the Greek muse of love and erotic poetry. The speaker reinforces her opening poke at a classical tradition embodied in Erato's "honeyed breast" by proposing the "gangster poet" as a joyful alternative, a jester of the sonnet.[60] Like court jesters who provided both entertainment for and critique of the aristocracy, Coleman is at once at home in the sonnet, her "court," and constantly dallying on the edge of outright exile, since she must carefully balance the entertainment (or aesthetic) value of her poetry with the political critique and commentary it offers. Daring the establishment to toss her out on her ear for offending the king and queen of the court, elsewhere figured as a "dated academic patriarchy,"[61] Coleman's jest, which sounds much like joust, represents her symbolic needling of the sonnet form and so-called arbiters of good taste as she elevates contrarian perspectives through the figure of the jousting jester.

As jousting jester, Coleman is more than minstrel: she is a trickster in control of her image whose "double-barrelled phrase[s]"[62] both entertain and critique. Moreover, the classical allusions in the first seven lines—the section that includes the poetry until the period following "galore"—serve a dual purpose in advancing the sonnet's central theme and affirming Coleman's ascendancy in the sonnet tradition. On the one hand, the allusions to female figures in Greek mythology, namely, Daphne, Athena, Terpsichore, and Coronis, confirm Coleman's mastery of the canon. On the other hand, by referring to magical and maligned women in Greek mythology, Coleman rewrites her foray into the sonnet tradition as yet another goddess being punished for asserting her gifts against patriarchy.

Consider line 4, where the potency of this "gangster poet's" "double-barrelled" "wordsport" is likened to "poisoned roses" or "a maddened potter's glaze" in a simile that suggests a deadly potency and wild brilliance behind even the most beautiful artefacts. Most likely a reference to Daphne, who was turned into the poisonous laurel when the gods responded to her pleas to be protected from Apollo's attempted rape, the "poisoned roses" are as beautiful as they are dangerous, perhaps even more so, since their appearance belies their toxicity. Athena, a goddess of wisdom and known for her beauty, is also the goddess of crafts and, by extension, pottery—a fact that allows the speaker to yoke her creative enterprise, her work that is like a "maddened potter's glaze," to a woman whose beauty disguised her fierceness. Attractive because of their beauty yet toxic because of their truth telling, Coleman's sonnets are tight and inviolate, fortified by the wisdom in their lines.

In the following sentence, comprised of all or most of lines 5, 6, and 7, Coleman makes an even more direct commentary on how, specifically, she contributes to a tradition of sonneteers. With the lyre as its dominant image, these lines feature a metaphor where this "gangster poet's . . . words abundant dance their meanings on / a thrilling floor, the stolen song of ravens and / purloined harps galore."[63] The reference to dance invokes Terpsichore, the muse who invented dance and is figured with a lyre; the "purloined harp" most likely refers to Hermes's pilfering of Apollo's cows, Apollo's decision to trade his cows for the lyre, and Apollo's role as conductor of the muses. This, with the reference to Coronis (a white crow turned black after cheating on her lover, Apollo) and the allusion to the "raven," combine to paint Coleman as a distinctly black sonneteer, a wordsmith of the little lyric cursed out of jealousy, yet defiant of the path cut by the class status of her birth.

Coleman's poetry is vengeful. But there is a violent subtext to the opening seven lines of "Sonnet #100." Without much distance between this "gangster poet's" "wordsport" and a lyrical bloodsport experienced by those facing the wrong side of Coleman's double barrels, her attack on the sonnet tradition is uncompromising in its expression. Allusions to Erato and Terpsichore affirm Coleman's interest in musically inspired artistic expressions, allusions that align with Coleman's interest in reshaping the little lyric of the sonnet so that it accommodates the experiences of the marginalized. Coleman also acknowledges that her poetry is vengeful, dangerous, and fierce. In "Sonnet #100," readers experience the anger of Coleman's poetry and the beauty of its artistry in a piece that represents what Malin Pereira calls the "apex" of her "sonnet achievement."[64]

Her so-called "gentle game," however, is misleading since the game Coleman plays with readers is blood sport, "wordsport," where Coleman fights for her life to receive the praise her sonnets deserve. Coleman writes the "black and luscious" language of the gangster poet with normative syllabics to normalize her poetic perspective as a black woman. Lines 1 and 2 of "Sonnet #100" have 15 and 8 syllables respectively, while lines 3 and 4 have 12 syllables apiece. This pattern of syllabic uniformity continues in the following couplet, lines 5 and 6, where both lines of 13 syllables seem to affirm the intentionality behind the regularity of lines 3 and 4. Reimagined in couplets, these lines become "double-barrelled," indeed: paired rhythmically by end-rhyme and connected thematically by double-voiced allusions linked to Greek goddesses. In couplets shaped by enjambment and slant rhyme, Coleman takes double-barrelled aim at an exclusionary tradition, a move that suggests the possibility of a blast of her critique from unexpected angles.

This critique may blindside from multiple angles, but the control Coleman exerts over the middle portion of "Sonnet #100" suggests that her rage, like her lines, is hardly random; that is, even when it overflows, it is still ordered, meticulous, and directed. With two commas that do little to slow the pace, the lines that read: "this is the gentle game of maniacs & queens, translations of the highly-souled into a dreamer's sputterings where dark gives voice into gazers light and writerly praise is blessed incontinence, the spillage of delight" rush readers through this middle section, providing little cause to pause and consider the relationship between, for example, "maniacs & queens," and "dreamer[s]" and "the highly-souled." But by pausing to gaze into the pool of poetry that collects at the midsection of the sonnet, readers might see themselves: whether manic or royalty, erratic or harmonious, dark or light. The poem's "incontinence"—which otherwise suggests physical failure or a lack of control—here provides a cacophony of voices with the opportunity, and the occasion, to come together. This is both an intended and inevitable outcome of what Coleman, in her essay "On Theloniousism," calls the jazz sonnet: a version of the traditional sonnet formed out of her "conscious attempt to level all creativity"[65] so that women, persons of color, and the so-called poor and unlettered can read themselves into, and assert themselves as heirs to, the tradition embodied in the form.

Coleman's choice to repeat "anthem," "liberate," and "glory" position "American Sonnet #100" as a poem that ironizes patriotism to write a new America, a new democracy, where excellence and virtuosity are appreciated in all their forms. Coleman's anguish, as an expression of the human condition, makes her poetry, especially her sonnets, necessary reading for the way they "hold a mirror up to us as a nation."[66] Coleman's open engagement with the sonnet, where she wrestles with its structural limits while welcoming it as a structure to work through her anger and rage, engages in a revolution guided by hope and possibility to prompt democracy. With metered and measured responses to antagonism against her person and her psyche, Coleman's sonnets reject the potential silencing wrought by tired and timeworn stereotypes of the angry black woman. They are compelling for the way they alter space and expand the contemporary sonnet tradition to include the unlettered and working class—those who express anger without filter, without pretense, and without restraint. Coleman democratizes the sonnet by claiming it for herself: a woman who has experienced life as a poor, single, working mother—but who positions herself as heir to American democracy nonetheless. With her intricate and improvisational textual compositions, Coleman crafts sonnets with the hope that her talent, despite her positionality, cannot be denied. Coleman takes up space within a form where there is, quite purposefully, little to work with. Through the language of gangster braggadocio, which refuses to be self-effacing about talent, Coleman demands that her peers and the poetic establishment give her credit where credit is due. This chapter calls for Coleman to be appreciated for her bold and intrepid effort to make inclusion available to all persons, regardless of race, gender, or class, thereby entitling those descendants of the children of the poor "to civilize a space / Wherein to play [their] violin with grace."[67]

Chapter 9

Bodies That Matter

Blackness, Social Symbolism, and the Affective Image

DEREK CONRAD MURRAY

> Why are today so many problems perceived as problems of intolerance, not as problems of inequality, exploitation, injustice? Why is the proposed remedy tolerance, not emancipation, political struggle, even armed struggle? The immediate answer is the liberal multiculturalist's basic ideological operation: the "culturalization of politics"—political differences, differences conditioned by political inequality, economic exploitation, etc., are naturalized/neutralized into "cultural" differences, different "ways of life," which are something given, something that cannot be overcome, but merely "tolerated."
>
> —Slavoj Žižek, "Tolerance as an Ideological Category"[1]

Blackness is all the rage these days. It is the en vogue fixation of the black intelligentsia, as well as the white liberal/progressive establishment: dominating the imaginations of scholars, artists, and the Left-leaning sectors of the media. It graces the glossy covers of magazines, academic journals, and the literary world—not to mention its increasing prevalence in the cinema and on television screens. In short, it is everywhere, yet the presence of racial disparity and anti-blackness (in all aspects of American life) are as ubiquitous and pernicious as ever before. This may sound like a cynical and pessimistic assessment, considering the incredible strides African Americans have made since the passing of the Civil Rights Bill in 1964, yet there is no denying the enduring presence of structural racism. Nevertheless, the contradiction between the resplendence of blackness (in representation) versus the stark realities of its cultural abjection is a phenomenon that is in much need of unpacking. Needless to say, the stubborn persistence of American racism continues to be contrasted by the great pacifier called progressive cultural politics. In our deeply polarized political moment, it is becoming an increasingly common sentiment that liberalism has turned institutionalized racism into a science: into a veritable marvel of social engineering. As I will discuss, even among Left-leaning scholars, a critique of liberalism has begun to take shape that characterizes it as disingenuous and too based upon the bureaucratizing of compassionate language, superficial anti-racist correctives, diversity mandates, and political correctness. While my assessment would be more charitable, we must begin to question the nature of our Left-leaning institutions, and the forms of social justice to which they claim to be committed.

In many respects, African American abjection is among the quintessential forms of American cool that ultimately defines notions of authentic blackness. In the visual realm, blackness is now a predictable and cliché-ridden genre of cultural production and a bastion of racial sermonizing, empty sentiment, and the pornographic reveling in black trauma, degradation, and comic folly. But the true obscenity of this phenomenon is that black cultural producers gleefully serve up racialized spectacle because it sells, because it has cultural currency, because it is expected, and because this is their socially defined role—not to mention their culturally and institutionally sanctioned playing field. Is the role of the black cultural producer to muse about how much the system has made them suffer: to aestheticize their deprivation into a beautiful, heart wrenching, resplendent, yet ennobled social spectacle? Is it their role to merely *love their wounds*? In the United States, the visual markers of blackness, what has been termed *black cultural distinctiveness*, are particularized attributes that, according to E. Patrick Johnson, have economic and/or social clout.[2] Johnson's writing on the problem of black authenticity have contested the notion that there is an essential black subject, but he has also productively argued that blackness is as much about exclusion as it is an armament against racial intolerance.

In my writing on the subject of contemporary black art, I have taken up the hetero-patriarchal dynamics of black authenticity, particularly as they relate to black queer subjectivity. Any engagement with the messiness of black representation (whether historical or contemporaneous) must contend with the manner in which sexuality and gender trouble its formations, values, and fantasies. Blackness is itself a fantasy: it is what Johnson calls, "a theatrical enterprise" that is the direct residue of the white racial imaginary.[3] To ponder blackness is to contend with both its discursiveness and its appropriation and codification into a set of reductions and legibilities. In that regard, it has always been a gated community: its boundaries fixed, its borders erected as a largely nebulous, yet nearly impenetrable set of exclusions—even while remaining porous and ultimately indefinable. If these contradictions tell us anything, they suggest that black authenticity is an exceedingly overdetermined cultural phenomenon in much need of interrogation, if not reimagining. The notion of authenticity has emerged as a major fixation in African American scholarship, not least because the phenomenon of blackness is itself illegible. It has no essence. It is entirely arbitrary, despite its mobilization as an armament against oppression. Johnson rightly argues that "when black Americans have employed the rhetoric of black authenticity, the outcome has often been a political agenda that has excluded more voices that it has included."[4] Perhaps the tendency to think of black authenticity as a marker of kinship and belongingness is ultimately flawed. Conversely, I tend to regard blackness as a set of restrictions that exclude. Much has been written about black essentialisms and their contestations, which I will not recount here, but I want to think about the manner in which blackness is mobilized to the exclusion of others: to think of it not as an affirming essence (as a symbol for self-love)—but rather as an expression of authenticity that is more concerned with erecting borders.

That said, I want to make a distinction between racialized blackness and racism, because the former (as I will argue) has merely become culture, while the latter is built into the ideological fabric of the United States. Racism is a system of brutal and all-encompassing discrimination that has defined the social, cultural, and economic life of America. As absurd as it may seem, this distinction needs to be drawn, because the *culturalization of blackness* has become shorthand for discussions of race and racism, rendering these distinct formations as interchangeable phenomena.

My mention of a *culturalization of blackness* refers to a range of intellectuals—most notably, the Slovenian philosopher Slavoj Žižek, British-Australian scholar Sara Ahmed, as well as American philosopher Wendy Brown, who have influenced my recent writings on liberal tolerance within the discourses of visual culture. In this chapter's opening quotation, Žižek has located what he characterizes as a liberal cliché: the facile identification with the Other as public performance, while either upholding or failing to challenge official structures of inequality. He has also termed this the *culturalization of politics*—the performance of political sentiment as cultural posturing.[5] If we define culture as the cumulative beliefs, values, attitudes, and meanings of a given society—the *culturalization* of politics suggests that anti-hegemonic sentiments have become just that: a collective set of cultivated behaviors and expressed attitudes that perform a kind of pleasing facsimile of political feeling. Within institutions, anti-racism and anti-homophobia (for example) have become a bureaucratically procedural and routinized form of political correctness.

In keeping with this notion, I believe that we must continually question our so-called liberal and progressive discourses—particularly, and most urgently, the multicultural justice they claim to be committed to. Along those lines, there continues to be a need to challenge the genteel and hushed political correctness of liberalism's bureaucratic approach to "diversity." The term "diversity" has become a kind of twenty-first-century symbol for the evils of institutionalized political correctness and the patronizing culture of trigger warnings, safe spaces, polite speech, tokenism, racial fetishism, and symbolic philanthropic gestures. If there is a politically correct expressiveness within the realm of American visual culture, it manifests itself in both intellectual and representational engagements with the visualization of *Othered* bodies. In certain respects, difference (as *the* subject of representation) has emerged as a kind of liberal cliché: one that allows for the performance of politically correct liberal sentiment. My point is that, while blackness has become shorthand for well-meaning and earnest discussions of race and racism, the truth is quite the contrary. Anti-black racism can remain structurally intact, even while blackness (as a cultural formation) is celebrated and made a spectacle. In other words, the cultural celebration of blackness (in its visual and representational fantasias) often functions as a salve, and a shield that preserves and maintains the institutional structures of anti-blackness.

The celebration of blackness by liberal institutions, which often takes the form of diversity-based programming and ritualized (if not also disingenuous) expressions of benevolence, function largely as optics that project an image of tolerance and good will—even while institutionally sanctioned forms of racial and gender-based inequality remain largely intact and unchallenged. The rise of #BlackLivesMatter (BLM), an international activist movement founded in 2013, has been instrumental in reigniting public interest in the obscenities of anti-blackness: bringing much-needed attention to the prevalence of violence against black people—particularly the disturbing frequency of racial profiling, police brutality, and the extrajudicial killing of unarmed African Americans by law enforcement. While BLM has been responsible for raising consciousness, it has simultaneously been the victim of attempts to pervert its agenda, as well as efforts to coopt and hijack its message—not to mention the sociopolitical urgency of its oppositional energy. Even so, the challenge posed by right-wing conservatives attempting to label #BlackLivesMatter a hate group is arguably less pernicious than the threat posed by liberal progressiveness, which has transformed the movement into a form of cultural appreciation and into a palatable social spectacle, largely drained of its oppositional force. In the introduction to a special issue of the journal *Black Camera*, Chip Linscott (in his summation of the various arguments advanced in the exposé) contemplated the manner in which popular media has impacted the #BlackLivesMatter movement, in many respects spawning an explosion of cultural forms:

> Rather, we contend that the same social, political, and cultural forces that have made the movement a necessity—black life and black death, black love, mourning and memorialization, anti-blackness, police violence and murder, racism *tout court*, misogyny, vast inequality, scarce representation in politics and media, etcetera—also inspire contemporary artistic, cultural-expressive, and mediatic productions.[6]

Linscott is correct in his assessment that we are witnessing what he calls a *mediatic* moment in American culture, where the spectacle of blackness is ubiquitous. However, this cultural fixation on the miseries of black life: the traumas brought about by discrimination and violence, are often misread as an earnest national conversation about racism. One of the contributors to the special issue, Michele Prettyman Beverly, made similar observations in her unpacking of the media response to the movement. However, she makes an important point that it was precisely the "spectacle of black death captured on video footage" that energized the #BlackLivesMatter movement, ultimately galvanizing its oppositional momentum:[7]

> #BlackLivesMatter as an advocacy and social media movement coalesced in the wake of the 2012 death of Trayvon Martin and the acquittal of George Zimmerman and became an organizing principle for those mobilizing after the murder of Michael Brown in Ferguson, Missouri, along with numerous subsequent

> tragic deaths. In response to the stunning number of incidents of police and civilian brutality leading to the deaths of often-unarmed men, women, and children, #BlackLivesMatter challenges the persistent devaluation and murder of black bodies and has developed a platform to inform, organize, connect, and advocate on behalf of black people and any dehumanized people. Both the civil rights and #BlackLivesMatter movements recognized and cultivated the need for collective and public mourning that extended beyond ceremony and ritual, beyond churches and other sanctioned spaces for memorializing. In the era of #BlackLivesMatter in particular, mourning transgresses physical, social, and spatial boundaries; grieving and eulogizing are virtual, mobile, shareable, disseminated, posted, and messaged . . . #BlackLivesMatter is inextricably connected to spectacles of violence and protest and an archive of imagery including a range of photographs, works of art, murals, videos, police camera images, and surveillance footage capturing conflict, memorials, confrontation, and rebellion.[8]

While Beverly aptly characterizes BLM's striking impact on the media landscape, the contradiction is that, it is this same tendency toward hyperbolic representation that forever traps black life in an endless cycle of ideological overdetermination, defined by misery, dysfunction, and death. This contradiction does not, however, negate the fact that American society has deep racial divisions and hierarchies that largely determine forms of social value and worth: "Our culture continues to decide which people matter and under what circumstances they are to be valued; whose lives and deaths are felt and affirmed; whose stories are told; which losses we will acknowledge and how that loss is quantified or whether it is even quantifiable at all."[9]

Both Linscott and Beverley agree that #BlackLivesMatter has spawned a cultural moment (for better or worse) that is profoundly visual: an imaged-based, social media movement that has globally defined the lives of black Americans as trapped by an all-encompassing and suffocating conglomeration of degradations and perils. Needless to say, this characterization is a misleading one, but it nevertheless persists largely unchallenged. My concern here is intellectually linked to the opening quotation by Žižek, which questions the disingenuous nature of liberalist and tolerance-based approaches to diversity. I tend to agree that liberal tolerance has been instrumental in the creation of so-called solidarity-based and anti-hegemonic sentiments that are ultimately cosmetic. This understanding has, in many respects, led me to challenge the manner in which I discuss race, and has encouraged me to question the social, intellectual, and institutional role that blackness (including my own presence and intellectual labor) occupies.

Over the past decade, I have spent considerable time unpacking the phenomenon of post-black: a terminology that has found a rather reluctant, yet persistent position within the discourses surrounding African American art and culture. Post-blackness (which in my formulation is a theory of representation) has enabled us to unpack the post–Civil Rights generation's satirical and rapidly shifting attitudes about race. Many in the African American artistic and intellectual communities have reacted to post-black with condemnation and hostility. These attitudes have largely been the result of two core misinterpretations. The first is its mischaracterization as a post-racial stance (an anti-black blackness). The second is a failure to understand that post-black is a theory of representation: it is a means to both understand and characterize a set of aesthetic, conceptual, political and artistic tendencies that are present in the creative practices of post–Civil Rights generation artists. It is not, in contrast to its rampant mischaracterization, a genre of art—nor should its critical reflection be regarded as a form of advocacy. The role of the critic (as a public witness) is to characterize cultural forms: to explicate them, and to render judgment—but not to promote them. Post-black functions as a means to unpack a shifting set of attitudes and expressive modalities about blackness that are steeped in satire.

I tend to regard the concept's emergence as an ethos concerned with constructing new interpretative possibilities around the visual representation of blackness. Divisive from its inception, the term "post-black" emerged in the early 2000s to describe the aesthetic and conceptual particularities of post–Civil Rights generation visual artists. Defined as a *queering* of blackness, post-black articulates how the political and visual emblems of normative blackness may not speak to the lived experiences and realities of those whose gender or sexual identities position them on the margins of society. Ultimately, post-blackness is a radical searching for new forms of self-definition that are deeply informed and enriched by the past, yet unencumbered by it. As a theory of representation, post-black can be described as both an aesthetic understanding of blackness as a modulation of an affective black sentience and a strategy that highlights expressiveness residing in materiality and form. By extension, it is more concerned with the visual and material sensuousness of blackness that take the form of fundamental ambiguities like: *l'informe*, abject materiality and formlessness. In doing so, the terminology gives a semiotic vulnerability to the overdetermined realm of black visuality. This chapter seeks to apply this terminology in service of challenging stilting racialized reductions, stereotypes, and representational forms of social symbolism—and further endeavors to develop more nuanced ways of attending to the expansive dimensions of racial representation, and the formal possibilities of the aesthetic production of blackness in visual culture. I find a type of unity between post-black and #BlackLivesMatter, as both are efforts to transcend racial reductions. This commonality is apparent, even while these formations might be characterized as competing ideological and political phenomena. Despite the misreading of post-black as annihilating, the terminology (and the cultural tendencies it describes) has productively acknowledged those constituencies who have fallen into the crevices of racial authenticity and legitimacy—those who have traditionally not been acknowledged by black resistance movements: LGBTQ and black queer communities, women, the undocumented, migrants, and the disabled. However, I tend to view both #BlackLivesMatter and post-black as attempts to resist the culturalization of politics, even while they find themselves beset by distortion, appropriation and exploitation. This may be an overly optimistic viewpoint, because these phenomena have been charged with reducing blackness to a series of limiting scripts that are too concerned with the fetishization of the black body. On the contrary, I see these efforts (despite their limitations) as sincere attempts to reimagine both the parameters of blackness (culturally, aesthetically, politically), as well as the manner in which it resists structures of intolerance.

My intellectual work has been concerned with the problem of racial difference within the disciplinary formation known as art history/visual studies. I call difference a problem because it functions in such a manner: as an unwanted or uninvited guest, as an intrusive presence that cheapens and distracts. Central to this disciplinary problem is the necessity to move beyond art history and visual culture's critical relationship to the representation of difference. This strain of research is concerned with two primary issues: the first being my discipline's antipathy toward difference, while it simultaneously ratchets up its stated commitments to diversity and equity. The other is the field's shabby and rather fetishistic treatment of racialized blackness, which has become *the* subject of representation for progressive scholarship. British-Australian scholar Sara Ahmed has discussed the recent rise in "diversity-based" discourses promoting racial equality (within academic institutions) and the simultaneous *extension* of institutional racism. In art history and visual studies, this contradiction is evidenced in the increasing prevalence of blackness as social symbolism (in representation), contrasted by the stunning lack of black scholars within the discipline itself. The black body within the milieu of institutionally dominant art history functions as one of its ultimate and most typifying reductions: the social symbol *par excellence*. As a result, the black body (as I previously advanced) has become shorthand for empty discussions of race.

Ahmed characterizes the function of "diversity work" within liberal institutions as generating the "right image" and correcting the wrong one: that perception is the problem, not the presence of structural inequity.[10] Bearing this in mind, my recent research on the intersection of art history and identity has turned away from the art object itself, directing critical attention to the discipline's methodological, ethical, and institutional complexities and contradictions. The intellectual rhetorics of diversity have an indelible impact on the ethics of art history, yet they do not intervene into the erasures and forms of racial marginalization that segregate the field. There is a contradiction between the discipline's stated ethics around diversity that take the form of what Ahmed calls "nonperformative speech acts": performative declarations of anti-racist sentiment and personal commitments that ultimately go unfulfilled.[11] My argument is that diversity is fundamentally about saying the right things, but it does not do enough to transform institutions, disciplines, and methods into more equitable spaces. The nonperformative failure of these speech acts, to borrow Ahmed's language, have become a crippling impediment to actual equitable change. The awareness of these slippery institutional speech acts and their disciplinary methods may create ruptures that open up new possibilities.

On university campuses, the impact of #BlackLivesMatter is widely felt and has ignited a spirit of activism among campus communities across the United States, including the institution where I teach. The visual signifiers of racial consciousness, anti-racist sentiment, and tolerance are everywhere and self-consciously emblazoned across office doors and windows: MLK quotations, emotionally wrenching images of civil rights protests, mixed with Coexist stickers and LGBTQ flags—all carefully curated for the optimal effect and visibility. Despite the glaring presence of these gestures, universities across the United States struggle with a striking lack of diversity and appallingly low numbers of underrepresented faculty, administrators, and students. While these performative acts are common, what do they mean within institutional systems that appear to devalue the very diversity they so passionately and visibly champion. The institutional values that #BlackLivesMatter has spawned (in their *culturalization of politics*) have made the curation of blackness the ultimate symbol of its tolerance. Put more bluntly, these nonperformative acts are meant to function as proof that the institution is not racist, or sexist, or homophobic, or transphobic, or a safe space for the undocumented. As a result, I've begun to consider how the often failing institutional politics of diversity and tolerance affect the values and methods of my chosen field, where difference similarly functions as a cosmetic distraction for the curation of diversity and politically correct sentiment.

The curation of blackness in the American art scene, in particular, has always been a fault line and an enduring source of institutional consternation. Case in point: the melée over artist Dana Schutz's painting *Open Casket* (a recreation of the notorious photograph of the slain Emmett Till), which caused a stir when included in the 2017 Whitney Biennial in New York. Schutz, a white American artist, was attacked for laying claim to an image of anti-black violence: an iconic photograph that many in the black arts community felt was the domain of African American culture. What ensued was a highly contentious and very public debate about the presence of such images in our media-saturated culture. While not taking a partisan position in this debate, I will say that I found it particularly generative that there was a public discussion about the proliferation of images of black suffering.

What do these images mean? And what is their social function? In many respects, both the images and the very predictable response to their presence, have become culture—and therefore, I am beginning to question the larger social role that blackness (as an imago and a positionality) plays within the cultural landscape. Nicole Fleetwood suggests that it is understood within visual culture scholarship, that "optical technologies have been used to discipline racialized bodies," and as she reminds us, "vision and visual technologies, in this context, are seen as hostile and violent forces that render blackness as aberration . . ."[12] Fleetwood effectively captures the inescapability of racial marking that is implicit to vision and visuality—and which functions as a powerful means to maintain power relations rooted in containment, repression, and social control. I'm also thinking here of Christian Metz's concept *scopic regime*, which has been instrumental in theorizations dedicated to unpacking the relation between looking and power, as well as the use of visual technologies within the realm of the imaginary—and as a means to produce desire.[13] Considering the relation between looking and power, vis-à-vis the representation of black bodies, there has not been a significant intracultural dialogue about the perpetuation and proliferation of what could be characterized as anti-black images by artists of African descent. Nor has there been a conversation about how black cultural producers self-position within the logics of anti-blackness in the United States.

American art historian Tanya Sheehan, in her essay entitled "A Time and a Place: Rethinking Race in American Art History," asked the important question: "where do we look for race?"[14] According to Sheehan's account, historians of American art in the second half of the twentieth century—particularly those concerned with the visual representation of race and identity—repeatedly returned to this question. In her assessment of this trend, scholars addressed this important query by turning their intellectual attention toward the black body—or more specifically, racialized blackness. Sheehan's model is a useful exemplar of a methodological problem within American art discourse toward the fetishization of difference. It is all too common for scholars within the fields of art history and visual culture to perpetuate a series of clichéd positions around difference—while not attending oppositionally (as the Slovenian philosopher Slavoj Žižek suggests) to the structural barriers that prevent equity from occurring.

Sheehan is correct that during this period, especially during the identity debates of the 1980s and early '90s, and within museum exhibitions and institutional art discourses, there was a rise in interest in contemplating the black body within the field of representation. These exhibitions, as the historian reminds us, were accompanied by published catalogues with a rather robust body of new scholarship exploring racial representation in the works of American artists like Thomas Eakins, John Singleton Copley, and Winslow Homer, as well as those of African American artists from the Harlem Renaissance to the era of multiculturalism.[15]

In her book *Regulating Aversion: Tolerance in the Age of Identity and Empire*, philosopher Wendy Brown takes on the politically leftist adherence to the cultural and institutional logics of tolerance, which forms the basis for current conceptions of liberalism. In *Regulating Aversion*, Brown argues that "tolerance is generally regarded as an un-problematized achievement of modern Western societies," but that regulation and marginalization rests at its core: that to tolerate is not an affirmation, but to conditionally allow the presence of the unwanted—a set of cultural and institutional practices she has termed: "mannered racialism."[16] Therefore, liberal tolerance both sustains and is invested in the marginality of certain subjects, and ultimately consolidates the power of the dominant. What is at stake here is the realization that liberal tolerance "produces, organizes, and marks subjects."[17] I have taken up what I consider the problems of liberal tolerance, specifically because they profoundly inform the manner in which cultural production is assessed, valued, and devalued. Along those lines, art produced by socially defined minorities, as well as the cultural production of a range of *Others* (whose work is dedicated to contesting the presence of inequity) find themselves in a marginal position within the histories and institutional structures of the arts. Liberal tolerance is fundamentally about saying the right things: polite speech, trigger warnings, anti-homophobic and anti-racist declarations, tokenism, symbolic events, and so on. However, my argument here (which is informed by Žižek and Brown) is that the institutional rhetoric of diversity often functions as a politically correct means to overtly disseminate the values of exclusion and management. Read through the logic of Brown's critique specifically, diversity means: "Yes, "our" institution discriminates. It regulates access to the institution and stringently controls certain constituency's ability to thrive. On the other hand, our discrimination is a polite one: it is rooted in tolerance and symbolic decency and manners. Under diversity, minorities may be demeaned or subordinated; yet they will be spared *homophobia*, *transphobia*, or *racism* (i.e., irrational brutal outbursts, physical violence, threats, etc.). Therefore structural bigotry (and its attendant forms of violence) is always something that occurs beyond the borders of liberal institutions and their stated values.

Ahmed's criticism of a "diversity work of perception" (the image game) is at play within disciplinary research method as well, where the presence of difference (both institutionally and representationally) is treated as an unwanted guest that is tolerated—and as Ahmed articulates, "they are temporary residents in someone else's home . . . they are welcomed *on condition* they return that hospitality by integrating into a common organizational culture, or by "being" diverse, and allowing institutions to celebrate their diversity."[18] The Othered body within the milieu of liberal academia functions as one of its ultimate and most typifying reductions: the social symbol *par excellence*. My argument here is that "social symbolism" is diversity's ultimate product: the reduction of difference as a legible and reducible imago. Put more bluntly, liberal tolerance produces an *ideal subject*, and it is this subject with which we must continually contend.

I have utilized Žižek's writings as an exemplar that has meaningfully taken up the structural logics of tolerance in liberal intellectual thought. Like Wendy Brown, Žižek's approach locates contradictions within liberal progressiveness that position difference in the role of social victimhood in both *discourse and representation*, only to fail these constituencies in larger efforts to bring about equitable change. If considered through the lens of

Žižek's and Brown's critique of liberal tolerance, in defending itself, American visual culture ultimately conceals its "innermost obscene secret": that within its institutional and representational frameworks and value systems are rituals and habits that marginalize, stereotype, and distort.[19] And according to Žižek, it is precisely this "obscene underground of habits" that is most difficult to change.[20] What takes the place of this change is a symbolic, liberalist, intellectual engagement with the representation of difference.[21]

Under this logic, difference enters into social consciousness only as objects of fantasy and spectacle, as stereotypes and projections. In psychoanalytic terms, when the body enters the realm of signification and becomes Other (in the Lacanian sense), it is simultaneously rendered a pathological subject, a symbol of lack. Several scholars have written about the perils of racial and ethnic fantasy from a psychoanalytic perspective, from Frantz Fanon and Homi Bhabha, to Stuart Hall and David Marriott, among many others. Žižek's critique of tolerance holds a particular fascination when unpacking the role that difference plays in the representational schemas of a society where racial division is fundamental to the social, economic, and political order. In his well-known investigation into the psychic effects of colonialism on the black subject, Homi Bhabha discusses the role of fantasy and racial fetishism:

> The black presence runs the representative narrative of Western personhood: its past tethered to treacherous stereotypes of primitivism and degeneracy will not produce a history of civil progress, a space for the *Socius*; its present, dismembered and dislocated, will not contain an image of identity that is questioned in the dialectic of mind/body and resolved in the epistemology of appearance and reality. The white man's eyes break up the black man's body and in that act of epistemic violence its own frame of reference transgressed, its field of vision disturbed.[22]

In *The Location of Culture*, Bhabha argues for the reading of stereotype in terms of fetishism. He suggests that the myth of historical origination—racial purity, cultural priority—produced in relation to the colonial stereotype functions to "normalize" these belief systems in the realm of representation.[23] The problematic of seeing/being seen elevates the act of looking as a key component in the policing of stereotypes in society: and by extension the maintenance of oppressive social relations. Following a similar thread, David Marriott discusses the paradoxical opposition between racial scopophilia and negrophobia—two acts of looking, one desiring and fetishistic, the other phobic and rooted in disavowal. In his writings on photography and lynching, Marriott discusses the viewing of lynching photography as functioning somewhere between pleasure and revulsion, fetishism and guilt. He continues this inquiry in his critical engagement with the late photographer Robert Mapplethorpe's controversial 1988 series, *Black Book*. The series, which consisted of images of mostly nude black men, received scrutiny for what many perceived to be fetishistic images that trafficked in racial stereotypes. Several of the more infamous images placed visual emphasis on the black male penis, playing into stereotypes and myths about sexual prowess, degeneracy, and pathology. This reading was heightened by the artist's decision to either crop out or obscure the subject's face: a gesture that removed the sitter's interiority and humanity. Two of the photographs, *Hooded Man* (1980) and *Man in a Polyester Suit* (1980), feature this obscuring by covering or omitting the face of the subject. In the first example, the subject's head is masked, with something reminiscent of a Ku Klux Klan mask. In *Man in a Polyester Suit*, the black male sitter is shown fully clothed, with head cropped out, and penis dangling oddly from his open trousers. As Marriott recounts, the image was received quite negatively, characterized as shocking and repulsive, inspiring a mix of voyeuristic fascination and revulsion. Much of the critical attention was directed toward the size of the subject's penis. Marriot cites art historian Arthur C. Danto and Andre Graham-Dixon's struggle to contend with the formal merits of Mapplethorpe's image:

> Mapplethorpe's photographs of the black male body and, in particular, the black penis, expose Danto to another fantasmatic scene, another limit to desire in looking, but here the disgust remains. It's a scene which appears to challenge the limits of the aesthetic invested by Danto who finds himself unable to follow Mapplethorpe in his feverish judgment of the 'photographical' form of the black male body . . .
>
> . . . "Sullen and heavy like the trunk of an elephant," muses Danto, reflecting on the "folkloric" tumescence of this penis (as if, like an elephant's trunk, it can feed the black man's mouth). Hanging, "veiny and pulpy" on the outside of the black man's suit, his penis is, to push the point, on the outside of the civilized. "His penises are so exotically weird," writes Andrew Graham-Dixon in response to the photograph, "they seem inhu-

> man, like some parasite species that has managed to graft itself on to the human form. . . . The penis looks like an elephant's trunk, not really human at all—certainly not civilized."[24]

In his edited volume *Representation: Cultural Representations and Signifying Practices*, Stuart Hall discusses how the spectacle of the Other (in the form of stereotype) functions in representation—inflicting a peculiar and potent form violence on the black subject, that is instrumental to the maintenance of social division and inequity. In keeping with Marriott's reading of Mapplethorpe's fetishistic images of black men, Hall unpacks the contradictory binarism of dueling stereotypes: one characterizing the black man as hyper-masculine and super-sexual, the other as passive, docile, and childish:

> The conscious attitude amongst whites—that "Blacks are not proper men, they are just simple children"—may "cover," or cover-up, for a deeper, more troubling fantasy—that "Blacks are really super-human, better endowed than whites, and sexually insatiable." It would be improper and "racist" to express the latter sentiment openly; but the fantasy is present, and secretly subscribed to by many, all the same. Thus when blacks act "macho," they seem to challenge the stereotype (that they are only children)—but in the process, they confirm the fantasy which lies behind or is the "deep structure" of the stereotype (that they are aggressive, over-sexed and over-endowed).
>
> . . . Stereotyping has its own *poetics*—its own ways of working—and its *politics*—the ways in which it is invested with power. We have also argued that this is a particular type of power—a *hegemonic* and *discursive* form of power, which operates as much through culture, the production of knowledge, imagery and representation, as through other means. Moreover, it is *circular*: it implicates "subjects" of power as well as those who are "subjected to it."[25]

In regard to the reception of African American art that deals in racial fetishism, my concern is that lingering deep within liberal multiculturalism is a postmodern racism rooted in tolerance. It is not an overt, or self-aware racism, nor is it one defined by ignorance and vulgarity. It is not crudely predicated on myths of cultural supremacy. On the contrary, it is steeped in the celebration and preservation of cultural differences and their specificities.

In this logic, minority cultures should retain their uniqueness by not being assimilated into the dominant culture. In essence, we must celebrate difference—maintaining its purity, while keeping it autonomous and separate. This is what Žižek means when he talks about liberal multiculturalism's tolerance and celebration of differences, but its lack of commitment to ending inequality, exploitation, and injustice. Racial pathology is perceived as a cultural difference to be tolerated, while the conditions (social, institutional, political, or otherwise) and root causes of that pathology go unacknowledged. Put more succinctly, pathology, degeneracy, and deficiency are so casually and uncritically grafted onto the black body that it has become *culture*, rather than a symptom of social inequity.

Wanting to devour and take something or someone in through the act of looking is not just a benign form of pleasure, or simply a means to make sense of the world. It is also a potent means to destroy: to project, distort, and indulge in fantasy. Looking is how differences are located and marked, how notions of Otherness are policed and maintained; it is how judgments are formed. It is a violent and penetrative act: invasive and scopophilic—yet seemingly banal and commonplace. How we look at difference is central to the social order. In many respects, the aim of this essay is to question the social function of racial representation, in an effort to counter or undo the damaging effects of negative and demeaning images. As Stuart Hall suggests, "to reverse the stereotype is not necessarily to overturn it,"[26] and American culture's fixation with black representation (even in its most progressive and tolerance-based politics) is self-consciously shifting this fixation toward the reification of its most troubling expressions—rather than committing its efforts toward their contestation. In his writings on the formation of difference, Homi Bhabha puts forth the notion that the ambivalent (and banal) nature of stereotypes is where these distorted perceptions become fixed upon subjects in a society where racial and ethnic discrimination is a central component of the social and political order. Difference must always be located in the matrix of seeing and being seen—and it is in these seemingly casual acts that "the object of discrimination is deemed natural and visible":[27]

> The role of fetishistic identification in the construction of discriminatory knowledges that depend on the "presence of difference," is to provide a process of splitting and multiple/contradictory belief at the point of enunciation and subjectification.[28]

Bhabha is rightly concerned with the construction and maintenance of Otherness in a colonialist and discriminatory cultural context. Stereotypes play an important role in the maintenance of social division and hierarchy—but my concern is not simply the manner in which visible and verifiable difference is used as a form of debasement and marginalization. I am also invested in understanding how tolerance-based discourses and value systems wield differences as both entertainment and as cultural capital, while simultaneously failing to disrupt a status quo. If it is true that difference must be made visible in a cultural climate of racial inequity, how are we then to gain insight into the types of images that continue to define blackness as a condition of violence, pathology, and deprivation?

Perhaps we are failing to adequately ponder, and ultimately resist, this ideological need in American society *to incorporate the spectacle of racial difference, to eat, through the eyes*, as David Marriott suggests. Even in this contentious moment, so impacted by #BlackLivesMatter, the black body is no less fraught and provocative as it has been at any other period in America's history. It holds a palpable sense of fear and fascination in the cultural consciousness. It is true that American society has a need to consume difference—often locking it into a perpetual state of lack that enables it to be approached altruistically, with tolerance, and with the appropriate amount of humanistic sympathy and moral outrage. But while these expressions of suffering become culture, other abuses are ignored. Looking at black bodies elicits a range of responses, from pleasure and revulsion, to condemnation and amused pity: but its presence must always be seen, because it functions as a visual testament that racial hierarchy is maintaining its integrity. And as a result, popular media is filled with images of black abjection: poverty, violence, buffoonery, and misery of all sorts, with few diverse or complex representations. I am concerned that all this progressive posturing has merely chosen to embrace the economic potential of the stereotype: to market it, and to capitalize on the economic viability of its enduring fascination—simultaneously reinforcing the conditions upon which blackness functions as a politically correct shorthand for well-meaning and tolerance-based discussions of race. This enduring challenge within American cultural life displaces responsibility for creating substantive structural change—in favor of celebrating the empty rhetorics, procedures, and representational regimes of diversity and tolerance.

PART III

MOVING FORWARD

Overcoming Fatigue with Rage and Joy

Chapter 10

A Eulogy in Two Parts

DOMINIQUE CHRISTINA

Ashton Sterling

Stipulation of fact:
Louisiana says every man for himself.
Carry a gun if you please.
This.
Is the South.
Aint no equivocating down here.
Steel and iron,
Iron and steel,
Red-clay conspiracy of color
Sky. Salt-edged and heavy
Sun wooed by clouds
Plump as babies
What part of red don't you get?

See Alton there?
Trying to be something
That knows pride for itself?
That good poetry—
He won't see 40.
How unoriginal.

How stamped with familiar tragedy—
We'll get to that.

In this faraway land
Women slide sons into coffins
That sit on top of the earth
Like brand new nickels
Swamps don't know how to keep corpses

Put a dead man's suit on the boy.
Something marked down,
Sleeves too long
Thrift Store bargain
Cry a river
Regular
Wave goodbye
Tradition
Some of em can't be in an open casket
Some of em can't be identified
Empty sockets
Buckshot mouth
What part of red don't you get?

July keeps a score sheet here.
You gon lose regardless.
Steel and iron
Iron and steel
Tenements with bad roofs
Leaking rain
Buckled under humidity—

We love a good funeral
Black folks I mean
Because we knew it was coming
Soon as a boy is born
We get ready for his return
To the earth
To God if you believe in Him
Got the casket picked before
He starts preschool

Ya'll did this.
You won't like hearing it.

No matter.
I gave up trying to explain.
This ain't that.
This is a requiem—
A birdsong anyhow.

See Ashton there?
A constituency of court dates and hard choices
Pockets swollen with blunt wraps and
The gun ya'll say he was reaching for . . .

That's a black man for you.
Always reaching
And dying because of it
Or the lie that he was

When maybe he was just human
Maybe he couldn't bend the way
You wanted him to
Maybe he couldn't let go of
Being a man just cuz you say so
Maybe his daddy's voice is still louder than yours
Even when you say
Freeze
Put your hands up
Get on the ground

What if these men know they are men?
Or maybe it's . . .
These boys need you to
Let em be boys
Ones who like toy guns and pretend
Like Tamir . . .
He was 12 when ya'll took him
But that's another story
About the same thing.

Alton is dying.

Tradition found him
The ordinary ferocity of
Steel and iron
Rattling bone
Hurrying blood

A man vanishing before our very eyes

Red shirt wet with his leaving,
Left arm trembling upwards
Like shaking a fist at God,
One last curse
Or prayer
Same difference

We die bad
And often
You see it
But call it something else.

You say:

He must've had it coming.
Police have always been good to me.

Philando Castile

Here
Again
The ache
The low growl of
Going from this place
To God knows where
(They call that heaven)
Here
Again
The pistoned shattered bone

Floating in a man
Until he slips from himself
Chases the one ghost that
Haunts churches and temples
Until somebody says amen

Here
Again
The woman as witness
Here
Again
The little girl
Made to watch a man
Bleed
Be jettisoned away

Here
Again
The gun
The scavenger bullets
That fret the body
To palsy

Here
Again
The spectacle
Of death
Performed on a loop
Until we forget how to
Grieve
Just another slaughtered
Negro
Just another weekday,

Here
Again
The marches
The rallies
The arrests
The hashtags

The vigils
The press conferences
The ceremonial apathy

I have forgotten how to cry in this country

I open my mouth,
I capsize.

I barely woman
I barely human
I wolf or something like it
I sugarcane and long memory
I cotton field and long blade
I eulogy
I suicide note
I manifesto
I rage
I grief
No tears left

Just teeth

I wild with it
I vengeful
I plotting heavy
I hanging on hanging on
I haunt myself
With every name
I hanging on
To every name
All their names
All their names
All their names
All their names
All their names
All their names

In response to the Question:
If 2017 was a poem, what would it be called?[1]

The year is no poem.
It won't be called anything
With light inside it—
It snatches milk from
The mouths of infants,
A lion devouring shrines and sunlight

2017 is a weapon.

A low groan in the dark,
A woman in the basement
With a wire hangar and a baby
No bigger than a mustard seed
That she will meet as an ooze in her palms
2017 is the lynch mob discography:
Girl bodies
Gay bodies
Trans bodies
Black bodies
Poor bodies
Nobodies
All strung up like
Mardi Gras beads on Main Street
The stench doesn't stop the parade

That's America.

2017 is a funeral procession.
A lunatic's marching orders

Conversion therapy
Celebrity Apprentice on
A terrible loop,

2017 is no poem.

It's the bastard child of
Interred bones in the Tallahatchie River
A severed spine in Baltimore
A boy's brain on the street in Ferguson
The last breath of a man in New York
Traffic stops that crescendoed to murder
2017 is a dustbin
Stacked with protest signs and court orders
The lickety split shudder
Of a nation that ran into its ghosts
And only the women were
Acquainted with being haunted.
Empty cupboard soliloquy queens
Snatching their children
From public schools and
Handing them switchblades
        Mommy is sorry.
        This is what the teacher won't show you.
        Take it.
        These bastards need mortality.

2017 is the state house glittered now in menstrual blood.

Girl children baying at the dawn limp moon
Oak trees decorated with brassieres
Nazis with their teeth knocked out
A linguistic resistance
With no room for words like "alt right"
When "white supremacy" is story enough.

2017 is no poem.

It's a pipeline trying
To breech an ocean,

A woman in a wheelchair
At a protest rally,
A tear gas canister on the steps of the Capitol.

2017 didn't bring my God with it.

Just hexes and hurricane winds
A democracy doomed by
The wrong weather wreckage of
Rich men and their crucifixion fetish
We gon all carry a cross
You better believe it
Let whatever happens be biblical then.
Let the locusts come if they must.

America is a murdered woman
Ghosting the world
With her cracked levees,
Her burned out mosque,
Her shot up church,
Her impossible promise
Her unmarked graves,
And I am dumb with calling her name.
Despite the yelps of history,
My wobbly faith splits heaven wide open
Reimagines God as mammy,
Starch white apron and a shotgun,
Babies suckling at her unremarkable breasts
Pushing scripture out from the rubble
Saying the battle is finally over and me,
War-walloped and heaving,
Rummaging through debris looking for
Something that glitters . . .

Oh America,
(If that is your real name)
Take these bones and perform
One last miracle
Take these hands and give me
Back my mouth

Take this mouth and give me back my feet
Take these feet and give me back my courage
Dazzle this uncaptured girl that I might
Live long enough to tell my grandchildren
About the year I stopped beseeching God and
In the trench grew my own temple.
God of the in-between,
God of the firing pin,
God of the slaughtered lamb,
God of a risen god,
Unspell me, here.

I am singing you the hymn of my skirt.
I am burning yellow dahlias on my
One good altar not splintered by shrapnel
Or singed with smoke . . .
If there is any prayer left
In this world let it be
What is left of our hearts,
Our coliseum hearts,
And the stupid hope that
Regulates the metronome
Of our blood machinery.

The orchestral thrumming,
The insistent rumble,
Of our broken, impossible hearts,
The only evidence I've ever had
That mountains can be moved.

Chapter 11

Puzzle Pieces on the Floor

Curriculum Gaps, White Fatigue, and Misunderstanding #BlackLivesMatter

JOSEPH FLYNN

In 2014, an African American teenage boy was visiting his father in a Florida gated community. During halftime of a football game, the teenager decided to walk to a nearby convenience store to get a bottle of tea and a bag of Skittles. While walking back, the neighborhood watch captain eyed the young man and found him "suspicious looking," due to the young man's hoodie and his walking in the rain. Although the local police dispatch operator told the watch captain, an older Latino man, to stay in his car and let law enforcement take over, the watch captain pursued the hoodie-wearing teen, resulting in an altercation and an eventual fatal shooting. The teenage boy, Trayvon Martin, was shot in the chest by neighborhood watch captain George Zimmerman. The act sparked nationwide protests and gave rise to the #BlackLivesMatter movement (#BLM).

As the movement gained steam, spreading like a wildfire across social media and then the popular media, a majority of White Americans expressed a range of reactions to #BLM, from full-on support of the idea to irrational anger and resistance. The response of many in the White American community was to begin the mantras "All Lives Matter" and "Blue Lives Matter" (a tribute to the truly dangerous job of police officers and a direct mocking of Black Lives Matter). As the two later slogans gained steam in the anti-protests and general sentiments that sought to embrace the notion of the sanctity of all life, the rift between the supporters of Trayvon Martin and the supporters of George Zimmerman widened and muddied the message, values, and goals of the #BLM movement. The frustration of many African Americans and their allies and accomplices deepened, for it became clear the detractors of #BLM were neither understanding nor appreciative of the unique, historic relationship between African Americans and law enforcement and other manifestations of White privilege and White supremacy. As Christopher J. Lebron opined, #BLM ultimately "seeks to undo this nation's murderous racial history."[1]

The #BLM movement was a response to both the death of Trayvon Martin and the historic desecration of the Black body across and throughout the history of Africans in America.[2] Despite that broad historical scope, many White Americans simply isolated and compartmentalized Trayvon's death, removing the tragedy from the larger historical context of violence perpetrated against African Americans. This disjuncture of contemporary events and larger historic trends reinforces frustrations between African Americans and White Americans, as it is evidence of the larger White community's inability to fully appreciate the historic institutional and systemic struggles of the African American community. Fully appreciating the African American struggle is a challenge for the irrational reactionary racist as well as for White folks who believe that racism is fundamentally wrong.

American education woefully underexposes students to the historic struggles against violence toward African Americans. This results in a disjuncture in the understanding of African American history and sews the seeds of misunderstanding, further decontextualizing the reality of Black struggles today. This disjuncture can lead to the phenomenon of White Fatigue[3] (Flynn 2015, 2018), or the tendency for White folks who may fundamentally believe racism is wrong yet grow frustrated with learning how racism functions due to focusing on interpersonal racism rather than systemic and/or institutional racism. That fatigue can foster other complications, such as connecting officer-involved shootings of unarmed Black men today with the larger historic trend of violence against Black bodies—regardless of gender.

To begin, this chapter will consider the lack of critical representations of African American history in textbooks and curricula. Next, the chapter will briefly explore historic violence perpetrated on African Americans—particularly the practice of lynching—in order to reflect the larger argument of the #BLM movement. The chapter will then consider how learning this obscured history can be challenging for White students (well, White people generally), and the engagement of that challenge can have the predictable outcomes of resistance, guilt, and fragility, further driving a wedge between White and African American communities.[4] However, it is essential to remember that there are many White students who feel racism is fundamentally wrong but struggle nonetheless, ultimately displaying White Fatigue, in light of what they did not learn and recognition of the horrific and terror-inducing phenomena—such as lynching—that shaped the Black experience and bolstered White supremacy. Ultimately, the chapter argues that as a society we must do a better job of educating our youth about the ways in which race and racism have functioned and the realities of systemic and institutional challenges that consistently negatively construct African Americans in the American imaginary, lest the fatigue, guilt, and fragility of White folks predictably produce a persistent rift between the resistant White community and the Black community along with its allies and accomplices.

The Black Hole of Textbooks

As the death toll of unarmed Black men began to receive national attention in the wake of the deaths of Trayvon Martin, Michael Brown, Eric Garner, Sandra Bland, Alton Sterling, Philando Castille, Laquan McDonald, and many others, the #BlackLivesMatter (or #BLM) movement took root. This forced Americans not only to observe the rash of deaths but also to engage and reckon with the historic and contemporary reality of ravaged black bodies. Furthermore, these events challenged the nation to consider how we reform criminal justice to be more fair and equitable.[5] Despite (or perhaps because of) #BLM protesters' pointed civil disobedience regarding officer-involved shootings of unarmed Black men and women, many White Americans were left scratching their heads, unable (and some unwilling) to acknowledge the notion that #BLM was considering both contemporary and historic trends of violence against Black bodies.

To deflect, the alternative hashtags #AllLivesMatter and #BlueLives Matter emerged from White and often politically conservative circles, transparent rhetorical strategies of backlash against the goals and ideals of #BLM. Detractors of #BLM promoted the idea that the movement was a self-righteous, anti-White, anti-police movement bent on promoting hateful, prejudiced ideals. However, that clearly missed the point of the movement and the nature of racism in America, historically and currently. American politics and foreign policy expert David Smith (2017) pointed out:

> "All Lives Matter" erases a long past and present of systemic inequality in the US. It represents a refusal to acknowledge that the state does not value all lives in the same way. It reduces the problem of racism to individual prejudice and casts African Americans as aggressors against a colourblind post-civil rights order in which White people no longer "see race."[6]

For a slightly deeper dive into the misunderstanding of White resisters of #BLM, an editorial from *The Economist* further clarified:

> Someone who says that black lives matter does not imply that other lives do not—*they are simply reminding people that for most of American history black lives have been valued less than white ones.* The days of slavery and de jure segregation have mercifully passed, but black Americans remain poorer, less healthy and more likely to be killed by police than whites. You can agree or disagree with BLM's platform, but nothing in it promotes hatred of any race or group (emphasis added).[7]

Although the points both Smith and *The Economist* make are spot-on, I must quibble with the notion of *reminding*. You cannot remind someone of something if they did not know it in the first place. Unfortunately, for many White folks the persistence of memory about anti-Black violence and the realities and legacies of institutional and systemic racism is hobbled by a curriculum and popular culture that promotes liberal notions of human diversity and cooperation over sustained, rigorous, critical examinations of U.S. history and society.[8] U.S. history curriculum, particularly through textbooks, tends to construct narratives of national progress, equality, and ethnic success, particularly the success of European ethnic groups.[9]

Before going further, White ignorance of the historic violence against African Americans must be considered. It is not so much that White folks en masse have never heard of lynchings or the depravity of slavery. Rather, it is argued that White folks, en masse, are not fully appreciative of the depths of that violent depravity and how that depravity cuts across the history of Africans in the United States (and throughout the Black diaspora). In my experience as a former high school English teacher and professor of both curriculum and instruction and Black Studies, when I engage these issues many students are shocked and dumbstruck at how extreme the violence has been. Knowing that something happened and critically appreciating what those events mean are two different issues. In short, many White students in my higher education classrooms have heard of these phenomenon but know little about them. As such, the narratives of slavery, lynching, Jim Crow laws and social practices, and other forms of anti-Black violence are cursorily understood while the deeper systemic, institutional connections are not fully formed. In addition, that experience is about what college students learn. Consider for a moment the millions of people who do not learn about these issues in the confines of a higher education setting. What do they learn about the historic violence perpetrated against African Americans? How much do they really know?

Simultaneously, these narratives all but silence critical and painful explorations of the depravity experienced by marginalized groups.[10] Although it is wonderful and important to our national identity to promote progress, equality, and the success of ethnic immigrants, that ought not happen at the expense of more robust (and dare I say honest) explorations of the damage and violence perpetrated against racial minoritized groups, in this case African Americans. To not be honest about that historic and current reality is to further a truncated story of (African) American history and further causes more collective dissonance about African Americans' continued struggle and collective sense of outrage after officer involved shootings of unarmed Black folks. The American curriculum and popular culture have tended to cursorily gloss over these realities that have persisted for centuries, and the depths of dehumanizing acts perpetrated against those of African descent are left to the historical dustbin with dismissals like, "Yeah, we know Black people were treated badly" or "Yeah, but we dealt with those issues in the '60s."

Although many Americans know of the broad strokes of African American history, they do not necessarily know the substance. Tosolt and Love (2012) point out "previous studies examining school textbooks argue that textbooks reaffirm the status quo and fail to help students understand the complicated structures of racism, sexism, and classism which are embedded within American society."[11] In effect, textbooks and the general curriculum fail to engage critical examinations of racism (and other forms of oppression) in a bait and switch of sorts that promotes notions of equality and progress that ultimately fall apart under heavier scrutiny.[12] It is not that Americans do not know that slavery existed, but that nationally our understanding of its history and legacy is minimal, trivial, and routinely controversial in

K–12 schools. Historian Susan Eva O'Donovan summarized the resistance to teaching slavery:

> Despite the proliferation of summer institutes, despite Congress's 2008 apology for the "fundamental injustices" of slavery, and despite ongoing revelations about slavery's ties to businesses, banks, and Ivy League institutions, America's slave past remains a tricky topic to teach. Tangled up with contemporary social and political issues and distorted by years of literary and cinematic treatments (including some of Hollywood's most lucrative productions), slavery continues to loom as something of a pedagogical minefield, one that many teachers are unprepared to deal with and consequently wish to avoid.[13]

Due to its horrors and the direct implication of White privilege and supremacy, slavery is the kind of topic that is easy for citizens—students—to think they "got it" by just hearing that it happened. Again, simply knowing that it happened precludes more critical considerations, especially the considerations about how the institution established race relations, sustained and cemented a racial hierarchy, provided an economic springboard for America (i.e., White America), *and* normalized violence against Black bodies.

When slavery is taken up, there is often miseducation abound. For instance, in 2015, the Texas State Board of Education—which has an incredible amount of power in determining what information is in textbooks—and textbook publisher McGraw-Hill were lambasted for adopting a textbook that reimagined slaves as "workers."[14] A few years later, in 2018, the Southern Poverty Law Center (SPLC) released a report that expressed some truly troubling findings. The SPLC report found: high school seniors struggle on the most basic questions about slavery in the U.S.; teachers, even those committed to teaching about slavery, struggle to dive deeply into the subject; textbooks do not comprehensively cover the topic; and, state standards do not set high expectations for teaching about the complexities of slavery.[15] This is staggering, considering the profound impact slavery has had on the United States. But to take it a step further, Ellen Bressler Rockmore (2015) offered a critique of the language of textbooks and how the real violence perpetrated against the enslaved can be minimized. She considered textbook authors' stylistic decisions, such as using passive voice, that ultimately produces the message to students that slavery was not so terrible. To illustrate she offered this example of textbook language:

> Some slaves reported that their masters treated them kindly. To protect their investment, some slaveholders provided adequate food and clothing for their slaves. However, severe treatment was very common. Whippings, brandings, and even worse torture were all part of American slavery.[16]

This gets at the heart of this chapter. Our nation—including its teachers and other education professionals—is so resistant to discuss the reality of slavery that contrarian and incomplete information about slavery persists. Whippings, branding, and even worse torture were not just part of American slavery, that violence was part and parcel to slavery. That violence sowed the seeds of normalizing violence against Black bodies. In effect, the protests of the #BlackLivesMatter movement begins with that obscured history. These gaps in the curriculum have an indelible and complicating effect on how we see the history of the United States, the history of African Americans, our national penchant for violence generally, and our national penchant for the desecration of Black bodies specifically.

Although the institution of slavery is woefully undertaught in American schools, we can safely assume that people do understand that violence against African Americans happened but not necessarily the depths of violence perpetrated against African Americans. A simple Google search can expose one to the many draconian torture devices used to discipline slaves, devices so monstrous even the Marquis de Sade would shudder. What is even less explored in the American curriculum is the horrific phenomenon of lynching.

An Ugly Pastime: The Trend of Mob Violence and Lynching

> Black bodies swinging in the southern breeze
> Strange fruit hanging from the poplar trees[17]
>
> —Louis Allan [pseudonym of Abel Meeropol] (1937)

Some of the most searing images of the Civil Rights Movement of the 1950s and 1960s come from the televised footage of German shepherds attacking innocent protesters in Birmingham, Alabama, in Ingram Park on May 3, 1963. It can be safely argued that the violence perpetrated in Ingram Park that iconic day has been seen by people across the globe since originally airing, especially here in the United States. In addition to vicious guard dogs, protesters were confronted with tear gas, batons, gun butts, fire hoses, and fists by the Birmingham Department of Public Safety (police). (And of course, this level of violence was not a unique phenomenon to Birmingham but occurred throughout the South and in many places in the North and West.) Equally powerful are the images of Black—and White—protesters sitting-in at lunch counters, or the footage of protesters fleeing bombed busses on Freedom Rides across the South. We consistently see these images on television documentaries, snapshots accompanying texts in textbooks, museum exhibits, and other popular spaces. So, the notion that violence has historically happened against African Americans is no national secret. However, as appalling as those images are, they serve as thumbnails for a much deeper, darker history of mob violence against African Americans.

Mob violence against African Americans was a regular occurrence throughout the history of Africans in America. Apart from the legal violence against Black bodies perpetrated through slavery there had also been routine mob violence against Black folks since Emancipation in 1865. Mob violence against African American slaves is a contested point. Some historians argue that mob violence against slaves was rare since they were considered the *property* of White men. On the other hand, some historians argue that mob violence and the lynching of slaves happened regularly and was intended to sustain the antebellum slave culture.[18]

Lynching historian Michael Pfeifer elucidates the reality of Southern White violence against African Americans and explains the genesis of the term lynching and the North's furthering of the practice despite its self-avowed disdain for the Southern ritual. Pfeifer states:

> Racially motivated violence against African Americans was not new in the 1860s. White southerners had collectively murdered African Americans during slavery, engaging in extralegal executions by having and burning at least forty-four slaves in the South from 1824–1862. In the antebellum era, Americans began to call this practice of southern racial violence "lynching," a term they also used to describe lethal and nonlethal summary collective violence that targeted whites in the South and whites, blacks, Indians, and Mexicans in regions outside the South. Southern extralegal executions of African Americans were frequently reported in the northern and abolitionist press, sometimes with editorial comment asserting that informal collective executions of slaves were an inevitable byproduct of the inhumanity and barbarity of the social relations of southern poverty. But racial violence was

> also a familiar phenomenon in the North. Groups of northern whites, often working class, had rioted against blacks in a variety of urban settings in the early republic and, especially, in the antebellum era, as social tensions rose in the wake of agitation for immediate abolitionism after 1830.[19]

Lynching, or extrajudicial violence perpetrated against an individual, grew to be one of the primary forms of racial terrorism employed by White Americans to maintain America's White racial hierarchy.

Dwight Murphey defined lynching and differentiated it from other acts of violence. He stated that lynching is

> an execution that is done outside the processes of established law by several or even many people in response to a perceived outrage, is motivated by a desire to vindicate the moral sense of the community, enjoys general public approval in the local community, and has as its target a specific person or persons.[20]

The Equal Justice Initiative has documented 4,084 racial terror lynchings occurring between 1877 and 1950, with the vast majority being African American men. What also cannot be dismissed is that according to records approximately 3 percent of those lynched between 1882 and 1930 (also known as the "lynching era") were females (and some of those were White women who cavorted with African Americans or showed anti-racist sentiments). The Equal Justice Initiative stated in their report *Lynching in America: Confronting the Legacy of Racial Terror*:

> Of the 4084 African American lynching victims EJI documented, nearly 25 percent were accused of sexual assault and nearly 30 percent were accused of murder. Hundreds more Black people were lynched based on accusations of far less serious crimes like arson, robbery, non-sexual assault, and vagrancy, many of which were not punishable by death if convicted in a court of law.[21]

What is even more disturbing is the fact that 4,084 represents *reported* lynchings, arousing the notion that many more could have happened, but it is impossible to surmise even a ballpark number.

Beginning in the Reconstruction period, White on Black extra-judicial violence and race riots grew to be widespread across the country between the late 1800s through the middle 1900s, and region was no guarantee of safety. Race riots erupted in Wilmington, North Carolina (1898); Atlanta, Georgia (1906); Springfield, Illinois (1908); East St. Louis, Illinois (1917); Tulsa, Oklahoma (1921); and the infamous Red Summer (1919) in which White on Black race riots ignited in over twenty-five cities, including Knoxville, Tennessee; Omaha, Nebraska; Chicago, Illinois; and Washington, DC. The primary reasons for these riots were often the accusation of rape of a White woman by a Black man (often unfounded), backlash against African American political empowerment, and economic strife.[22] No matter the reason for the spark, there was always a foundation of terrorism and the attempt to keep "the Blacks" in their "place," and extreme outbursts and constant threat of horrific violence was an essential tool in the maintenance of the Southern racial caste system and the Northern disdain for African Americans.

In contrast, during the race riots of the 1960s and beyond, the lion's share of those riots were African Americans *responding* to persistent police brutality and/or economic unrest, as wanton White mob violence slowed. For example, the Watts and Detroit riots of 1965 and 1967, respectively, the Los Angeles riots of 1992, and the Baltimore riots of 2015 were direct responses to historic police brutality and economic divestment in predominantly Black communities, among other issues. To wit, many do not call these riots but uprisings because they were events of protest and not merely senseless violence. Regardless, White on Black riots were not the only times lynching was employed. Lynchings could happen with hundreds to thousands of onlookers, or in the dead of night with only a few witnesses.

Lynching was and is nothing to trivialize. If there is anything in human history that can be labeled the zenith of inhumanity it is lynching. These were some of the most grotesque acts of violence, and many of the participants included not only White men but also White women and children and so called God-fearing people. Many folks memorialized the events with photographs, smiling, reveling, and pointing. Photographs were circulated widely as mementos and postcards, and that served to bolster the point of lynchings: keeping African Americans in their place.[23] It is a testament to how pernicious racism is that so many people could be involved with lynching without batting an eye to the depravity and inhumanity. Perloff (2000) informs that "public opinion and elites, particularly in Southern communities, frequently viewed lynchings as necessary mechanisms to enforce racial norms."[24] And without doubt, lynchings were in fact terrifying.

I do not want to belabor the issue or turn this chapter into a series of lynching recounts. Rather, my intention here is to consider how this part of our history not being essential to school curriculum results in the ways in which many White folks fail to comprehend why so many African Americans are frustrated about officer-involved shootings and, by extension, supportive of the #BlackLivesMatter movement. But when considering what a lynching was like, they could be as simple as someone being hanged from a tree (horrifying enough) to much more grotesque displays of wanton violence. Curriculum theorist William Pinar retold a lynching account from Marianna, Florida, in 1934 by Howard Kester, a White NAACP investigator. Kester's informant recounted:

> After taking the nigger to the woods about four miles from Greenwood, they cut off his penis. He was made to eat it. Then they cut off his testicles and made him eat them and say he liked it. (I gathered that this barbarous act consumed considerable time and that other means of torture were used from time to time on Neal.) Then they sliced his sides and stomach with knives and every now and then somebody would cut off a finger or toe. Red hot irons were used on the nigger to burn him from top to bottom. From time to time during the torture a rope would be tied around Neal's neck and he was pulled up over a limb and held there until he almost choked to death when he would be let down and the torture began all over again.[25]

As humanly aberrant as this eye-witness description sounds, it is actually typical for a lynching.

This description is nothing short of macabre, reported with a peculiar objectivity. Press reports of lynchings often detailed such horror, and they were especially damning of African American victims. As professor of communications Richard M. Perloff explained:

> Articles on Black lynchings had a special vitriolic quality. Newspaper stories identified the race of the accused; assumed without question that the accused person was guilty; used a number of dehumanizing terms to label the Black victim—for example, *wretch*, *fiend*, and *desperado*; assumed the Black person's race predisposed him to commit violent crimes, particularly rape; and sometimes self-righteously defended lynching of Black individuals. These descriptions would unquestionably fall under the category of racist discourse.[26]

What must be stressed here is that when it is said that many would come to watch and/or actively participate in a lynching, law enforcement was there too. Lynchings happened with White police officers actively participating or complicity standing idly by. That is not to say no White police officers ever stopped a lynching. Although exact numbers cannot be pinned down, research suggests that between half to two-thirds of lynchings were foiled, usually by law enforcement[27] (Griffin, Clark, and Sandberg 1997; Pinar 2001). Even so, a significant number of lynchings occurred with the participation of police, often erasing public records of the event.[28] Frankly, if the data suggest that anywhere between one-third to half of all *recorded* lynchings happened, that means law enforcement either did not stop and/or participated in lynchings. This leaves a sour feeling in the collective memory of African Americans, and begs the question that if law enforcement can participate in lynchings, can we ever trust them to protect and serve the Black community? Moreover, this question has to be asked in the context of law enforcement's historic mandates to capture fugitive slaves, contain or push African Americans into particular designated spaces, and participate in White supremacist organizations, among other activities.

This is a crucial point in learning this past through our curricula and textbooks. It helps us understand the nature of systemic and institutional racism and why African Americans would feel that they receive inequitable and unjust—let alone disrespectful—treatment from law enforcement today. It is difficult to summarily dismiss any racial group's skepticism of an institution such as law enforcement if we know how historically law enforcement has aided and abetted racial mob violence and extrajudicial summary executions (with no due process, let alone evidence). Likewise, that malfeasance can be clearly traced from then to now, especially in light of the high-profile federal investigations of Ferguson, Missouri; Chicago; and Baltimore police departments. Collectively, their findings show rampant deplorable acts against African Americans that include torture, profiling and targeting African American citizens, forced confessions, routine excessive force, rampant disrespect when engaging African American citizens, spreading racist jokes and paraphernalia through departments, and not promoting African American officers through the ranks.[29]

In turn, when an officer-involved shooting or killing of an unarmed African American happens, the practice of lynching and law enforcement's tacit or direct involvement is an indelible part of the collective memory of the African American experience. It becomes *another example* of how African Americans are marginalized, as a noun and a verb. Furthermore, the reactions of White folks who assumed the lynched victim was "up to no good anyway" are the roots of suspicion toward contemporary White folks who criticize the victim for past indiscretions or showing any frustrations about treatment from officers. Like Michael Brown stealing a handful of cigars, Eric Garner illegally selling loosies (single cigarettes), Trayvon Martin playfully posing like a "thug" in a picture on Facebook, or Amadou Diallo reaching for what "looked" like a gun. That urge to justify the killing over privileging the humanity of the victim is a cultural wolf whistle that beckons that history of violence against Black folks. Although the history of White police brutality against African Americans is also essential to understanding the prelude that foregrounds the current state of affairs #BLM stands against, I know that other chapters in this volume adeptly explore that troubled history.

My intention here, again, is to introduce a topic that is fundamental to the ways in which the grotesque practice of lynching is equally profound to the African American experience, but it is also neglected in the American curriculum. The full scope of that history must be conveyed to the critical mass of Americans in order to understand why so many African Americans are wary of law enforcement and supportive of protests, policies, and action that question authorities and challenge our law enforcement institutions to implement thoughtful and effective reforms, the ultimate goal of the #BlackLivesMatter movement. Also, this exposure helps create a stronger understanding of how institutional racism works, for lynching was legitimated by the media, law enforcement, slow-to-act policymakers, and other institutions. But, learning about these issues can cause a great deal of cognitive and spiritual dissonance for White students. After all, this is deeply challenging and painful information. That dissonance can lead to White Fatigue and further hamstring progress between White and Black communities.

White Fatigue and the Trouble with Racial Violence

Let's be honest. Learning about race and racism is challenging. Intellectually. Psychologically. Spiritually. It is intellectually challenging because there is an intense amount of history, ideas, and theories that ought to be engaged in order to have enough objective information to make sense of things. It is psychologically challenging because we often tell painful stories about racism that can cause cognitive dissonance and make folks question how race impacts them personally. And that needs to happen. If people are not provided the space and respect to speak their truths, reconciliation is deferred. Oftentimes for White learners, especially those who fundamentally believe racism is wrong, feelings of guilt can settle in. People can get lost in or resign to guilt, never moving beyond that space of hollow confusion about why and how did racism happen and it all seems too big for one to change. That leads to the spiritual challenge. Engaging in learning about race and racism forces us to ask essential questions about the nature of humanity, what does one mean by justice, how did these . . . events, atrocities, exclusions . . . have an impact on who I am and how I got here? When that complexity is coupled with K–12 curriculum that merely engage these issues on the surface, deeper learning about these issues can be overwhelming to many White students. Again, it's complex. That complexity can lead to fatigue.

White fatigue is "a temporary state in which individuals who are understanding of the moral imperative of anti-racism disengage from or assume they no longer need to continue learning about how racism functions due to a simplistic understanding of racism as primarily an individual's problem."[30] When it comes to a phenomenon like officer-involved shootings of unarmed Black men and women, many White folks who say they are not racist, and truly mean it, cannot actively see the workings of systemic and institutional racism in real time.

A June 2018 Pew Research Center survey showed that 57 percent of White respondents felt that the United States' growing diversity was making the nation a better place, while only 14 percent reported growing diversity is making it worse.[31] At the same time, Gallup polling also shows that White respondents have a skewed view about the reality of the African American struggle.[32] Gallup's polling demonstrated that 75 percent of Whites think Black kids have as good a chance at a good education, while 49 percent of Blacks do. 75 percent of Whites think Blacks have as good a chance at finding housing they desire compared to 46 percent of Blacks. 79 percent of Whites think Blacks are treated fairly at work compared to 46 percent of Blacks. 80 percent of Whites think Blacks are not treated less fairly in stores compared to 46 percent of Blacks. And, 55 percent of Whites think Blacks are not treated less fairly in dealing with police compared to 32 percent of Blacks. What is striking about these numbers is between 1997 and 2016 they have fluctuated only slightly. This indicates an important point. White folks en masse tend not to see the reality of social conditions of African Americans, begging the question of why these gaps in perceptions persist.

A significant part of the problem is the lack of sustained, critical explorations about how the histories of racial groups in the United States are divergent histories and our institutions—government, law enforcement, the courts, real estate, media, education, and others—continue to produce inequitable outcomes for African Americans. When it comes to the relationship between the African American community and law enforcement, the lack of historicity regarding the relationship between the African American community and law enforcement—specifically the ways in which law enforcement has been complicit in the marginalization of Black folks, of which lynching is a part of that history—can prevent the White community from fully appreciating how and why the Black community can have the frustrated reactions they do when another unarmed Black person is killed by police. All this despite a majority of White folks (56%) believing racism against African Americans is widespread in the United States, according to the same Gallup polling.[33] This displays the need for more substantive exploration and deeper understanding about the history of racist practices perpetrated against the African American community, the depth of trauma and frustration for African Americans about that treatment, and how those phenomena are part and parcel to current realities. Even though we do see a majority of White Americans understanding that racism is real and wrong, learning those dynamics is a complex and frustrating activity, for such critical explorations directly challenges status quo narratives about personal responsibility, the sanctity of our public institutions, and the ways in which struggle is rooted in the histories of different racial communities. I submit that the intellectual, psychological, and spiritual dissonance caused by such explorations can produce White fatigue, and that fatigue further impedes racial understanding and healing.

Concluding Thoughts

The points raised in this chapter are not to say that these lessons are *never* taught in schools. After all, I personally know history, social studies, and English/Language Arts teachers who successfully engage their students in this stream of American history. However, they are not the lion's share of teachers, and no specific standards demand this material and these connections be taught in elementary, middle, or secondary schools in the United States. As pointed out above, there is a national head-nod to historic violence against

African Americans, but the critical connections of those historic trends to current police violence against African Americans is not as robust. After all, if it were, it would be difficult to cavalierly declare "all lives matter" over "Black lives matter." Figuratively speaking, it is as though the nation is looking at a complex puzzle, one in which the final picture can be guessed, but since significant pieces of the puzzle are missing we cannot see the full reality of why "Black lives matter."

To be Black in America is to eternally struggle to uncover the truth. Not only struggle to discover the source of one's lineage, but also struggle to have the story of the race told—properly, honestly, and with the dignity it deserves. Without doubt, the history of African Americans is a history of struggle, perseverance, ingenuity, and progress. Simultaneously, it is a story of reaction—reaction to the dehumanizing and often violent marginalization of African Americans through law, policy, and social practice across the history of the nation.

Meanwhile, to be White in America is to struggle to catch up to the reality and depths of the marginalized histories of marginalized groups. That struggle to understand race, racism, and the role of Whiteness is challenging intellectually, psychologically, and spiritually, to say the least. This is a perennial challenge, even for a White person who knows racism is wrong but continues to struggle to understand the connections, realities, and repercussions of systemic and institutional racism nonetheless. In this process of learning, White fatigue for them can often translate into Black frustration, rage, and the declaration that Black lives matter.

Chapter 12

"We're Going to Have to Do It Ourselves"

Banking Black in the United States

ANDREW J. PADILLA

Introduction

Since the founding of the United States, Black bodies have been under attack. So too has black wealth. This article looks at the movement of money during the Black Lives Matter protests—specifically, the millions spent on surveilling communities after the Black Lives Matter protests and the millions divested from White-owned institutions and reinvested into Black banks. The trail of money reveals a history of resistance, and ingenuity often ignored in the story of U.S. race relations. I trace this history through a media review and interviews with Bank Black USA lead organizer Justin Garrett Moore (figure 12.1), and with Me'Lea Connelly, the director of the Association for Black Economic Power (ABEP).

There is a difference between divestment from existing White-owned structures that are harming our communities, supporting people of color lead structures that are struggling today, and creating new structures for the world we wish to see. The pain of the Black Lives Matter protests has inspired all three. Over the last few years, our bodies have spent so much time on the front lines. The initiatives I cover in this chapter have offered community space to reflect, educate, heal emotionally, mentally, and plan

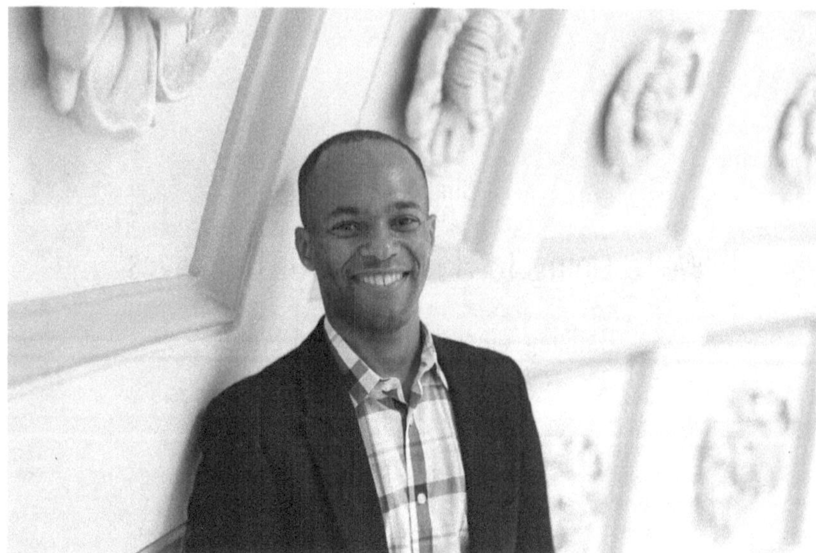

Figure 12.1. Andrew Padilla, *Justin Garrett Moore*, lead organizer for Bank Black USA, 2017. © Andrew Padilla.

long term for the future. As someone who was deeply involved in the Black Lives Matter protests and the Bank Black movement, I speak in the first person for much of this piece.

There's "No Money"

I opened Twitter and saw the video of NYPD officer Daniel Pantaleo choking Eric Garner to death. I was stunned into silence. I knew police violence existed; the only time I had been held at gunpoint was by NYPD's finest. But I had never watched someone die on video before. Enraged, I spent the summer of 2014 protesting with tens of thousands of New Yorkers to call for Officer Pantaleo's arrest and prosecution. On December 3, 2014, a New York grand jury declined to press charges against the officer, just days after Mike Brown's killer, Officer Darren Wilson, escaped prosecution in Ferguson, Missouri.[1] Through our anger, we called for many things. In addition to punishment for Officer Pantaleo, many called for the police to be defunded, money re-routed to support the communities they had historically targeted. Not one person at the Eric Garner protests demanded police body cameras. We all watched Eric Garner die on a cell phone video, and no justice was served. The only person to see jail time was the cameraman himself. Over the coming months and years, body cameras would be proposed by the media, political elites, as a technological revolution in police accountability.[2] In 2015, the Obama administration proposed a $75 million program to equip agencies across the United States with 50,000 cameras. By February of 2019, some 20,000 body cameras, one for every uniformed patrol officer, had been distributed to the NYPD, the world's largest police force.[3] Funding for new police and jails would rise throughout this same period.

While the state was investing in our surveillance and incarceration, activists throughout the United States began to focus on their own individual investments. From civil rights, South African apartheid, anti-tobacco campaigns to current-day environmental movements, activists have long used divestment to economically sanction those that seek to harm their communities and invest in their own growth. Over the last few years, thousands of U.S. citizens who aligned with Black Lives Matter began to fight back against policing and predatory financiers. We believed that by divesting from institutions that harm our communities and investing in our growth we had the potential to not only help us sustain our movement but also the ability to magnify changes in policy that could benefit our people.

Growing up in East Harlem, the phrase I heard most often in our politics was that there was "no money." The lack of funds for basic societal needs was always only partially true. Over the last three decades, communities of color in the United States have seen a precipitous decline in the resources in social safety net programs and infrastructure. At the same time, these same communities have seen a dramatic increase in the funds used to support policing that facilitates their own criminalization and mass incarceration.[4] As Michele Alexander notes in "The New Jim Crow,"[5] much of this increase in funding for police was justified through the "war on drugs," a political project with its roots in the segregationist "law and order" period of the 1950s and 1960s. The "war on drugs" narratively altered how communities of color could be attacked in the post-segregation political climate, without having to mention race explicitly. John Ehrlichman, Nixon's former domestic policy advisor, speaking in 1994 on drug prohibition politics, explained:

> The Nixon campaign in 1968, and the Nixon White House after that, had two enemies: the antiwar left and Black people. You understand what I'm saying? We knew we couldn't make it

> illegal to be either against the war or Black, but by getting the public to associate the hippies with marijuana and Blacks with heroin, and then criminalizing both heavily, we could disrupt those communities. We could arrest their leaders, raid their homes, break up their meetings, and vilify them night after night on the evening news. Did we know we were lying about the drugs? Of course we did.[6]

Since Richard Nixon declared the "war on drugs" in 1971, over $1 trillion has been spent on incarcerating a generation of fathers, brothers, mothers, sisters and more. The incarceration of Black bodies and the introduction of tanks and military equipment to civilian police inevitably seeded contemporary tensions between community and police. Chants like "NYPD KKK how many kids have you killed today?" and "Back up back up we want freedom freedom all these killer ass cops we don't need um need um!" were generations in the making.

For many on the right of U.S. politics and those hoping to maintain the status quo, our chants did not sit well. Protesters were called "cop haters," "communists," and "criminals." Many who have spoken out, like the man who recorded Eric Garner's death, were eventually pursued by the state. The death of Eric Garner's daughter, activist Erica Garner, shed light on just how many Black Lives Matter activists we have lost to heart attacks, suicide, and suspicious circumstances.[7] The stress of being a part of such a traumatic movement has consequences. In 2018 the medical journal *The Lancet* confirmed what activists and organizers already knew, that police killings of unarmed Black Americans had adverse effects on the mental health of Blacks in the United States.[8]

Amidst this climate in the summer of 2015, organizers from throughout the United States converged in Cleveland for the first National Convening of the Black Lives Matter movement. Thousands of activists and organizers gathered to build relationships and protest. Organizers described the conference's original goal as strategizing to find ways the Movement for Black Lives could hold law enforcement accountable for their actions on a national level.[9] Eventually, the focus of the organizers broadened to include many forms of violence directed against Black and Brown communities.

> Neither our grievances nor our solutions are limited to the police killing of our people—it includes the systemic underinvestment in our communities the caging of our people, predatory state

> and corporate practices targeting our neighborhoods, government policies that result in the poisoning of our water and the theft of our land, failing schools that criminalize rather than educate our children, economic practices that extract our labor, and wars on our Trans and Queer family that deny them their humanity.[10]

The conference sparked a year-long process of convening local and national groups to create a national front for Black Lives Matter. The result of this process was the policy platform, "A Vision for Black Lives." Drafted by over fifty organizations working on the Movement for Black Lives, the platform was a visionary agenda aimed not at reforming but at transforming the United States into a country that actually supports, protects, and preserves Black life. Some goals, like the workers right to organize and progressive restructuring of the tax code, generally aligned with mainline Democratic party talking points and policy proposals. One of the platform's most contentious goals, investment, and divestment, did not.

Divestment as a Tactic

From taking on tobacco companies to ending apartheid in South Africa, divestment campaigns are wildly considered historically successful tactics. In the 1970s and 1980s, students protesting apartheid staged major protests at corporations and universities across the United States. By 1988, 155 colleges had divested, at least in part, from South Africa.[11] Corporations like Coca Cola and IBM had also engaged in divestment. The U.S. Congress even sanctioned the South African government, one of its staunchest allies, a country the United States relied heavily upon for mineral wealth.[12, 13] Thatcher and Reagan, who long accused Mandela and his ANC party of being communists and terrorists, were forced to support Mandela's release.[14, 15] Some argued that such divestment could hurt South African jobs.[16] Some later argued the overall financial impact of the South African divestment campaign was minimal.[17] But it is clear today that divestment helped raise the public's awareness of apartheid, moral standards, gave legitimacy to protest demands, and helped ratchet up the political pressure to change policy.[18]

In the late 1980s and 1990s, public health officials leaders began to vigorously target tobacco companies, using divestment as one of the main tools. There have been multiple waves of tobacco divestment since, all of which have placed public pressure on tobacco companies to confront the reality that their product kills their long-term consumers. Tobacco companies like Phillip Morris often confronted divestment threats by hiring firms to create alternative facts.[19] Despite the efforts of big tobacco, in 2005, the UN Framework Convention on Tobacco Control came into force. A total of 168 countries signed the treaty, which called on a number of reforms, including further taxation of cigarettes, regulation of smoking in public, and restriction of sales to minors.[20] In California, CalPERS, the United States' largest public employee pension fund, divested from their tobacco holdings and voted to expand those divestments as recently as 2016. Few nations have successfully divested from the tobacco industry, and most of the major tobacco companies exist today. Still, divestment has helped inspire an array of other policy changes. Divestment's potential to shift policy has led to its use in environmental movements and the Black Lives Matter movement. As Justin Garrett Moore, lead organizer of Bank Black USA stated in our 2017 interview:

> This is not only about empowerment, supporting Black financial intuitions, it's also about economic sanctions. That's what we've done historically. The Montgomery bus boycott was an economic sanction that was used as leverage to push a social good, to promote a social narrative to advocate for policy change. We are sanctioning these institutions because they are mistreating us.

Divesting from Policing

Divesting from policing has become one of the more contested positions of the Black Lives Matter movement. In the wake of state killings, Black Lives Matter advocates and organizers have effectively pressured the state to invest in their communities. Still states and municipalities throughout the United States have largely chosen to invest in policing. The right-wing of U.S. politics has routinely compared the simple act of boycotting to "economic terrorism," calling those who wage economic boycotts "terrorists."[21] U.S. states have passed laws restricting divestment from Israel for their violations of international law and Palestinian human rights.[22] The restrictions are not unrelated to Black Lives Matter, as large numbers of U.S. police receive training by Israeli forces.[23] The groundbreaking 2017 report "Freedom to

Thrive: Reimagining Safety and Security in Our Communities" explains why recent divestment campaigns have triggered such an intense backlash:

> These invest/divest campaigns, which advocate for investments in supportive services and divestment from punitive institutions, challenge the very roots of mass criminalization and inequity. They demand elected officials and decision-makers acknowledge that the lack of investment in communities of color and the over-investment in their criminalization is emblematic of governmental disregard for Black and Brown life.[24]

The 100-page report, spearheaded by the Center for Popular Democracy, the Law for Black Lives, and the Black Youth Project 100, focused on the budgets of twelve cities and counties throughout the United States with large percentages of people of color and Black Lives Matter protests. The report, created through the collaboration of over twenty-five grassroots and community-based organizations throughout the United States, used the budgets to reveal these municipality's priorities and which groups benefited the most from these investments. The data, ending in 2017, showed that despite increasing demands by Black Lives Matter activists for education, health care, mental health services, jobs, and various other improvements, municipalities continued to prioritize funding for police, even as these forces had long been accused of discrimination, brutality, and corruption and were increasingly becoming militarized. The report was striking because it went against the "there's no money" narrative we hear when advocates call for funding programs or initiatives to support Black and Brown people.

As Jennifer Epps-Addison, co-executive director of the Center for Popular Democracy, noted, their report was able to prove that "there is an incredible amount of investment going into Black and Brown communities. But it's going into criminalizing them."[25] In Detroit, 30 percent of the city's $1 billion dollar general fund went to their police department. Just 1.6 percent of expenses went to the Department of Health and Wellness Promotion. In Houston, for every .05 cents spent on libraries, one dollar was spent on the Houston police department.[26] The year after Eric Garner was choked to death by the NYPD, the department received 1,300 new officers, costing the city close to $100 million.[27] Out of the new hires, hundreds were set aside to create a counter-terrorism squad that would go on to routinely monitor communities of color and peaceful protests with machine guns.[28] [29] Most recently, the New York City Council voted to spend close to $11 billion on the construction of New Jails despite widespread grassroots protests.[30]

Investment: Banking Black

As organizers pushed cities and large institutions to divest from policing, Bank Black USA began urging individuals to change their own investment decisions to align with their values. Just days after the deaths of Philando Castile, who was killed by police after notifying them he was carrying a licensed firearm (in an open carry state) and Alton Sterling, who was shot to death while pinned to the ground, rapper Killer Mike spoke at a BET MTV town hall meeting entitled "What Now?":

> "If you are truly able," Killer Mike said, "keep your big bank account with one of the national banks because you may need to travel and out of state and out of the country. But make sure you take a portion of your money you put in a small Black bank or credit union, and for the next two-three-four years, you watch that money accumulate. What I would like is to see one million people instead of buying Jordans or caps or whatever thing is cool this month, instead of us doing that one million Black people find one Black banking institution. If you're in the southeast, you can go to Citizens Trust Bank. You can go to Citizens Trust and start a 100 dollar or more account, you can go as cheap as 20, but 100 is where I'd like you to start. One million people do that Black or White. We have 100 million dollars moved into that bank. That bank can then start doing small home loans in areas that are being gentrified so Black people can move into those areas also. It also can be small business loans 15 to 18 thousand dollars can float a small business for a year, larger banks will not float those types of loans to minorities, and I know this because I own a small business. And I have tried to apply for those. This bank will start to do that. That means the bank will make money and they will be able to give more loans, collect more money as we will open more accounts."[31]

The day after Killer Mike's call, more than 350 people opened new accounts at Unity National Bank. Many waited in line for hours, traveling across state lines from parts of the country where Black banks had since closed.[32] In just five days, 8,000 people submitted applications to join Atlanta's oldest Black bank, Citizens Trust Bank. It was the largest wave of account applications in such a short timeframe in the bank's ninety-seven-year history.[33]

In the weeks after the shootings, I was contacted by Justin Garret Moore, lead organizer of Bank Black USA. I first met Justin in 2013 when he asked me to co-teach his urban design course at Columbia University. As usual, our conversation turned quickly from random internet memes to politics to what we were doing to advance our own visions of equity and justice. Justin asked me to transfer my money into a Black bank, reminding me that

> Long held discriminatory practices have denied or made riskier lending and financial services to people of color communities. The majority of these big banks do not serve our communities. You've seen the discrimination, and predatory practices on financial services be they, lending, mortgages, loans, credit cards, where these banks time and again have charged people of color more for loans.

I respected the call to divest from White-owned banks and build wealth for our communities, but I was busy and did not want to be bothered with the process of transferring my money. Justin explained that the process of transferring my money would not be that time consuming or difficult and that I could ease into the process, as Killer Mike had suggested. It was not until I began protesting the pipeline at Standing Rock that I realized I had to move my money. In 2016, protesters from across the country descended on North Dakota to protest an oil pipeline being built near the Standing Rock Sioux Reservation. Unable to afford the time off from work, I joined New York City protests in solidarity. Shortly after, Justin texted me, "You know TD Bank is one of the biggest investors in the pipeline?" I had no idea. I had many close friends at the protest camp in North Dakota, getting attacked by SWAT teams in the freezing North Dakota winter. Every day they would update me and the rest of the world to the conditions they were facing. Every day I wished I could do more. Every two weeks, I gave my check over to TD Bank, which thanks to $360 million in financing, was one of the pipeline's largest investors.[34] When I asked employees at my bank about the pipeline investments, they told me off the record that they were explicitly barred by higher-ups from telling customers about it. Protesters like myself, thanks to organizers like Justin, began to realize they were financially supporting many of the wrongs we were physically protesting. More from Justin Garrett Moore:

> Today, fights for social justice are at global scale, so too are the values of these banks and what they do with their money. At NODAPL protests, wasn't just Black people, it was people across the spectrum were upset with these banks doing things that were harmful to people to the environment, with their money. Another big one on the spectrum was the funding of things like for-profit prisons. Many of the big banks support businesses that run prisons, detention centers, that don't align with the values of many Americans. Disinvestment was happening during OWS, so bank transfer protests like Bank Black is in many ways continuing protests that were started back then, its roots go back generations.

Despite the clear ethical reasons to switch banks, I, rather shamefully, rather privately, wondered if I would receive substandard service at a Black bank. Would I be charged more ATM fees? Would I get the same type of points rewards? Would my money be as safe there, as in a larger, White-owned bank? The more I researched, the more I learned how deeply rooted my lack of trust in Black banking was. As Justin explained to me, "the distrust of Black financial intuitions in America starts with the 1st one"—the Freedman's Savings and Trust Company, whose foundation and failure can be traced to the arch of progress in post–Civil War America.

Freedman's Bank

In 1863, President Abraham Lincoln signed the Emancipation Proclamation, declaring all slaves (within the Confederate states) free. At the time of the signing, Blacks owned less than 1 percent of all wealth in the United States. Over a century and a half later, Blacks still own just about 1 percent of U.S. wealth.[35] People of color in the United States are still, as Martin Luther King Jr. described in a 1963 letter from a Birmingham jail cell, caught "smothering in an airtight cage of poverty in the midst of an affluent society."[36] Part of the reason Black wealth is relatively unmoved over 150 years after the civil war is that Blacks were long prohibited from engaging in many of the wealth-building activities that federally backed financial structures offered whites. Blacks had few places to grow their wealth outside of mutual aid societies revolving most often around the church. Another reason Black wealth has remained stagnant is that former slaves never received the land confiscated from southern oligarchs—land that the U.S. government promised them after the Civil War. Instead of a redistribution of land, a federally chartered bank is where much of the post–Civil War promise lay for newly freed slaves.

In 1865, Congress chartered the "Freedman's Savings and Trust Company," a savings bank designed to serve millions of newly emancipated American slaves and help them navigate their financial lives. As the Bank's pamphlets proclaimed:

> The whole institute is under the charter of Congress, and received the commendation and countenance of the president, Abraham Lincoln. One of the last official acts of his valued life was the signing of the bill which gave legal existence of the bank.[37]

The Freedman's Savings Bank boasted thirty-seven branches in seventeen states, including the District of Columbia. For the first time, slaves had somewhere they could place their money to gather interest safely. By 1873 the bank had received just over $50 million in deposits from 70,000 depositors.[38] But the bank did not receive initial capital from the federal government; it was funded through deposits. Maintaining so many small accounts, across so many branches, for the nation's poorest citizens, incurred expenses that were hard to sustain. It was extremely difficult for the bank to earn enough on deposits to pay substantial rates of interest. High costs and lack of funds led to the hiring of substandard bookkeepers. The pressure was constantly on to take on riskier investments, and a lack of transparency at the top of the bank led to a litany of risky investments.[39] The bank would eventually fail due to mismanagement of funds, largely due to its structural position in the financial sector and the bank's White leadership.

The banking house charged with investing the savings of freed slaves was Jay Cooke & Company. Cooke & Company founder, Jay Cooke, a former abolitionist, became involved with the bank through his brother Henry. Henry was a member of the post–Civil War Republican political machine, first governor of the District of Columbia, and a board member of Freedman's Bank. As part of his role in the Republican political machine, Henry doled out loans to the politically connected whose influence the Cookes desired. He gave unsecured loans to the soon-to-fail Seneca Sand

Stone Company, a company for which he was also a board member.[40] He also played a major role in investing the bank's deposits. In a push for higher returns than those offered by government bonds, Henry pushed for a change of the bank's charter, converting it from a savings bank into an investment bank. This change allowed the bank to engage in more speculative investments. The brothers pushed the Freedman's Bank to buy railroad bonds that Jay Cooke had not been able to sell as collateral, for which they also received a commission.[41, 42] As Cooke's losses mounted, they increased advertisements to freedmen in order to encourage more deposits.[43] When the market crashed on September 18, 1873, Jay Cook & Company failed. The savings of hundreds of thousands of former slaves were decimated.

Frederick Douglas was brought in to be the bank's (first) Black president in 1874 and soon realized the extent of the bank's prior mismanagement. He looked to Congress to save the bank, but they would not. Frederick Douglas soon realized he was "married to a corpse."[44] The congressional investigation into the bank's failure recommended Cooke and others be indicted, but there was never any follow-up.[45] Depositors lost almost all of the money they placed in Freedman's bank. The sting of this initial failure lingered in the hearts and minds of African Americans for generations.

As the short-lived reconstruction period ended, and Jim Crow segregation took hold of the nation, Black banking again saw a resurgence. The first banks actually organized and operated by African Americans were Capital Savings Bank from 1888 to 1903 and True Reformers Bank from 1889 to 1910.[46, 47] In 1903, Maggie Walker became the first woman bank president to charter a bank in the United States, the St. Luke Penny Savings Bank in Richmond, Virginia. Walker led the bank through the great depression, and through its merger to become Consolidated Bank and Trust, until her death in 1934. Until being purchased by Abigail Adams National Bank in 2005, Consolidated Bank and Trust was believed to be the oldest continuously Black-owned bank in the United States.[48]

But these early banks were not anomalies. Even after fighting in World War I, Blacks still could not deposit their money in White-owned institutions. They had to start their own institutions and support their own institutions. By default, Black dollars remained in Black communities. Communities like "Black Wall Street" in Tulsa, Oklahoma, became a testament to Black ingenuity. Just over a half-century after slavery ended, the community of Greenwood was the epicenter of Black wealth and entrepreneurship in the United States—an economically thriving community of well over 300 Black-owned businesses, hospitals, hotels, theaters, and banks, all created in the era of Jim Crow. As Tulsa native and poet Phetote Mshairi so eloquently put it, "Greenwood was Wakanda before Wakanda"[49] Unfortunately, like many Black communities attaining economic success in the United States, it would not be allowed to thrive. Moore lamented:

> Historically, there's this sort of interesting pattern in America. When there's a certain degree of success or independence or wealth that's created in Black communities, it becomes a problem. So it's been difficult to find good examples of economic models to follow because when they start to get to that point, there is some sort of thing that comes in and compromises them.

As the community continued to build wealth, White animus grew with it. Racial animus eventually grew to animalistic violence. From May 31 to June 1, 1921, a White mob attacked homes and businesses in the neighborhood of Tulsa. Aided by the National Guard, Whites burned the Tulsa Greenwood community to the ground, while also looting houses and businesses. An elderly couple was killed on their way home from church. Homeowners were shot dead in their yards. One White rioter even commandeered an airplane and used it to drop bundles of dynamite on the Greenwood community. Tulsa became the first U.S. city to be bombed by an airplane.[50] After the smoke settled, the American Red Cross estimated as many as 300 had been killed, and nearly 9,000 were left homeless[51] Days later, Adjutant General Charles J. Barrett—sent in to suppress the massacre—described what he saw:

> In all of my experience, I have never witnessed such scenes as prevailed in this city when I arrived at the height of the rioting. Twenty-five thousand whites, armed to the teeth, were ranging the city in utter and ruthless defiance of every concept of law and righteousness. Motorcars, bristling with guns swept through your city, their occupants firing at will.[52]

The Tulsa Massacre remains one of the worst and least-known incidents of racial violence in the history of the United States, mainly because it was covered up. Monetary damages claimed by Greenwood residents were denied by insurance companies because they deemed the killings a "riot."[53] The *Tulsa Tribune* ripped the front-page story from its bound volumes before sending them to be microfilmed. Police and State militia also removed any mention of the massacre from their archives.[54] It wasn't until the fall of 2019 that state officials, prodded by a truth commission, added study of the massacre to Oklahoma's school curriculum.[55]

Even less known than the massacre itself was the resilience displayed by the people of Greenwood. The rebuilding began almost immediately after the burning. Within one year, the majority of structures in Greenwood had been rebuilt, most of them resembling those that had stood pre-massacre. Greenwood again thrived, reaching its economic apex in the 1940s.[56] But, like many communities of color in the 1950s and 1960s, it was decimated by highway construction and urban renewal. An interstate overpass ripped through the center of Greenwood, standing today where the Dreamland Theater once stood.[57] Many were displaced; communities once held together through racial segregation were now spread out, their economic power diluted. The poor became concentrated in ghettos, while many upper-income people of color attempted to move out into suburban areas. This had a tremendous impact on Black business, and particularly on Black banking. Now that some Blacks could go to White schools and put their money in White-owned banks, Black-owned banks began to decline. As Justin explained, integration had some downsides for the Black community:

> Higher numbers of White-owned companies began to hire people of color and allow them to move into their communities and open accounts in their banks. As people of color left, their money did as well. The idea of integrating has its positives, but it was difficult for a lot of these Black-owned banks which tended to be smaller banks, to compete as society integrated and became less connected to a particular place. That flight of affluent Blacks from the cities and movement of Blacks from the south to the north during the great migration, all impacted Black Banking and the places they were rooted in.

Martin Luther King Jr. understood the role of Black banking in liberation and the danger it faced. In his final speech before his assassination, he called for a "bank-in" movement. Speaking in Memphis, Tennessee, King called on audience members to divest their money from the "banks downtown," that is, White-owned banks, and deposit their dollars into Black-owned Tri-State Bank. He saw these as practical steps to begin building a greater economic base, while at the same time, "putting pressure where it really hurts."[58] Fifty years after King's call to invest and divest, the accumulation of Black wealth continues to suffer severe structural impediments. Over the last two decades, more than half of all Black banks have been lost. According to Bank Black USA, today just twenty Black-owned banks remain—only eighteen if your definition of Black bank is a bank that is majority Black-owned. The decline follows a broader trend, which has seen the number of MDIs (Minority Depository Institutions) fall by 9.1 percent and community banks by 42.2 percent.[59] Today, Black banks in the United States control an estimated $5 billion, compared to banking giants like JPMorgan Chase and Bank of America, which in early 2019 held well over $2 trillion in assets each.[60]

This decline in Black banks occurred alongside continued discrimination against people of color by White-owned financial institutions. Outright denial of loans to people of color, the red-lining of communities of color, and denying anyone proximate to them financing was the reality of MLK's time. And these practices are not a thing of the past. Economists at the Federal Reserve Bank of Chicago recently found that red-lining communities based on race has had a casual and persistent effect on the development of neighborhoods and their access to credit through to the present day.[61] In 2012, Wells Fargo was forced to pay $175 million after allegations it pushed people of color toward more expensive mortgages and charged them higher rates and fees than their White borrowers with similar credit histories. [62] Facing similar allegations, Bank of America Corp also agreed to pay a historic $335 million in settlement.[63] Citigroup and JPMorgan Chase have also been sued for discriminatory lending practices.[64]

Are Black Banks More Accountable?

A bank is not more ethical or capable simply because people of color run it. But statistically, Minority Depository Institutions (MDI)'s use a far greater share of their resources to serve communities of color than White-owned banks do. A 2011 study by the Federal Deposit Insurance Corp (FDIC) revealed that Black banks made almost 67 percent of their mortgage loans to Black borrowers.[65] Black-owned banks offer a far higher median share of mortgage and small business loans to Black borrowers than do White-owned banks. The gap in service people of color can expect from White-run banks goes beyond financing. Over 25 percent of U.S. households are currently "unbanked" or "underbanked."[66] Many of these citizens do not qualify for accounts in the major banks. They do not have access to savings or checking accounts and thus must rely heavily on payday lenders and check-cashing places that can charge usury rates. Basic access to a bank account and tools to gain financial literacy are gaps that MDIs, Black banks in particular, routinely fill.

Different Visions: A Credit Union in Minnesota

Not every Black bank is the same. Most have more traditional investor-based business models, but there are alternatives. One week after the murder of Philando Castile at the hand of Minneapolis Police in 2016, Blexit, a grassroots economic disruption movement, organized over 200 residents to attend a meeting addressing inequity in Minnesota and the United States more broadly. As residents weighed in on what they saw were the most important priorities for their community, they landed on a Black-led financial institution for the North Side of Minneapolis.[67] It made sense to Me'Lea Connelly, director of the Association for Black Economic Power (ABEP), that the community would ask for such a service. As Connelly reminds all who ask about Blexit's efforts, her neighborhood in North Minnesota is filled with payday lenders and predatory financiers:

> You practically can't throw a rock without hitting a payday lender. They are cash checking outfits and are extremely predatory. I say predatory because their target market is poor people. Black poor people, especially in North Minneapolis, are the last people that can afford to pay a 200-percent interest rate on a payday loan, and it puts people in extreme debt.[68]

Blexit's 2016 meeting was the beginning of what has now come to be known as the Village Trust Financial Cooperative. ABEP began raising funds and organizing to create a federally chartered Black-lead credit union, and in the winter of 2018, the Village Financial Cooperative received conditional approval from the Minnesota Department of Commerce. Organizers hope to encourage Black business owners to establish cooperative businesses and use the credit union to support those emerging cooperatives.[69] As Connelly explained to me:

> Typical banks, unless they are mission-driven in their bylaws and have a specific set of commitments to their community, are simply for-profit entities. Shareholders and the CEO are the main benefactors. Banks extract wealth and make money off of your

> deposit. Credit unions are member-owned. They are structured to create velocity and distribute wealth within a community.

Currently, only 0.78 percent of credit unions in the United States are Black led. Connelly and her organizers believe a cooperative model can better insulate her community from the ebbs and flows of the market than investor-based business models. She believes they will be able to take risks that large banks would not, as well as be able to offer relevant financial literacy skills and advice, which large white-owned banks normally do not bother with. Connelly sees the Village's role as standing "in the gap":

> We can't put up the same barriers the big corporate banks do. Some existing credit unions are great but you need a credit score of like 650 to become a member. That isn't sustainable for who we are and why we are starting. We are here for people who don't meet the traditional requirements. We don't believe in denying people products and services. When you come here you get approved or a plan. We will walk with you on the path towards goals you have for yourself and your family. If your income to debt ratio is not responsible for us to loan you money we will help you get through those challenges and get you to approval. We believe in a clean all access checking and savings accounts, removing all sorts of barriers to access. Is it going to be easy? Of course not. But we have to accept our identity. We stand in the gap. That's our purpose.

Standing in the gap is not easy, and Blexit's movement for Black economic independence has not come without contention. In November of 2018, Candice Owens, the Trump-supporting, (then) communications director for the right-wing nonprofit Talking Point USA, announced she'd come up with her own, completely unrelated, "Blexit movement." Owens's Blexit does not look to divest from the systems that benefit from Black pain and invest in ones that support communities of color. Owens uses her new Blexit platform to encourage people of color to leave the democratic party and unite behind Trump's vision for "Making America Great Again." The real Blexit has served Candace Owens with multiple cease-and-desist letters for co-opting their name, but Owens has pressed on.[70]

Throughout 2019, Owens's version of Blexit has held rallies in major U.S. cities she claims Democrats have destroyed. Connelly and the original

Blexit movement wholly acknowledge the oppression of people of color in the United States has been a bipartisan affair. By 2053, the median Black household income is projected to hit zero.[71] But in Los Angeles, Dallas, Richmond, and Atlanta, the focus of Owens's Blexit events was not structural changes needed to improve the lives of people of color, as much as calling people of color to "wake up" and see how good they have it in America. Speakers like Ann Coulter and former Tucson police officer Brandon Tatum thrill the crowd by rooting the problems people of color face in how they have been taught to see their current situation by liberals. Each time the camera cuts to the crowd, one cannot help but notice that many (if not most) Blexit attendees are White people wearing Make America Great Again hats.[72, 73] Speakers and attendees embrace what they call "Freethinking," a change in mindset that dismisses the police brutality and systemic racial and economic inequality Connelly's Blexit was founded to combat.

Despite the continued, intentional confusion on the part of a well-connected Trump to depress the opposition vote effort, the original Blexit is thriving. As of this writing, the Village Financial Cooperative has reported 1,900 members, representing over $5 million in pledged deposits. In addition, the mayor of Minneapolis has promised to invest $500,000 for the continued development of this "transformational entity."[74] The first and only Black-owned credit union and financial cooperative to open in Minneapolis is an accomplishment organizers have dedicated to the family of Philando Castile, saying "this is a movement whose origins lay at our deepest sorrows."[75]

"We're Gonna Have to Do It Ourselves"

In the year after Castile's death, close to $60 million was moved into Black-owned banks.[76] These are millions that, instead of going into white-owned institutions, went to Black-owned banks that make the vast majority of their loans to people of color. Holding the momentum proved more difficult. In the years since, attention to Black banking has waned, and many of the gains in assets have declined. Why new accounts and interest in Black banking declined after the initial surge is an important topic of further research.

At the end of 2019, Village Financial faced a dramatic setback, as Me'Lea Connelly was ousted as executive director of (ABEP), along with CFO Joe Riemann. Both were accused of mismanagement and gross negligence. Me'Lea accused the board of discrimination for removing Joe Riemann, the only white person at Village Financial.[77] The ABEP board of directors took their allegations to the Minneapolis Police Department, the same department responsible for the death of Philando Castile. As of this writing, the investigation by the Minnesota Bureau of Criminal Apprehension has not been completed. The ABEP board has since rescinded its state charter application for Village Financial Trust and is focusing on reorganizing the cooperative before reapplying for a state charter.[78]

The individual and structural difficulties that small banks, credit unions, and co-operatives face (minority-owned or otherwise) are immense. Simply put, these are groups of imperfect people with limited means deciding to take on the responsibility of their communities' limited resources—a burden most often carried out by large corporations with far more structural power. Divestment and banking Black are not a means to an end; they will face challenges, and are just one part of a larger economic strategy for a broader liberation movement. However, as the Montgomery bus boycott revealed, it is hard to have a boycott if you don't have the funds to support its participants. Like the divestment from Apartheid South Africa campaign and the boycotts of big tobacco, divesting from institutions that maintain our current system of mass incarceration means building power. Whether its policing or predatory financiers, divesting from institutions that harm our communities and investing in our growth can help sustain our movement and magnify changes in policy that could benefit our people.

Shortly before being shot to death by Chicago police, revolutionary Black Panther leader Fred Hampton said, "you don't fight capitalism with no black capitalism; you fight capitalism with socialism."[79] But this did not, however, mean that we should fail to acknowledge how we invest our money. Irrespective of whether you approve of or dismiss banking Black as Black capitalism, we have to build our own power. We have to ask if how we spend our money aligns with the values we profess, and at least attempt to act accordingly. Bank Black USA has played a crucial role in doing this work.

The White supremacist state that has put us into the position we are in will not save us. We did not march from New York to Ferguson so that police departments across the United States could receive hundreds of millions of dollars in funding for surveillance equipment. We did not march to attain more funding for incarceration. We were marching for our liberation. Divesting from institutions that benefit from our pain and investing in our communities is one necessary step toward our liberation. In the words of Fannie Lou Hamer: "The time has come now when we are going to have to get what we need ourselves. We may get a little help, here and there, but in the main, we're going to have to do it ourselves."[80] That "we" is key. Fighting for our liberation does not rely on any one structure or person, but all of us, moving beyond our pain, to create a more just future.

Chapter 13

Black Joy in the Time of Ferguson

JAVON JOHNSON

> So little is known of our past, we can imagine damn near anything.
>
> —Terrance Hayes, "We Should Make a Documentary about Spades"[1]

In the wake of this country's most recent displays of structurally violent anti-blackness—including the acquittal of murderer George Zimmerman and the refusals to indict murderer officers Darren Wilson, Daniel Pantaleo, and Sean Williams, or murderer Sergeant David Darko—we witnessed a wave of responses, from peaceful marches, strategy meetings, die-ins, social media campaigns such as #BlackLivesMatter, uprisings, riots, a litany of think pieces, poems, songs, art work, and so many others. As a spoken-word poet, I penned a number of pieces in a series of attempts to find a place to put all of this bubbling rage, hurt, and fear. In one poem, "(Un)titled Black," I wrote simply, "I want to live in a world where police do not murder Black people" over and over, as if my basic request was a punishment unto itself. In another, I demanded a move away from peaceful protests, which ended:

> Pay close attention
> WHEN the State says,
> "This is a time for peace."
> They are admitting

that when they first
fired the gun
it was a time of war.
Do not sit quiet.
Do not whisper, unless it's for strategy.
Do not make another beautiful Black ballad
to be used in the soundtrack to
yet another shitty movie about racism
three decades from now. Do not go gentle.
Do not turn the other check.
Yell. Scream. Show them
your claws. Your fangs.
Be the monster
they always thought you were.
Show them the anger.
The hurt.
IT HURTS.
IT HURTS.
IT HURTS.
WHEN the State decides to murder
its next Black child,
remind them of the shotgun
show them the hurt . . .

I struggle mightily with my poetic call for the "shotgun," as I truly want to be a pacifist, but how can I continue to desire that in the face of all this black death? How can I turn the other cheek when my people are murdered, comedic songs are made, "I can breathe" t-shirts are produced? All while painting us as the violent ones in the media? If anything, black folks have been overly patient and overly nonviolent, as it is not just these few cases that have received national attention. It is the all-too-forgotten black women and black queer folks, it is twelve-year-old Tamir Rice, Tarika Wilson, shot in her home while holding her baby, seven-year-old Aiyana Jones, unconscious Tyisha Miller, ninety-three-year-old Kathryn Johnston, and the too many names I do not have the space to list here that are corporeal reminders of the "vulnerability of [our] own black bodies."[2]

In her brilliant essay, " 'Can you be BLACK and Look at This?' Reading the Rodney King Video(s)," Alexander locates what she

> calls a "bottom line black-ness."[3] For her, in the midst of high anti-essentialist discourses, violence often "erases other differentiations and highlight race."[4] Ultimately she argues that black pain is made both invisible and inaudible to many with crucial judicial, cultural, and political consequences. But, given that "Black bodies in pain for public consumption have been an American national spectacle for centuries," I do not want to think about invisibility and inaudibility as antithetical to visibility and audibility.[5] The in/visibility and in/audibility of black pain are often one and the same, establishing orders and essentially communicating/dictating place and boundaries in service of the nation-state that uses anti-black racism as the foundation for white supremacy. How else can we make sense of murderer Darren Wilson's testimony that he feared for his life because Mike Brown "had the most intense aggressive face" that could only be described as "a demon?"[6] In our God-fearing country, which historically constructs black people as innately violent, Mike Brown was not portrayed as a prospective college student, not even a human, but a demon that needed to be exorcised so that this un/holy house could be made.

Black pain is used in service of the nation-state because we have been historically constructed as threatening by virtue of being loud, excessive, unruly, illegible, pathological, and outside the comfortable confines of white neoliberal, liberal, and conservative structures alike. In other words, black people are a threat to safety simply because we are black, "and the resistance to enslavement," or perhaps resistance in general "is the performative essence of blackness," which, in a white supremacist, anti-black world, must be reined in.[7] Hell, gay safe spaces,[8] prison (not justice) systems,[9] HIV/AIDS discourses,[10] and this entire country were built on the logic that black bodies are inherently unsafe and must be reeled in.[11]

But, "what does it mean," asks Moten, "to suffer from political despair when your identity is bound-up with utopian political aspirations and desires?"[12] Danez Smith beautifully pens his "Dinosaurs in the Hood," which might offer us some insight to Moten's query.[13] Riffing and improvising, which for Moten is black performance, on Terrance Hayes's unapologetically black ekphrastic poem, "We Should Make a Documentary about Spades,"[14] Smith writes:

> Don't let Tarantino direct this. In his version, the boy plays with a gun, the metaphor: black boys toy with their own lives,

> the foreshadow to his end, the spitting image of his father. Fuck that, the kid has a plastic Brontosaurus or Triceratops & this is his proof of magic or God or Santa.

He later writes:

> This movie can't be a metaphor for black people & extinction. This movie can't be about race. This movie can't be about black pain or cause black people pain. This movie can't be about a long history of having a long history with hurt. This movie can't be about race. Nobody can say nigga in this movie who can't say it to my face in public.[15]

Smith's film of reference, "*Jurassic Park* meets *Friday* meets *The Pursuit of Happyness*," is an imagined place that is undeniably black, fun, and has redemption at the end.[16] In addition, in refusing Tarantino, Smith consequently refuses white directorship, ensuring the film is not about anything but "a neighborhood of royal folks—children of slaves & immigrants & addicts & exiles—saving their town. . . ."[17] With breathtaking line breaks, a kind of punctuation that Jennifer Brody might say "performs as a type of (im)material event," Smith poetically imagines a cinematic world that refuses to be about and/or cause black pain.[18] And, it is here, somewhere *In the Break* (from linearity) that we can, and perhaps must, continually imagine black possibility outside the conditions of white supremacy. And, rather than thinking squarely about black pain in response to the most recent wave of state-sanctioned anti-black violence and terrorism, I wonder how we might also think about black joy as a theory, a method, and a political device. Thinking about black joy beyond Ferguson, beyond the continual pain of being denied basic human rights, beyond, and perhaps outside of, structural racism, anti-blackness, white supremacy, and state-sanctioned terror have allowed black people to continue on, despite every reason to not. In addition, black joy, a real and imagined site of utopian possibility, must also be an important part of Alexander's "bottom line blackness" and Moten's radical "freedom drive that animates black performances."[19] More than a method to endure, however, black joy allows us the space to stretch our imaginations beyond what we previously thought possible and allows us to theorize a world in which white supremacy does not dictate our everyday lives. House parties, backyard cookouts, and other spaces where black bodies gather in celebration produce rich and profound moments in which black love and laughter "lifts everyone slightly above the present" and allows to feel, to know in our bones, what black utopia might be like.[20] I firmly believe that our bodies harbor knowledge, and in these moments every smile, head nod, hip shake, and high-five is an exchange of embodied truths that black joy is phenomenally transformational. In this way, black joy provides another set of political tactics to "make do" and use the in/visibility and in/audibility of black joy as a site with which to operate outside of white supremacy.

On the night it was announced there would be no murder trial for Darren Wilson, I decided not to protest. Instead, I fell asleep listening to Stevie Wonder, Nina Simone, Roberta Flack, Donny Hathaway, and others because I wanted to be happy *and* black. In the weeks following the decision not to indict the officer who killed Eric Garner, I attended a few protests in Los Angeles. I marched and chanted through some of the busiest streets in Los Angeles, not because I believe these demonstrations necessarily work, as the very fact that the streets were blocked off for us by and in coordination with the LAPD means we were operating within the same structures that murders black people without any accountability. I remember seeing waves and waves of black (and other) people brought together by a "bottom line blackness," animated by an unwavering "freedom drive," and made somewhat whole again through black joy—that is, the black love, laughter, hugs, and smiles that for a moment offer us glimpses of radical democracy, freedom, and utopia. And, I want a theory about that, one powerful enough to "imagine damn near anything," as Hayes put it, one about what to do with all of this black joy just bursting at the seams.[21]

> Thick, Black, and unapologetic like
> big momma's chili just spilling over
> the top, too much spice for most people to stomach
> but we like it that way.
> Black like a fish fry,
> like a backyard
> cookout with
> some Maze playing.
> Where ALL (but not really all)
> the Black folks know the dance
> before it was even created, and
> we look at each other with that
> "White folks cook in their backyards too but they don't
> know nothing bout this"

look. That Black.
And isn't that we are all fighting
for, the right to be joyfully Black.
The audacity of it all.
That in spite of Ferguson, or Staten Island,
or Ohio, or Mississippi, or Alabama, or Louisiana,
or Texas, or anywhere else
that makes racism sound like it's "over there,"
that in spite of it all
we still smile and laugh and dance.
That Black.
Not that we laugh to keep from crying Black,
but sometimes we laugh because it's just funny.
That Black.
And, aint that why they think we magical
in the first place?
That despite every reason not to
we still have joy, Black joy.
We smile, and live, and love. We love.
We love.
We Black.
We love.[22]

Notes

Introduction

1. Brittney Cooper, "In Defense of Black Rage: Michael Brown, Police and the American Dream," *Salon* (August 11, 2014), http://www.salon.com/2014/08/12/in_defense_of_black_rage_michael_brown_police_and_the_american_dream.

2. It should be noted that McKesson was never a member of a Black Lives Matter chapter. DeRay McKesson, "I Am Running for Mayor of Baltimore," *Medium.com*, http://www.medium.com/deray-for-mayor/i-am-running-for-mayor-of-baltimore-34b4e214d582.

3. Sarah Ahmed, *The Cultural Politics of Emotions* (London: Routledge, 2014).

4. Josh Eidelson, "Black Lives Matter Leader Says Even Great People Can Be Part of the Problem," Bloomberg.com, http://www.bloomberg.com/features/2016-alicia-garza-interview-issue.

5. bell hooks, "Killing Rage," *Killing Rage: Ending Racism* (New York: Henry Holt, 1995).

6. Cited in Brigit Katz, "Due to Repeated Vandalism, Emmett Till Memorial to Be Replaced With Bulletproof Sign," *Smithsonian Magazine*, July 29, 2019, http://www.smithsonianmag.com/smart-news/emmett-till-memorial-be-replaced-bulletproof-sign-due-repeated-vandalism-180972753.

7. Cited in Brian Duignan, "Brown v. Board of Education Topeka," *Encyclopedia Britannica*, http://www.britannica.com/event/Brown-v-Board-of-Education-of-Topeka.

8. Jeanne Theoharis, *A More Beautiful and Terrible History: The Uses and Misuses of Civil Rights History* (Boston: Beacon Press, 2018), 25.

9. Barbara Ransby, *Making All Black Lives Matter: Reimagining Freedom in the Twenty-First Century* (Berkeley: University of California Press, 2018), 101.

10. Ransby, *Making All Black Lives Matter*, 103.

11. Rashawn Ray, Melissa Brown, and Wendy Laybourn, "The Evolution of #BlackLivesMatter on Twitter: Social Movements, Big Data, and Race," *Ethnic & Racial Studies* 40, no. 11 (September 2017): 1795. See also Rashawn Ray, Melissa

Brown, Neil Fraistat, and Edward Summers, "Ferguson and the Death of Michael Brown on Twitter: #BlackLivesMatter, #TCOT, and the Evolution of Collective Identities," *Ethnic & Racial Studies* 40, no. 11 (September 2017): 1797–1813.

12. Ray et al., 1807.

13. Patrice Khan-Cullors and Ashe Bandele, *When They Call You a Terrorist: A Black Lives Matter Memoir* (New York: St. Martin's Press, 2018), 166.

14. Psychologist Drew Westen points to the increasing emotionality of our political landscape, arguing that maintaining a steadfast belief in the dispassionate mind and the dominance of rationality in contemporary politics today is actually an irrational emotional commitment to rationality. As the selection of the word "post-truth" for word of the year for 2016 by the Oxford English dictionary suggests, truth and factual accuracy no longer are seen as the dominant register of meaning-making in society. While all politicians might have lied throughout the ages, the difference now is that such lies are not ideological, meant to offer a false view of the world that could be later discredited. Rather, lies today often bypass truth claims by being anchored in deeply felt personal beliefs. A speaker's deep emotional commitment to a topic, rather than their knowledgeable discussion of the issue, forges empathetic bonds between their selves and intended audience. A study of post-election surveys conducted by the Public Religion Research Institute and *The Atlantic* revealed that voters in the 2016 election tended to vote according to their fears of cultural displacement, rather than economic woes. www.prri.org/research/white-working-class-attitudes-economy-trade-immigration-election-donald-trump

15. Robin Kelley, "Black Study, Black Struggle." Boston Review (March 7, 2016), http://www.bostonreview.net/forum/robin-d-g-kelley-black-study-black-struggle.

Chapter 1

1. Dominique Christina, "In response to the Question If 2017 was a poem what would it be called?" (see chapter 10, this volume).

2. Note that McKesson was never a member of a Black Lives Matter chapter. See also DeRay McKesson, "I Am Running for Mayor of Baltimore," *Medium.com*, http://www.medium.com/deray-for-mayor/i-am-running-for-mayor-of-baltimore-34b4e214d582.

3. Yomaira C. Figueroa-Vásquez and Jessica Marie Johnson, "Hoodrat Praxis in a Time of Love and Fury" (chapter 4, this volume).

4. The conversation around the 2017 Whitney Biennial and Dana Schutz's *Open Casket* is a case in point.

5. See Erin Stephens's "Emotion, Race, and Cultural Trauma in #BlackLives Matter" (chapter 3, this volume).

6. Sarah Ahmed, *The Cultural Politics of Emotions* (London: Routledge, 2014).

7. Barbara Ransby, *Making All Black Lives Matter: Reimagining Freedom in the 21st Century* (Berkeley: University of California Press), 95.

8. Kameelah Janan Rasheed, "How to Suffer Politely (and Other Etiquette)," http://www.kameelahr.com/howtosufferpolitely.

9. bell hooks, "Killing Rage," *Killing Rage: Ending Racism* (New York: Henry Holt, 1995).

10. Interview with Alicia Garza in Liz Adetiba and Jordie Davies, "Alicia Garza on What's Missing from the Black Lives Matter Movement," *Black Youth Project* (October 5, 2016), http://www.blackyouthproject.com/exclusive-alicia-garza-on-what-is-missing-in-the-black-lives-matter-movement.

11. AD Win, "We Are Not Well: The Effects of Stress, Racism, and Depression," *Blavity* (April 29, 2017). Win also notes that "When African-Americans experience psychological trauma due to the stress of racism, factors such as racial violence, discrimination, and microaggressions may be ignored as contributors to depression," http://www.blavity.com/affects-of-stress-racism-depression.

12. Leah Lakshmi Piepzna-Samarasinha, "A Modest Proposal for a Fair Trade Emotional Labor Economy," *Bitch Magazine* 75 (2017), http://www.bitchmedia.org/article/modest-proposal-fair-trade-emotional-labor-economy/centered-disabled-femme-color-working.

13. Simone Leigh as quoted in Andy Battaglia, "The Doctor Is In, at the New Museum: New York artist Simone Leigh explores health and wellness in 'The Waiting Room,'" *Wall Street Journal* (June 27, 2016), http://www.wsj.com/articles/the-doctor-is-in-at-the-new-museum-1467070910 and http://www.sdrubin.org/new-grantee/nyt-simone-leighs-exhibition-reviewed-new-museum.

14. Joe Osmundson, "How Many Black Histories We Still Don't Know: An Interview with Simone Leigh," *The Feminist Wire* (October 3, 2014), http://www.thefeministwire.com/2014/10/many-black-histories-still-dont-know-interview-simone-leigh.

15. See http://www.realclearpolitics.com/video/2014/12/09/oreilly_a_conversation_about_race_means_bloviating_about_things_that_happened_150_years_ago.html.

16. Al Sharpton, Eulogy for Michael Brown, transcribed at "Watch Al Sharpton Bring the House Down at Michael Brown's Funeral: 'This Is Not About You! This Is About Justice!'" by Joe Coscarelli, New York Mag, August 24, 2014, http://www.nymag.com/daily/intelligencer/2014/08/al-sharpton-eulogy-michael-brown-funeral.html. Sharpton's comments here mirror the reaction I received from a college president where I was completing a community project celebrating the lives of black people who were killed by state violence in 2015. She argued that instead of focusing on state violence that we should be looking at black-on-black violence instead.

17. Garnette Cadogan, "Black and Blue," in *The Fire This Time* (New York: Scribner, 2017), 142.

18. Claudia Rankine, "The Condition of Black Life Is One of Mourning," in *The Fire This Time*, 147.

19. Sharpton eulogy. See note 16.

20. Brittney Cooper, "Al Sharpton Does Not Have My Ear: Why We Need New Black Leadership Now," *Salon*, http://www.salon.com/2014/08/26/al_sharpton_does_not_have_my_ear_why_we_need_new_black_leadership_now.

21. See http://www.washingtonpost.com/posteverything/wp/2015/08/24/i-was-a-civil-rights-activist-in-the-1960s-but-its-hard-for-me-to-get-behind-black-lives-matter/?postshare=5221440433170944&utm_term=.8e81e4194eb6.

22. Marc Lamont Hill, *Nobody: Casualties of the War on America's Vulnerable, From Ferguson to Flint and Beyond* (New York: Atria Books, 2016), 80.

23. W. Kamau Bell, "Face Full of Flour," 2010, http://www.wkamaubell.com/blog.

24. Gates as quoted in Huma Khan and Michelle McPhee, "Obama Defends Criticism of Cambridge Police in Arrest of Gates," ABC News, July 23, 2009, http://www.abcnews.go.com/Politics/story?id=8153681.

25. President Barack Obama during the national town hall "The President and the People: A National Conversation," which aired July 14, 2016.

26. Hill, *Nobody*, 12. My emphasis.

27. Javon Joy, "Black Joy in the Time of Ferguson" (chapter 13, this volume).

28. Donna Austin, "Recalled to Life: On the Meaning and Power of a Die-in," http://www.anthronow.com/online-articles/recalled-to-life-on-the-meaning-and-power-of-a-die-in.

29. Howard Kurtz, "How a False Media Narrative Made Ferguson Worse," Fox News, November 26, 2014, http://www.foxnews.com/politics/2014/11/26/how-false-media-narrative-made-ferguson-worse.html.

30. Ta-Nahesi Coates, *Between the World and Me* (New York: Spiegel and Grau, 2015), 9.

31. Brittney Cooper, "I Am Utterly Undone: My Struggle with Black Rage and Fear after Ferguson," *Salon*, November 25, 2014, http://www.salon.com/2014/11/25/i_am_utterly_undone_my_struggle_with_black_rage_and_fear_after_ferguson.

32. Brittney Cooper, "In Defense of Black Rage," *Salon*, August 12, 2014, http://www.salon.com/2014/08/12/in_defense_of_black_rage_michael_brown_police_and_the_american_dream.

33. James Baldwin, "The Negro in American Culture," *Cross Currents* 11 (1961): 205.

34. Xandria Phillips, "Director's Note," in *Love Letters to Spooks*: special issue, *Winter Tangerine*, http://www.wintertangerine.com/llts-director-note.

35. Phillips, *Winter Tangerine.*

36. Carol Anderson, *White Rage: The Unspoken Truth of Our Racial Divide* (New York: Bloomsbury, 2016).

37. Helen Molesworth, "Only Connect: The Year in Shock," *Artforum* (December 2016): 239.

38. See Judith Butler, "Rethinking Vulnerability and Resistance," in *Vulnerability in Resistance*, eds. Butler, Gambetti, and Sabsay (Durham, NC: Duke University Press, 2016), 12–27.

39. The Panthers PFMC were a centerpiece of their program to "serve the people, body and soul" by providing general care such as screening for illness and diseases such as sickle cell anemia, as well as minor surgeries, and in some instances dental care. They were a mandated community service, required by president Bobby Seale of all chapter groups by 1970. Alondra Nelson has written about the Panthers' health advocacy that they served as "bio-cultural brokers" who mediated between underserved black communities distrustful of the racism and sexism built into mainstream medicine and health experts who had to participate in required Panther-led political education programs before volunteering at the free (or low cost) clinics. Their existence, Huey Newton noted, exposed the contradiction between what the panthers could achieve with so few resources in comparison with the little achieved by the state's plenty. This contradiction was confirmed by Leigh's focus on self-determination in her project—and her use of sandbags in the next iteration of her Free People's Medical Clinic at the New Museum of Contemporary Art in NYC that ran from June to September 2016. See Nelson, *Body and Soul: The Black Panther Party and the Fight against Medical Discrimination* (Minneapolis: University of Minnesota Press, 2011). See also the interview with Leigh conducted by Rizvana Bradley, "Going Underground: An Interview with Simone Leigh." *Art In America*, August 20, 2015, http://www.artinamericamagazine.com/news-features/interviews/going-underground-an-interview-with-simone-leigh.

40. LaTasha N. Nevada Diggs as quoted in Jillian Steinhauer, "Reflections from Black Women Artists for Black Lives Matter," *Hyperallergic*, September 15, 2016, http://www.hyperallergic.com/322742/reflections-from-black-women-artists-for-black-lives-matter.

41. Javon Johnson, "Black Joy in the Time of Ferguson" (chapter 13, this volume).

42. Deborah King, Multiple Jeopardy, "Multiple Consciousness: The Context of a Black Feminist Ideology," in *Words of Fire: An Anthology of African-American Feminist Thought*, ed. Beverly Guy-Sheftall (New York: New Press, 1995), 298.

43. Gina Dent, "Black Pleasure, Black Joy: An Introduction," in *Black Popular Culture*, G. Dent, ed. (New York: New Press, 1998), 18.

44. Sara Ahmed, *The Cultural Politics of Emotions* (New York: Routledge, 2013), 202.

45. Adaku Utah as quoted in Lauren Barber, "Harriet's Squad: Black Women Using Ancient Healing Methods as Resistance." *Elle*, July 26, 2017, http://www.elle.com/culture/career-politics/a46954/harriets-apothecary-ancient-healing-resistance.

46. The Black Lives Matter Global Network has a full-time staff member dealing with issues of healing. In Chicago, the Black Youth Project 100 (BYP100), organized by Charlene Carruthers, has created a healing and accountability committee.

Chapter 2

1. Eric Foner, "Introduction," in Rayford W. Logan, *The Betrayal of the Negro from Rutherford Hayes to Woodrow Wilson* (Boston: Da Capo Press, 1997 [1954]), xiii.

2. Here and throughout the chapter I will not capitalize the term "black" because I do not believe it should be viewed as an identity. To my mind, the term "black" remains an adjective, an inaccurate one at that. While I accept it as a racial identity, one with which I identify stridently, its limitations should not be ignored in the name of racial solidarity. Black refers to brown skin color and invokes mythologies about demons that lurk in dark places. Historian Winthrop Jordan has traced the origin of these "black" myths to fourteenth- and fifteenth-century English Pagan and Christian superstitions. When English travelers started calling West African people "blacks," they conflated the so-called "savages" they encountered along the coast with the devils they imagined in their religious art and literature. To capitalize "Black" is to champion a color as an identity and, with it, a long history of demonizing the very people it marks in the United States. I see the same problem with the n-word, and while I grew up using the n-word warmheartedly with friends and loved ones, I have since ceased because current usage does not erase or eradicate its historical legacy. In any case, I exalt Black Power, proclaim Black Is Beautiful, and demand that Black Lives Matter, but I do not see an anti-racist future in a society where millions of United States citizens continue to define themselves as "Black" people. The next step, in my opinion, is not increased racialization but, rather, deracialization and rehumanization based on a cultural commonality that transcends phenotype.

3. Logan, *The Betrayal of the Negro*, 11.

4. Logan, 314.

5. Logan, 315.

6. In a report titled "Foreclosed," Ryan Cooper and Matt Bruenig of the People's Policy Project argued that Obama's presidency destroyed black wealth, particularly housing wealth, by passing foreclosure policies that benefitted lending institutions while refusing to use executive powers to provide financial relief to black American households targeted racially for abusive lending practices like subprime loans. Ryan Cooper and Matt Bruenig, "Foreclosed: Destruction of Black Wealth during the Obama Presidency," *People'sPolicyProject.org*, www.peoplespolicyproject.org/wp-content/uploads/2017/12/Foreclosed.pdf.

7. There are legitimate questions about whether the numbers of extrajudicial killings are increasing in number. Journalist and cultural critic Ta-Nehisi Coates has argued persuasively that police killings are not increasing but, rather, receiving more media attention because black Americans are using camera phones and social media to expose these killings. Current black activists join a rich history of black American muckrakers and whistleblowers like Ida B. Wells, William Patterson, and Paul Robeson, who shone light on lynchings by white terrorist mobs and police officers. See Ida B. Wells, *On Lynchings* (New York: Humanity Books, 2002); and

William L. Patterson, ed., *We Charge Genocide: The Historic Petition to the United Nations for Relief from a Crime of the United States Government against the Negro People* (New York: International Publishers, 1951).

8. In fact, scholars like Cornel West and Brittany Cooper have harped on black leaders' failure to fight structural inequality and to empathize with the plight of black Americans in the U.S. West, for example, argued that Obama showed a "lack of courage" when confronting the Wall Street financial institutions that tanked the U.S. economy in 2008, a financial recession that disproportionately devastated black homeowners. "And not one Wall Street criminal executive went to jail," he lamented. Cooper criticized Al Sharpton for assuming the mantle of "black spiritual leader" while blaming black Americans for not helping themselves in the search for progress. She characterized him as a "safe truths" type of leader, one who does the bidding of the Obama administration, which includes "the placating of the people by ostensibly affirming their sense of injustice, while disaffirming their right to a kind of righteous rage in the face of such injustice." Both West and Cooper share a distrust for black leaders in high politics who promote piecemeal reforms of political and economic structures that, in their view, need radical dismantling. They also resent that these leaders "suggested that the real turning point needed to be first within black communities," when in fact it is the United States as a nation that must be held accountable for the persistence of socioeconomic inequality and racial discrimination.

9. Maki Becker, "AG's Wardel Davis probe clears officers, faults lack of body cams," *Buffalo News*, December 13, 2017; Omar Fetouth and Mike Desmond, "Buffalo police officers cleared in shooting death of unarmed man," *WBFO*, February 1, 2018, news.wbfo.org/post/buffalo-police-officers-cleared-shooting-death-unarmed-man.

10. Michelle Alexander, *The New Jim Crow: Mass Incarceration in the Age of Colorblindness* (New York: The New Press, 2012), 21.

11. Alexander, *The New Jim Crow*, 30–31.

12. Carol Anderson, *White Rage: The Unspoken Truth of Our Racial Divide* (New York: Bloomsbury, 2016), 3.

13. Anderson, *White Rage*, 3–4.

14. Keeanga-Yamahtta Taylor, *From #Blacklivesmatter to Black Liberation* (Chicago: Haymarket Books, 2016), 9.

15. Taylor, *From #Blacklivesmatter to Black Liberation*, 10.

16. Harris, "Coming of Age," 110.

17. Harris, 116.

18. Harris, 116.

19. Harris, 109.

20. Harris, 116.

21. Harris, 110.

22. Harris, 116.

23. Harris, 110.

24. C. Matthew Snipp and Sin Yi Ceung, "Changes in Racial and Gender Inequality since 1970," *Annals of the American Academy, AAPSS* 663 (January 2016): 88 (esp. table 2).

25. George L. Kelling and James Q. Wilson, "Broken Windows: The Police and Neighborhood Safety," *The Atlantic Monthly* (1982), 29, 30–31, and 38, cited in Jones, "He's a Black Male," 1047.

26. D. Marvin Jones, "'He's a Black Male . . . Something Is Wrong with Him!' The Role of Race in the Stand Your Ground Debate," *University of Miami Law Review* 68 (2014): 1034.

27. James Kilgore, "Mass Incarceration: Examining and Moving Beyond the New Jim Crow," *Critical Sociology* 41, no. 2 (2014): 284.

28. Kilgore, "Mass Incarceration, 284.

29. Mauer, "Addressing Racial Disparities in Incarceration," 89s.

30. Mauer, 88s.

31. Mauer, "Addressing Racial Disparities in Incarceration," 96s.

32. Ben Brucato, "Big Data and the New Transparency: Measuring and Representing Police Killings," *Big Data & Society* (January–June 2017): 2.

33. Brucato, "Big Data and the New Transparency," 3.

34. "Fatal Force: Police Shooting Database," *Washington Post*, 2018, www.washingtonpost.com/graphics/2018/national/police-shootings-2018/?utm_term=.752ff2c01342.

35. "Quick Facts: United States," *United States Census Bureau*, www.census.gov/quickfacts/fact/table/US#viewtop.

36. "Fatal Force."

37. "Quick Facts."

38. Jones, "He's a Black Male," 1034.

39. Jones, 1029.

40. Jones, 1030.

41. Khalil G. Muhammad, *The Condemnation of Blackness: Race, Crime, and the Making of Modern Urban America* (Cambridge: MA: Harvard University Press, 2010), 16.

42. Muhammad, *The Condemnation of Blackness*, 16.

43. Gunnar Myrdal, *An American Dilemma: The Negro Problem and Modern Democrac*, 20th ann. ed. (New York: Harper & Row, 1962), 529, cited in Muhammad, *The Condemnation of Blackness*, 276.

44. The myth of the content slave was so dominant in contemporaneous literature that slavery historians reproduced this mythology in studies well into the twentieth century. W. E. B. Du Bois, Carter G. Woodson, Herbert Aptheker, Raymond A. Bauer, and Alice H. Bauer were among the earliest historians to challenge this myth with studies of slave resistance. See Raymond A. Bauer and Alice H. Bauer, "Day to Day Resistance to Slavery," *Journal of Negro History* 27, no. 4 (1942): 389.

45. Jones, "He's a Black Male," 1034.

46. Jones, 1045–1046.

47. *City of Chicago v. Morales*, 527 U.S. 41 (1999), cited in Jones, "He's a Black Male," 1046.

48. In a brilliant essay, "Black and Blue," Garnette Cadogan starkly differentiates his pedestrian experiences in Kingston, Jamaica, New Orleans, and New York, three cities where he spent time walking. In Kingston, Cadogan could disappear in the black majority population, enjoying the sights, sounds, and smells of the city, and resting assured that the police would not harass and harm him. In New Orleans, he learned to dress "unthreatening" and stay clear of white Americans, who feared him and might have him arrested. In New York, he felt hunted by police officers and in one incident was stopped, frisked, and cuffed for running to the train station. "Walking—the simple, monotonous act of placing one foot before the other to prevent falling—turns out not to be so simple if you're black," Cadogan lamented. "Walking alone has been anything but monotonous for me; monotony is a luxury." See Jesmyn Ward, ed., *The Fire This Time: A New Generation Speaks about Race* (New York: Scribner's Sons, 2016), 142–143.

49. Alexander, *The New Jim Crow*, 100.

50. Alexander, 4.

51. Martin Luther King Jr., "'I Have a Dream,' Address Delivered at the March on Washington for Jobs and Freedom," *The Martin Luther King, Jr. Research and Education Institute*, Stanford University, kinginstitute.stanford.edu/king-papers/documents/i-have-dream-address-delivered-march-washington-jobs-and-freedom.

52. "Civil Rights Act (1964)," http://www.ourdocuments.gov/doc.php?flash=false&doc=97&page=transcript.

53. "Voting Rights Act (1965)," http://www.ourdocuments.gov/doc.php?flash=true&doc=100&page=transcript.

54. Michael Omi and Howard Winant, *Racial Formation in the United States*, 3rd ed. (New York: Routledge), 165.

55. Omi and Winant, *Racial Formation in the United States*, 192.

56. Omi and Winant, 192.

57. Michelle Alexander, *The New Jim Crow*, 40.

58. Goldwater, quoted in Alexander, 42.

59. H. R. Haldeman, cited in Alexander, 44.

60. Taylor, *From #Blacklivesmatter to Black Liberation*, 62.

61. Taylor, 15.

62. Taylor, 102.

63. Taylor, 15.

64. Taylor, 87.

65. Taylor, 142–143.

66. A 2015 ACLU report, for example, explained that "during the 2009–2011 period . . . the typical white family's losses [due to the recession] slowed to zero, while the typical black family lost an additional 13 percent of its wealth." While

white households recover from the economic downturn, black households will feel the effects reverberate well into the future, as the racial disparities that were decreasing before the downturn became more stark after it. See Sarah Burd-Sharps and Rebecca Rasch, *Impacts of the US Housing Crisis on the Racial Wealth Gap Across Generations*, Social Sciences Research Council, American Civil Liberties Union, 2015, 3.

67. Ella Baker, "Bigger than a Hamburger," *History is a Weapon*, http://www.historyisaweapon.com/defcon1/bakerbigger.html.

68. Taylor, *From #Blacklivesmatter to Black Liberation*, 103.

69. Logan, *The Betrayal of the Negro*, xix.

70. Dr. Martin L. King Jr., "The Ethical Demands for Integration," in *Martin Luther King, Jr., Malcolm X, and the Civil Rights Struggle of the 1950s and 1960s: A Brief History with Documents*, ed. David Howard-Pitney (New York: Bedford / St. Martin's, 2004), 60–64 passim.

71. Ta-Nehisi Coates, *Between the World and Me* (New York: Spiegel and Grau, 2015), 11–12.

72. James Baldwin, "A Letter to My Nephew," *Progressive*, December 1, 1962, http://www.progressive.org/magazine/letter-nephew.

73. Barbara Ransby, *Making All Black Lives Matter: Reimagining Freedom in the 21st Century* (Berkeley: University of California Press, 2018), 3.

Chapter 3

1. Louwanda Evans and Joe R. Feagin, "The Costs of Policing Violence: Foregrounding Cognitive and Emotional Labor," *Critical Sociology* 41, no. 6 (2015): 890.

2. Jeffrey C. Alexander et al., *Cultural Trauma and Collective Identity* (Berkeley: University of California Press, 2004); Ron Eyerman, *Is This America?: Katrina as Cultural Trauma* (Austin: University of Texas Press, 2015); Ron Eyerman, *Cultural Trauma: Slavery and the Formation of African American Identity* (Cambridge: Cambridge University Press, 2001).

3. Hiro Saito, "Reiterated Commemoration: Hiroshima as National Trauma," *Sociological Theory* 24, no. 4 (2006): 353–376.

4. John Postill and Sarah Pink, "Social Media Ethnography: The Digital Researcher in a Messy Web," *Media International Australia* 145 (2012): 123–134.

5. Paolo Gerbaudo, *Tweets and the Streets: Social Media and Contemporary Activism* (London: Pluto Press, 2012), 14.

6. Gerbaudo, *Tweets and the Streets*, 117.

7. "They Killed Her. They Fucking Killed Sandra Bland," *VSB*, 2015, http://www.verysmartbrothas.com/they-killed-her-they-fucking-killed-sandra-bland.

8. Jenna Wortham, "Black Health Matters," *New York Times*, 2016, http://www.nytimes.com/2016/08/28/fashion/black-lives-matter-wellness-health-self-care.html?_r=0.

9. Liz Adetiba and Anna Almendrala, "Watching Videos Of Police Brutality Can Traumatize You, Especially If You're Black," *Huffington Post*, 2016, http://www.huffingtonpost.com/entry/watching-police-brutality-videos_us_577ee9b3e4b0344d514eaa5d.

10. Kenya Downs, "When Black Death Goes Viral, It Can Trigger PTSD-like Trauma," *PBS Newshour*, 2016, http://www.pbs.org/newshour/rundown/black-pain-gone-viral-racism-graphic-videos-can-create-ptsd-like-trauma/.

11. Imani Brammer, "Must-See: Do You Ever Want to 'Call in Black' from Work?" *Essence*, July 2015, http://www.essence.com/news/call-black-work-evelyn-from-internets/.

12. "Calling in Black" brings to mind Talcott Parson's theorization of the sick role, wherein the sick individual is released from social responsibility through sanctioned deviance. Of course, "Call in Black" is not an acceptable excuse from productivity for the majority of work places; the sufferer instead must make use of the sanctioned sick role to be excused from their responsibilities.

13. Philomena Essed, *Understanding Everyday Racism: An Interdisciplinary Theory* (Newbury Park: SAGE, 1991); Amy C. Wilkins, " 'Not Out to Start a Revolution': Race, Gender, and Emotional Restraint among Black University Men," *Journal of Contemporary Ethnography* 41, no. 1 (2012): 34–65.

14. Audre Lorde, *Zami, Sister Outsider, Undersong* (New York: Quality Paperback Book Club, 1993); Sarita Srivastava, "Canadian Journal of Sociology Emotion Fears and Careers: And in Social Movement Organizations," *Canadian Journal of Sociology* 31, no. 1 (2006): 55–90.

15. Robin Diangelo, *White Fragility: Why It's so Hard for White People to Talk About Racism* (Boston: Beacon Press, 2018); Ruby Hamad, "How White Women Use Strategic Tears to Silence Women of Colour," *Guardian*, 2018, http://www.theguardian.com/commentisfree/2018/may/08/how-white-women-use-strategic-tears-to-avoid-accountability.

16. BYP100, "In Defense of Black Rage and Black Resistance," 2016, http://byp100.org/byp100-in-defense-of-black-rage-and-black-resistance/.

17. Lily Workneh, "#BlackLivesMatter Co-Founders on Baltimore Uprisings: 'We Stand in Solidarity,' " *Huffington Post*, 2015.

18. Patricia Hill Collins, *Black Feminist Thought: Knowledge, Consciousness, and the Politics of Empowerment* (New York: Routledge, 2000).

19. Mary Holmes, "Feeling Beyond Rules: Politicizing the Sociology of Emotion and Anger in Feminist Politics," *European Journal of Social Theory* 7, no. 2 (May 1, 2004): 209–227; Cheryl Hercus, "Identity, Emotion, and Feminist Collective Action," *Gender & Society* 13, no. 1 (1999): 34–55.

20. Audre Lorde, "The Uses of Anger: Women Responding to Racism," in *Sister Outsider: Essays & Speeches by Audre Lorde* (Berkeley, CA: Crossing Press, 2007), 127.

21. Bianca C. Williams, "The Anthropoliteia #BlackLivesMatterSyllabus Project, Week 8: Bianca C. Williams On 'The Uses of Anger' by Audre Lorde," *Anthropoliteia*,

2016, http://www.anthropoliteia.net/2016/11/03/the-anthropoliteia-blacklivesmatter syllabus-project-week-8-bianca-c-williams-on-the-uses-of-anger-by-audre-lorde.

22. Julia S. Jordan-Zachery, "Beyond the Side Eye: Black Women's Ancestral Anger as a Liberatory Practice," *Journal of Black Sexuality and Relationships* 4, no. 1 (2017): 61–82.

23. " 'Assume the Position . . . You Fit the Description': Psychosocial Experiences and Racial Batlle Fatigure Among African American Male College Students," *American Behavioral Scientist* 51, no. 4 (2007): 551–578.

24. Deborah Douglas, "Did Racism Kill Erica Garner?," *Vice*, 2018, http://www.vice.com/en_us/article/vby7qy/did-racism-kill-erica-garner; Alexis Dent, "Eric Garner Died Because of Systemic Racism. Unfortunately, His Daughter Suffered the Same Fate," *Medium*, 2017, http://www.medium.com/@alexisdent/eric-garner-died-because-of-systemic-racism-unfortunately-his-daughter-suffered-the-same-fate-a9f9d27766855; Jessica Roach, "Sickened By Oppression," *Rewire News*, 2018, http://www.rewire.news/article/2018/01/03/sickened-by-oppression-mourning-erica-garner.

25. *I'm Judging You: The Do-Better Manual* (New York: Holt Paperbacks, 2016), 79.

26. Anna Orso, "How Black Lives Matter Philly Is Responding to 36 Hours of Right-Wing Media Attacks," *BillyPenn*, 2015, http://www.billypenn.com/2017/04/05/how-black-lives-matter-philly-is-responding-to-36-hours-of-right-wing-media-attacks.

27. Downs, "When Black Death Goes Viral."

28. *The Managed Heart: Comercialization of Human Feeling* (Berkeley: University of California Press, 1983).

29. Jamelle Bouie et al., "I'm Not Your Racial Confessor," *Slate*, 2016, http://www.slate.com/articles/news_and_politics/politics/2016/12/the_black_person_s_burden_of_managing_white_emotions_in_the_age_of_trump.html.

30. "A Homegirl Reflecting on Charlotte Uprising," tressicmc.com, 2016, http://www.tressiemc.com/uncategorized/a-homegirl-reflecting-on-charlotte-uprising.

31. Lori Lakin Hutcherson, "What I Said When My White Friend Asked for My Black Opinion on White Privilege," GoodBlackNews.org, 2017, http://goodblacknews.org/2016/07/14/editorial-what-i-said-when-my-white-friend-asked-for-my-black-opinion-on-white-privilege.

32. Landess Kearns, "The Incredible Reason You Might Start Seeing Safety Pins Everywhere," Huffington Post, 2016, http://www.huffingtonpost.com/entry/safety-pin-trump-brexit_us_58251b53e4b0c4b63b0c11a9.

33. Shane Paul Neil, "Is Saftey Pin Box the Gift for 'White Allies'?" NBC News, 2016.

34. Michal Jones, "5 Reasons We Need Black-Only Spaces (And No, Reverse Racism Isn't One of Them)," Everyday Feminism, 2015, http://www.everydayfeminism.com/2015/09/why-need-black-only-spaces.

35. *Scandalize My Name: Black Feminist Practice and the Making of Black Social Life* (New York: Fordham University Press, 2017), 9.

36. "A Love Letter to Black People," 2017, http://www.medium.com/@BYP100/a-love-letter-to-black-people-3d5e49ee890e#.nd9nmih21.

37. Black Lives Matter, "Healing in Action: A Toolkit for Black Lives Matter Healing Justice & Direct Action," 2017, http://www.blacklivesmatter.com/resource/healing-justice-toolkit.

Chapter 4

1. NCADV: National Coalition Against Domestic Violence, "The Nation's Leading Grassroots Voice on Domestic Violence," http://www.ncadv.org/statistics; J. C. Campbell, D. Webster, J. Koziol-McLain, C. Block, D. Campbell, M. A. Curry, and K. Laughon (2003), "Risk Factors for Femicide in Abusive Relationships: Results from a Multisite Case Control Study," *American Journal of Public Health* 93, no. 7: 1089–1097.

2. Carolyn M. West, "Black Women and Intimate Partner Violence: New Directions for Research." *Journal of Interpersonal Violence* 19, no. 12 (2004): 1487–1493; "The Legal System Has Failed Black Girls, Women, and Non-Binary Survivors of Violence," American Civil Liberties Union, March 21, 2019, http://www.aclu.org/blog/racial-justice/race-and-criminal-justice/legal-system-has-failed-black-girls-women-and-non; E. Petrosky, J. M. Blair, C. J. Betz, K. A. Fowler, S. P. Jack, and B. H. Lyons, "Racial and Ethnic Differences in Homicides of Adult Women and the Role of Intimate Partner Violence—United States, 2003–2014," *Morbid Mortality Weekly Report* 66 (2017): 741–746.

3. Richard Fausset, Richard Pérez-Peña, and Campbell Robertson, "Alton Sterling Shooting in Baton Rouge Prompts Justice Dept. Investigation," *New York Times*, July 6, 2016, http://www.nytimes.com/2016/07/06/us/alton-sterling-baton-rouge-shooting.html; Eyder Peralta and Cheryl Corley, "The Driving Life and Death of Philando Castile," NPR, http://www.npr.org/sections/thetwo-way/2016/07/15/485835272/the-driving-life-and-death-of-philando-castile.

4. Cindy Cruz, "LGBTQ Street Youth Talk Back: A Meditation on Resistance and Witnessing," *International Journal of Qualitative Studies in Education* 24, no. 5 (October 1, 2011): 547–558.

5. With the aid of British abolitionists, in 1824, flogging enslaved women was banned in the colonies. The British Abolition Act of 1834 wrote this prohibition into law, but it didn't stop the practice. It transferred the power to whip from the hands of individual slaveowners and placed it in the arms of the state and continued to exempt black women from corporeal punishment.

6. For scholars exploring the hoodrat, ratchet, and crunk as Black feminist praxes, see Kendall, Mikki. *Hood Feminism: Notes from the Women That a Movement Forgot* (New York: Viking, 2020); intellectual work generated by I'Nasah Crockett, creator of the "Ratchetness as Praxis" clothing line (http://www.patreon.com/sotreu);

Brittney C. Cooper, Susana M. Morris, and Robin M. Boylorn, eds., *The Crunk Feminist Collection* (New York: Feminist Press at CUNY, 2017).

7. Names have been changed.

8. "After the Hurricane: Decolonial Feminisms & Destierro," *Hypatia, a Journal of Feminist Philosophy* 35, no. 1 (February 2020).

9. Cherríe Moraga. *This Bridge Called My Back, 4th Edition: Writings by Radical Women of Color*, translated by Gloria Anzaldúa (Albany: State University of New York Press, 2015); Chela Sandoval, *Methodology of the Oppressed* (Minneapolis: University of Minnesota Press, 2000); María Lugones. "Heterosexualism and the Colonial/modern Gender System," *Hypatia* 22, no. 1 (2007): 186–219; Anibal Quijano, "Coloniality of Power and Eurocentrism in Latin America," *International Sociology* 15, no. 2 (2000): 215–232.

10. Jennifer L. Morgan. "Accounting for "the Most Excruciating Torment": Gender, Slavery, and Trans-Atlantic Passages," *History of the Present* 6 (2016): 184–207.

11. Yomaira C. Figueroa-Vásquez. "Faithful Witnessing as Practice: Decolonial Readings of Shadows of Your Black Memory and the Brief Wondrous Life of Oscar Wao," *Hypatia* 30, no. 4 (2015): 641–656.

12. Stephanie Farr, "Police: Ex-Temple Cops Killed Roommate Because "She Would Not Submit," http://www.philly.com/philly/blogs/dncrime/Police-Ex-Temple-cops-conspired-to-murder-roommate-.html.

Chapter 5

1. First published in Lauren Alleyne, *Difficult Fruit* (Leeds: Peepal Tree Press, 2014).

2. First published in *One*, August 2015, no. 6.

3. First published in *The Mighty Stream: Poems in Celebration of Martin Luther King* (United Kingdom: Bloodaxe Books, 2017).

4. First published in *Los Angeles Review of Books*, Winter 2014.

5. First published in *Split This Rock Poem of the Week*, September 9, 2016.

Chapter 6

1. For a historical view, see Louis-Georges Schwartz *Mechanical Witness: A History of Motion Picture Evidence in US Courts* (New York & Oxford: Oxford University Press, 2009). For an excellent account of the range of activist strategies developed to counteract police violence against black and immigrant populations in the wake of Mr. Garner's death, see Jeffrey Skoller, "iDocument Police: Contingency, Resistance, and the Precarious Present," *World Records*, ed. Jason Fox, vol. 1, 2018.

2. See Alicia Garza, "A Herstory of the #BlackLivesMatter Movement" *Feminist Wire*, October 7, 2014, http://www.thefeministwire.com/2014/10/blacklivesmatter-2.

3. One reviewer found this open format together with the focus on the female body to detract from what he saw as the central significance of the vulnerable black *male* body in recent activism. See Seph Rodney, "An Exhibition about Black Lives with a Gender Focus," *Hyperallergic*, May 7, 2016, http://www.hyperallergic.com/297075/an-exhibition-about-black-lives-with-a-gendered-focus. For an alternative review of the exhibition that explicitly engages with and challenges Rodney's account, advocating for the feminist perspective, see Florencia San Martin Ruitort, "Feminismo, #blacklivesmatter," *Artishock*, July 7, 2016, http://www.artishockrevista.com/2016/07/07/i-cant-breathe-arte-contemporaneo-feminismo-black-life-matters.

4. There are three other works not discussed in this essay. The two videos in the exhibition by Walker, *An Audience* (2015) and *Rhapsody* (2015), were made in relation to her installation, *A Subtlety*, at the Domino Sugar factory (2014). This centered on an enormous sugarcoated figure of a sphinx that was rendered with stereotypical "Mamie" features and enlarged, exposed genitals. *An Audience* was shot on the last day of the installation and focused on viewers' interaction with the work with a particular emphasis on African American visitors. The installation, widely popular with black and white audiences alike, became controversial because of the number of viewers who took selfies and posted them on social media platforms. *Rhapsody* showed the destruction of the sculpture after the exhibition closed. Wolukau-Wanambwa's *A Short Video about Tate Modern* (2003) shows the artist, against a plain white wall. There is no sound, only a scrolling first-person text that recounts an incident at an artists' workshop at the Tate Modern in London. She became doubly aware of how unusual it was for a black artist to participate in this event when she finds herself the object of open scrutiny by the black service workers watching nearby.

5. The idea of a "visual economy" was first theorized by Deborah Poole in relation to Andean image culture. She developed this approach to challenge the widespread influence of cinematic gaze theory for the analysis of photography. Poole's important intervention marks a shift in theorizing photography to suggest a more dynamic and mobile relation to images. See Deborah Poole, *Vision, Race, and Modernity: The Visual Economy of the Andean Image World* (Princeton, NJ: Princeton University Press, 1997).

6. Katherine McKittrick, "Mathematics Black Life," *Black Scholar* 44, no. 2 (Summer 2014): 17.

7. See Molly Rogers, *Delia's Tears: Race, Science and Photography in Nineteenth Century America* (New Haven, CT: Yale University Press, 2010).

8. Elizabeth Edwards, "Anthropology and Photography: A Long History of Knowledge and Affect," *Photographies* 8, no. 3:240.

9. Rogers, *Delia's Tears*, 6.

10. Edwards, "Tracing Photography," in *Made to be Seen: Perspectives on the History of Visual Anthropology*, ed. Marcus Banks and Jay Ruby (Chicago: University of Chicago Press, 2011), 180.

11. Edwards, "Tracing Photography," 179.

12. Weems recounts these behind the scenes events in a PBS TV series segment of *art21* about her work, http://www.art21.org/watch/art-in-the-twenty-first-century/s5/compassion.

13. Jennifer Doyle, *Hold It Against Me: Difficulty and Emotion in Contemporary Art* (Durham, NC: Duke University Press, 2013), 120.

14. See Ranjana Khanna *Algeria Cuts: Women and Representation, 1830 to the Present* (Stanford, CA: Stanford University Press, 2008), 59–60.

15. Saidiya Hartman, "Venus in Two Acts," *Small Axe* 26 (June 2008): 13.

16. Eve Kosofsky Sedgwick "Paranoid Reading and Reparative Reading, or, You're so Paranoid, You Probably Think this Essay Is About You," in *Touching Feeling: Affect, Pedagogy, Performativity*, ed. Sedgwick (Durham, NC: Duke University Press, 2003), 128. Original italics.

17. The department had been embroiled in an earlier censorship scandal over a student production of Holly Hughes's *Well of Horniness*. See Jim Dwyer "OffStage, A Farce gets a Second Act," *New York Times*, April 28, 2009, http://ww.nytimes.com/2009/04/29/nyregion/29about.html.

18. This pattern of silencing and obfuscation can be traced back to the college administration's response to the unprovoked killing of black auxiliary worker, Corey Holmes, by a New York police officer on the campus in November 2011. See "Corey Holmes Caught Smoking Pot at College of Staten Island and Dies after Struggle with Police," *Huffington Post*, November 30, 2011, http://www.huffpost.com/entry/cory-holmes-caught-smokin_n_1121010.

19. For a close analysis of the different use of images from the Civil Rights Movement in the black and white press, including an excellent discussion of the coverage of Emmett Till's funeral, see Maurice Berger, *For All the World to See: Visual Culture and the Struggle for Civil Rights* (New Haven, CT: Yale University Press, 2010).

20. In an untitled public presentation at the Whitney Museum organized in response to the Schutz scandal, see Gaines in *Perspectives on Race and Representation: An Evening with the Racial Imaginary Institute*, April 9, 2017.

21. For a powerful critique of formalist strategies in contemporary poetry, a perspective that has influenced my thinking here, see Ken Chan, "Authenticity as Obsession, or Conceptual Poetry as Minstrel Show," *Asian American Writers Workshop*, http://www.aaww.org/authenticity-obsession.

22. For a discussion of the social spaces of the lynching spectacle, see Leon F. Litwack's "Hellhounds" in James Allen, ed., *Without Sanctuary: Lynching Photography in America* (Santa Fe, NM: Twin Palms, 2000), 8–37. My understanding of lynching photography is indebted to Dora Apel *Imagery of Lynching: Black Men, White*

Women and the Mob (New Brunswick, NJ: Rutgers University Press, 2003); and Dora Apel and Shawne-Michelle Smith, *Lynching Photographs* (Berkeley: University of California Press, 2007).

23. On the relationship between the footage of the Rodney King beating and the Emmett Till image, see Elizabeth Alexander, "Can You Be Black and Look at This?" *Public Culture* 7 (1994): 77–94.

24. Shianne Ngai, *Ugly Feelings* (Cambridge, MA: Harvard University Press, 2005), 10.

25. I am grateful to Nicky Bird and Nancy Proctor for this insight. For a powerful art historical discussion of rendering black women invisible, see Griselda Pollock, "A Tale of Three Women: Seeing in the Dark, Seeing Double, at Least, with Manet," in *Differencing the Canon: Feminism and the Writing of Art's Histories*, ed. Pollock (London & New York: Routledge, 1999), 247–315.

26. Michael Rothberg, *Multidirectional Memory: Remembering the Holocaust in the Age of Decolonization* (Stanford, CA: Stanford University Press, 2009).

27. Christina Sharpe *In the Wake: On Blackness and Being* (Durham, NC: Duke University Press, 2016), 10, 3, 4.

28. Sharpe discusses this analysis in an interview with Siddhartha Mitter. See Mitter and Sharpe, "What Does It Mean to Be Black and Look at This? A Scholar Reflects on the Dana Schutz Controversy," *Hyperallergic*, March 24, 2017, http://www.hyperallergic.com/368012/what-does-it-mean-to-be-black-and-look-at-this-a-scholar-reflects-on-the-dana-schutz-controversy.

Chapter 8

1. The #blacklivesmatter movement emerged to draw attention to the killing of unarmed black men and women and the ongoing disenfranchisement of African Americans in the United States. With a slate of demands and action items organized around the desire to have the human rights of black people recognized and protected, #blacklivesmatter provides allies of the movement with an opportunity to organize, protest, and fight against white supremacy and its institutionalized legacy.

2. "Profoundly Disappointed: Michael Brown Family Reacts to Lack of Indictment," *NBC News*, November 24, 2014.

3. "Obama Calls on Nation to Accept Ferguson Decision, Protest Peacefully," *NBC News*, November 24, 2014.

4. Jennifer D. Ryan, "'Come. Glory in My Wonder's Will': An Interview with Wanda Coleman," *MELUS* 40, no. 1 (2015): 195–205.

5. Krista Comer, "Revising Western Criticism through Wanda Coleman," *Western American Literature* 33, no. 4 (1999): 358.

6. Jennifer Ryan, *Post-Jazz Poetics: A Social History* (New York: Palgrave Macmillan, 2010), 131.

7. Ryan, *Post-Jazz Poetics*, 280.

8. Ryan, 113.

9. Anna Julia Cooper, *A Voice from the South* (New York: Oxford University Press, 1988 [1892]), 31. My emphasis.

10. Cooper, *A Voice from the South*, 187.

11. Cooper, 187.

12. Cooper, 193.

13. Cooper, 193.

14. Notwithstanding the fact that much of the #blacklivesmatter movement has failed to mobilize behind the murders of unarmed black women—Tanisha Anderson, Yvette Smith, and Renisha McBride are three in a heartbreakingly long list of black women murdered while seeking assistance from everyday citizens or law enforcement.

15. "Bougie" is a colloquial term that has traditionally described individuals who present an elitist, snobbish, and sometimes affected performance of middle-class or upper-middle-class values (or what one perceives as middle-class or upper-middle-class values) whether one is middle class or not. "Ratchet" describes behavior or dress that is loud, excessive, brash, and/or fails to display modest modes of comportment. Both are traditionally derogatory terms despite having been reclaimed and reappropriated in certain circles and in particular contexts. For example, while my use of "ratchet" invokes the term according to its negative connotations, in "Shoving aside the Politics of Respectability," Therí A. Pickens "recuperates the derogatory term 'ratchet' as a performative strategy that secures a liberatory space for black women" (1).

16. Michelle Wallace, *Black Macho and the Myth of the Superwoman* (New York: Verso, 1990 [1979]), 91.

17. Wallace, *Black Macho and the Myth of the Superwoman*, 12. Even though hooks follows this sentence with a statement about black folks who have "made it" skillfully express their rage, it is unclear whether the "folk" to which she refers in this passage are black or white.

18. Comer, *Landscapes*, 90.

19. Malin Pereira, "Wanda Coleman," in *Twenty-First Century American Poets. Dictionary of Literary Biography*, vol. 372, ed. John Custasis (Detroit: Gale, 2013), 87.

20. Lakesia Johnson, "The Myth of the Angry Black Woman," in *Iconic: Decoding Images of the Revolutionary Black Woman* (Waco, TX: Baylor University Press, 2012), 2.

21. Johnson, "The Myth of the Angry Black Woman," 1.

22. Gina Athena Ulysse, "She Ain't Oprah, Angela, or Your Baby Mama: The Michelle O Enigma," *Meridians: Feminism, Race, Transnationalism* 9, no. 1 (2009): 174.

23. J. Beth Mabry and K. Jill Kiecolt, "Anger in Black and White: Race, Alienation, and Anger," *Journal of Health and Social Behavior* 46 (2005): 85.

24. J. Celeste Walley-Jean, "Debunking the Myth of the 'Angry Black Woman': An Exploration of Anger in Young African American Women," *Black Women, Gender, and Families* 3, no. 2 (2009): 68.

25. Chavella T. Pittman, "Getting Mad but Ending Up Sad: The Mental Health Consequences for African Americans Using Anger to Cope with Racism," *Journal of Black Studies* 42, no. 7 (2011): 1107.

26. hooks, bell, "Revolutionary Black Women: Making Ourselves Subject," in *Black Looks: Race and Representation* (Boston: South End, 1992): 42.

27. Michelle Wallace, "Anger in Isolation: A Black Feminist's Search for Sisterhood," *Invisibility Blues: From Pop to Theory* (New York: Verso, 1990), 23.

28. Elizabeth Alexander, *The Black Interior: Essays* (Minneapolis, MN: Gray Wolf, 2004), x.

29. Audre Lorde, "The Uses of Anger," *Women's Studies Quarterly* 9, no. 3 (1981): 8. The prevalence and popularity of Lorde's essay suggests that black women's rage is inappropriately expressed in poetry but appropriately expressed through prose.

30. David Orr, "Adrienne Rich, Beyond the Anger," *NYTimes*, March 30, 2012.

31. hooks, "Killing Rage," 19.

32. "Flipping the bird" describes the gesture of thrusting one's middle finger in the direction of another as a sign of disgust. In many American contexts it translates easily to "Fuck you."

33. Malin Pereira, "Interview with Wanda Coleman," in *Into a Light Both Brilliant and Unseen: Conversations with Contemporary Black Poets* (Athens: University of Georgia Press, 2010), 31.

34. Wanda Coleman, *Bathwater Wine* (Santa Rosa, CA: Black Sparrow, 1998), 271.

35. Wanda Coleman, "Letters to E. Ethelbert Miller," *Callaloo* 22, no. 1 (1999): 105.

36. Coleman, "Letters to E. Ethelbert Miller," 105.

37. Coleman, 105.

38. Wanda Coleman, *American Sonnets* (Milwaukee: Light and Dust, 1994), 1.1.

39. Coleman, *American Sonnets*, 1.7.

40. Coleman, 1.7.

41. Coleman, 1.8.

42. Coleman, 1.1, 1.2.

43. Coleman, 1.5.

44. Coleman, 1.5. My emphasis.

45. Ralph Waldo Emerson, "Nature," in *Nature and Selected Essays* (New York: Penguin Classics, 1993), 35.

46. Coleman, *American Sonnets*, 1.4.

47. Coleman, 1.

48. Craig Hansen Werner, *A Change Is Gonna Come: Music Race and the Soul of America* (Ann Arbor: University of Michigan Press, [1998] 2006), 131.

49. Coleman, *American Sonnets*, 1.3 and 1.4.

50. Jennifer Ryan, *Post-Jazz Poetics: A Social History* (New York: Palgrave Macmillan, 2010), 112.

51. Coleman, *American Sonnets*, 1.6–1.10.

52. Coleman, 1.12.

53. Werner, *A Change Is Gonna Come*, 69.

54. In Werner, 69.

55. "Covering" describes the practice of performing a song originally sung or written by someone else.

56. Coleman, *American Sonnets*, 1.14.

57. Coleman, 1.11.

58. Coleman, 1.12.

59. Wanda Coleman, *Mercurochrome* (Santa Rosa, CA: Black Sparrow, 2001), 105.

60. Coleman, *American Sonnets*, 1.2.

61. Pereira, "Interview," 31.

62. Coleman, *American Sonnets*, 1.3–1.4.

63. Coleman, 1.4–1.7.

64. Pereira, "Interview," 19.

65. Wanda Coleman, "On Theloniousism," *Caliban* 4 (1988): 68.

66. Tony Magistrale and Patricia Ferreira. "Sweet Mama Wanda Tells Fortunes: An Interview with Wanda Coleman," *Black American Literature Forum* 24, no. 3 (1990): 491.

67. Gwendolyn Brooks. *Annie Allen* (Westport, CT: Greenwood, 1971 [1945]), 38.

Chapter 9

1. Slavoj Žižek, "Tolerance as an Ideological Category," *Critical Inquiry* 34, no. 4 (2008): 660.

2. E. Patrick Johnson, "Introduction," in *Appropriating Blackness: Performance and the Politics of Authenticity* (Durham, NC: Duke University Press, 2003), 2.

3. Johnson, "Introduction," 8.

4. Johnson, 3.

5. Žižek, "Tolerance as an Ideological Category," 660.

6. Charles "Chip" P. Linscott, "Introduction: #BlackLivesMatter and the Mediatic Lives of a Movement," *Black Camera* 8, no. 2 (Spring 2017): 77.

7. Michele Prettyman Beverly, "'No Medicine for Melancholy': Cinema of Loss and Mourning in the Era of #BlackLivesMatter," *Black Camera* 8, no. 2 (Spring 2017): 87.

8. Beverly, "'No Medicine for Melancholy,'" 83.

9. Beverly, 82.

10. Sara Ahmed, "Institutional Life," in *On Being Included: Racism and Diversity in Institutional Life* (Durham, NC: Duke University Press, 2012), 34.

11. Sara Ahmed, "The Nonperformativity of Antiracism," *Meridians* 7, no. 1 (2006): 104–126.

12. Nicole Fleetwood, "Introduction," in *Troubling Vision: Performance, Visuality, and Blackness* (Chicago: University of Chicago Press, 2011). 17.

13. Christian Metz, *The Imaginary Signifier: Psychoanalysis and the Cinema* (Bloomington: Indiana University Press, 1986).

14. Tanya Sheehan, "A Time and Place: Rethinking Race in American Art History," in *A Companion to American Art*, ed. John Davis, Jennifer A. Greenhill, and Jason D. LaFountain (New York: Wiley-Blackwell, 2015), 49.

15. Sheehan, "A Time and Place," 49.

16. Wendy Brown, "Tolerance as a Discourse of Depoliticization," in *Regulating Aversion: Tolerance in the Age of Identity and Empire* (Princeton, NJ: Princeton University Press, 2008), 1.

17. Wendy Brown, "Tolerance as a Discourse of Power," in *Regulating Aversion: Tolerance in the Age of Identity and Empire* (Princeton, NJ: Princeton University Press, 2008), 29.

18. Ahmed, "The Nonperformativity of Antiracism," 43.

19. Žižek, "Tolerance as an Ideological Category," 682.

20. Žižek, 682.

21. Žižek, 660.

22. Homi Bhabha, "Interrogating Identity," in *The Location of Culture* (London: Routledge, 1994), 60.

23. Bhabha, "Interrogating Identity," 106.

24. David Marriott, "Photography and Fantasy," in *On Black Men* (Chicago: University of Chicago Press, 2000), 25.

25. Stuart Hall, "The Spectacle of the Other," in *Representation: Cultural Representations and Signifying Practices* (London: Sage Publications, 1997), 263.

26. Hall, "The Spectacle of the Other," 272.

27. Homi K. Bhabha, "The Other Question," in *The Location of Culture* (London: Routledge, 1994), 115.

28. Bhabha, "The Other Question," 114.

Chapter 10

1. Previously published in *The Huffington Post*, February 28, 2017.

Chapter 11

1. Christopher J. Lebron, *The Making of Black Lives Matter: A Brief History of an Idea* (New York & Oxford: Oxford University Press), xii.

2. Lebron, *The Making of Black Lives Matter*, xii; Patrisse Khan-Cullors and Asha Bandele, *When They Call You a Terrorist: A Black Lives Matter Memoir* (New York: St. Martin's Press, 2018).

3. Joseph Flynn, *White Fatigue: Rethinking Resistance for Social Justice* (New York: Peter Lang, 2018), 31; Joseph Flynn, "White Fatigue: Naming the Challenge in Moving from an Individual to a Systemic Understanding of Racism," *Multicultural Perspectives* 17, no. 3 (2015): 115–124.

4. Robin DiAngelo, "White Fragility," *International Journal of Critical Pedagogy* 3, no. 3 (2011): 54–55; Jeff Hitchcock, *Lifting the White Veil: An Exploration of White American Culture in a Multicultural Context* (Roselle, NJ: Crandall, Dostie & Douglass Books, 2002).

5. BBC News, "Black Lives Matter Activists Outline Policy Goals," http://www.bbc.com/news/world-us-canada-34023751.

6. David Smith, "The Backlash against Black Lives Matter Is Just More Evidence of Injustice," *The Conversation*, October 31, 2017, http://www.theconversation.com/the-backlash-against-black-lives-matter-is-just-more-evidence-of-injustice-85587.

7. "*The Economist* Explains: The Misplaced Arguments against Black Lives Matter," The Economist, August 18, 2017, http://www.economist.com/the-economist-explains/2017/08/18/the-misplaced-arguments-against-black-lives-matter.

8. Christine Sleeter and Carl Grant. *Making Choices for Multicultural Education: Five Approaches to Race, Class, and Gender*, 6th ed. (Hoboken, NJ: John Wiley & Sons, 2011); Peter McLaren, *Life in Schools: An Introduction to Critical Pedagogy in the Foundations of Education*, 2nd ed. (Harlow, UK: Longman, 1994); James Banks, *Multicultural Education: Theory and Practice* (Boston: Allyn and Bacon, 1988).

9. Stuart Foster, "Whose History? Portrayals of Immigrant Groups in U.S. History Textbooks, 1800–Present," in *What Shall We Tell the Children? International Perspectives on School History Textbooks*, ed. Stuart Foster and Keith Crawford (Greenwich, CT: Information Age Press, 2006), 155–178; Bruce VanSledright, "Narratives of Nation-State, Historical Knowledge, and School History Education," *Review of Research in Education* 32, no. 1 (2008): 109–146.

10. Joseph O'Brien, Tina M. Ellsworth, and Duane Fleck, "Equality in US history: Where Great Persons, Literacy, and Historical Evidence Intersect," *History Teacher* 49, no. 3 (2016): 359–382.

11. Brandelyn Tosolt and Bettina L. Love, "Racial Harmony & Heroes: A Content Analysis of the Pearson Reading Program 'Good Habits, Great Readers,'" *Critical Questions in Education* 2, no. 1 (2012): 47.

12. Anthony L. Brown and Keffrelyn D. Brown, "Strange Fruit Indeed: Interrogating Contemporary Textbook Representations of Racial Violence toward African Americans," *Teachers College Record* 112, no. 1 (2010): 31–67; James Lowen, *Lies My Teacher Told Me: Everything Your American History Textbook Got Wrong* (New York: Touchstone, 2007); Christine E. Sleeter and Carl Grant, "Textbooks and Race,

Class, Gender, and Disability," in *The Politics of the Textbook*, ed. Michael Apple and Linda Christian-Smith (New York: Routledge, 1991), 78–110.

13. Susan Eva O'Donovan, "Foreword: Teaching Slavery in Today's Classroom," *OAH Magazine of History* 23, no. 2 (April 2009): 7.

14. Manny Fernandez and Christine Hauser, "Texas Mother Teaches Textbook Company a Lesson on Accuracy," *New York Times*, October 15, 2015, http://www.nytimes.com/2015/10/06/us/publisher-promises-revisions-after-textbook-refers-to-african-slaves-as-workers.html; Ellen Bresler Rockmore, "How Texas Teaches History," *New York Times*, October 21, 2015, http://www.nytimes.com/2015/10/22/opinion/how-texas-teaches-history.html.

15. Kate Shuster, *Teaching Hard History* (Report), Southern Poverty Law Center, January 31, 2018, http://www.easybib.com/guides/citation-guides/chicago-turabian/how-to-cite-a-report-chicago-turabian; Stella M. Chávez, "American Slavery Isn't Taught Well in Schools in Texas or across the U.S., Report Says," *KERA News*, February 1, 2018, http://www.keranews.org/post/american-slavery-isnt-taught-well-schools-texas-or-across-us-report-says.

16. Rockmore, "How Texas Teaches History."

17. Lewis Allan [pseudonym of Abel Meeropol], *Strange Fruit* (New York: Commodore Records, 1939).

18. Eugene Genovese, *Roll, Jordan, Roll: The World the Slaved Made* (New York: Vintage, 2011); Clemet Eaton, "Mob Violence in the Old South," *Mississippi Valley Historical Review* 29, no. 3 (1942): 351–370; Kenneth M. Stampp, *The Peculiar Institution: Slavery in the Ante-Bellum South*, reissue ed. (New York: Vintage, 1989).

19. Michael J. Pfeifer, "The Northern United States and the Genesis of Racial Lynching: The Lynching of African Americans in the Civil War Era," *Journal of American History* 97, no. 3 (2010): 622–623.

20. Dwight D. Murphey, "Lynching: History and Analysis," Council for Social and Economic Studies, Washington, DC, 1995.

21. *Lynching in America: Confronting the Legacy of Racial Terror*, 3rd ed., Equal Justice Initiative, part 3,

para 9 and 10, http://www.lynchinginamerica.eji.org/report.

22. Scott Ellsworth, *Death in a Promised Land: The Tulsa Race Riot of 1921*, 8th ed. (Baton Rouge: Louisiana State University Press, 1992); Claire Hartfield, *A Few Red Drops: The Chicago Race Riot of 1919* (New York: Clarion Books, 2018); Senechal de la Roche, *In Lincoln's Shadow: The 1908 Race Riot in Springfield, Illinois* (Carbondale: Southern Illinois University Press, 2008); Cameron McWhirter, *Red Summer: The Summer of 1919 and the Awakening of Black America* (New York: Henry Holt, 2012).

23. Linda Tucker, "Not Without Sanctuary: Teaching about Lynching," *Transformations: The Journal of Inclusive Scholarship and Pedagogy* 16, no. 2 (2005): 70–86.

24. Richard M. Perloff, "The Press and Lynchings of African Americans," *Journal of Black Studies* 30, no. 3 (2000): 318.

25. William Pinar, "The Gender of Racial Politics and Violence in America: Lynching, Prison Rape, and the Crisis of Masculinity," *Counterpoints* 163 (2001): 49.

26. Perloff, "The Press and Lynchings of African Americans," 326–327.

27. Larry J. Griffin, Paula Clark, and Joanne C. Sandberg, "Narrative and Event: Lynching and Historical Sociology," in *Under Sentence of Death: Lynching in the South*, ed. Fitzhugh Brundage (Chapel Hill: University of North Carolina Press, 1997), 24–47; Pinar, "The Gender of Racial Politics and Violence in America," 49.

28. Joe R. Feagin, Hernán Vera, and Pinar Batur, *White Racism: The* Basics, 2nd ed. (New York: Routledge, 2000).

29. United States Department of Justice Civil Rights Division, *Investigation of the Ferguson Police Department* (Washington, DC: Author, 2015); United States Department of Justice Civil Rights Division, *Investigation of the Baltimore Police Department* (Washington, DC: Author, 2016); United States Department of Justice Civil Rights Division, *Investigation of the Chicago Police Department* (Washington, DC: Author, 2017).

30. Joseph Flynn, *White Fatigue: Rethinking Resistance for Social Justice* (New York: Peter Lang, 2018), 31.

31. Hannah Fingerhut, "Most Americans Express Positive Views of Country's Growing Racial and Ethnic Diversity," http://www.pewresearch.org/fact-tank/2018/06/14/most-americans-express-positive-views-of-countrys-growing-racial-and-ethnic-diversity.

32. "In-depth topics A–Z: Race relations," Gallup, http://news.gallup.com/poll/1687/race-relations.aspx.

33. "In-depth topics A–Z: Race relations."

Chapter 12

1. Adam Chandler, "Eric Garner and Michael Brown: Deaths without Indictments," *Atlantic*, December 4, 2014, http://www.theatlantic.com/national/archive/2014/12/eric-garner-grand-jury-no-indictment-nypd/383392.

2. Rocco Parascandola, "60 NYPD Cops Set to Begin Wearing Body Cameras in Pilot Program," *New York Daily News*, September 5, 2014, http://www.nydailynews.com/new-york/50-nypd-cops-set-wearing-body-cameras-pilot-program-article-1.1927876.

3. "De Blasio Administration, NYPD Announce All Officers on Patrol to Wear Body Cameras by End of 2018," City of New York, January 30, 2018, http://www1.nyc.gov/office-of-the-mayor/news/071-18/de-blasio-administration-nypd-all-officers-patrol-wear-body-cameras-end-2018.

4. David Cloud, "On Life Support | Vera Institute," Vera, 2014, http://www.vera.org/publications/on-life-support-public-health-in-the-age-of-mass-incarceration.

5. Alexander Michelle, *The New Jim Crow: Mass Incarceration in the Age of Colorblindness* (New York: New Press, 2012).

6. Dan Baum, "Legalize It All: How to Win the War on Drugs," *Harpers*, April 2016, http://www.harpers.org/archive/2016/04/legalize-it-all.

7. John Eligon, "They Push. They Protest. And Many Activists, Privately, Suffer as a Result," *New York Times*, March 26, 2018, http://www.nytimes.com/2018/03/26/us/they-push-they-protest-and-many-activists-privately-suffer-as-a-result.html; E. J. Dickson, "Mysterious Deaths Leave Ferguson Activists 'On Pins and Needles,'" *Rolling Stone*, March 18, 2019, http://www.rollingstone.com/culture/culture-news/ferguson-death-mystery-black-lives-matter-michael-brown-809407.

8. Jacob Bor, Atheendar S. Venkataramani, David R. Williams, and Alexander C. Tsai, "Police Killings and Their Spillover Effects on the Mental Health of Black Americans: a Population-Based, Quasi-Experimental Study," *Lancet* 392, no. 10144 (2018): 302–310.

9. Jane Morice, "Thousands of 'Freedom Fighters' in Cleveland for First National Black Lives Matter Conference," Cleveland, July 26, 2015, http://www.cleveland.com/metro/index.ssf/2015/07/thousands_of_freedom_fighters.html.

10. M4BL, "About Us," The Movement for Black Lives, n.d., http://policy.m4bl.org/about.

11. "Divestment Action on South Africa by US and Canadian Colleges and Universities," Michigan State University, the Africa Fund, August 1988, http://www.kora.matrix.msu.edu/files/50/304/32-130-E6E-84-AL.SFF.DOCUMENT.acoa000194.pdf.

12. US Congress. House, "Comprehensive Anti-Apartheid Act of 1986," H.R. 4868, 99th Cong., 2nd Sess, introduced in House May 21, 2001, http://www.govinfo.gov/content/pkg/STATUTE-100/pdf/STATUTE-100-Pg1086.pdf#page=30.

13. Walter Cronkite, "Excerpts from an Interview with Walter Cronkite of CBS News: Ronald Reagan Presidential Library—National Archives and Records Administration," Reagan Library, March 3, 1981, http://www.reaganlibrary.gov/research/speeches/30381c.

14. Becky Little, "Why Nelson Mandela Was Viewed as a 'Terrorist' by the U.S. until 2008," Biography, June 25, 2019, http://www.biography.com/news/nelson-mandela-terrorist-reagan-thatcher 9.

15. Olivia B. Waxman, "Why Nelson Mandela Was on Terror Watch Lists Until 2008," *Time*, July 18, 2018, http://time.com/5338569/nelson-mandela-terror-list.

16. Paul Lansing and Sarosh Kuruvilla. "Business divestment in South Africa: In Who's Best Interest?" *Journal of Business Ethics* 7, no. 8 (1988): 561–574.

17. Siew Hong Teoh, Ivo Welch, and C. Paul Wazzan. "The Effect of Socially Activist Investment Policies on the Financial Markets: Evidence from the South African Boycott," *Journal of Business* 72, no. 1 (1999): 35–89.

18. Stephen Kaufman, "Pressure to End Apartheid Began at Grass Roots in U.S.," US Mission to International Organizations in Geneva, April 20, 2018, http://www.geneva.usmission.gov/2013/12/17/pressure-to-end-apartheid-began-at-grass-roots-in-u-s.

19. Nathaniel Wander and Ruth E. Malone, "Making Big Tobacco Give In: You Lose, They Win," *American Journal of Public Health* 96, no. 11 (2006): 2048–2054.

20. World Health Organization, *WHO Framework Convention on Tobacco Control: Guidelines for Implementation*, art. 5.3, articles 8 to 14.

21. Fox News, "Mike Huckabee: The Left Is Trying to Commit 'Acts of Terror,' " Fox and Friends, July 7, 2018, http://www.video.foxnews.com/v/5806520436001/?#sp=-show-clips Fox News.

22. "US: States Use Anti-Boycott Laws to Punish Responsible Businesses," Human Rights Watch, April 23, 2019, http://www.hrw.org/news/2019/04/23/us-states-use-anti-boycott-laws-punish-responsible-businesses.

23. Sari Bashi, "For U.S. Police, Refusing Israeli Training Is Not BDS—It's Common Sense: Opinion," Haaretz, December 4, 2018, http://www.haaretz.com/opinion/.premium-for-u-s-police-refusing-israeli-training-is-not-bds-it-s-common-sense-1.6718491.

24. "Freedom to Thrive: Reimagining Safety in Our Communities," Center for Popular Democracy, 2012, http://www.populardemocracy.org/sites/default/files/FreedomToThrive.

25. Brentin Mock, "What Happens If Cities Stop Spending on Police?" *CityLab*, July 14, 2017, http://www.citylab.com/equity/2017/07/the-price-of-defunding-the-police/533232.

26. "Freedom to Thrive," 39–40.

27. Michael M. Grynbaum and Matt Flegenheimer, "Mayor De Blasio Poised to Hire Nearly 1,300 Police Officers," *New York Times*, June 22, 2015, http://www.nytimes.com/2015/06/23/nyregion/mayor-de-blasio-poised-to-hire-hundreds-of-police-officers.html.

28. Oliver Laughland, "New NYPD Unit Armed with 'Machine Guns' Criticised by Reform Advocates," *Guardian*, January 30, 2015, http://www.theguardian.com/us-news/2015/jan/30/nypd-bill-bratton-anti-terror-unit-black-lives-matter.

29. Ashoka Jegroo, "NYPD Unit That Monitored Proud Boys Event Has Troubled History," *The Appeal*, October 19, 2018, http://www.theappeal.org/nypd-unit-that-monitored-proud-boys-event-has-troubled-history.

30. "Close Rikers NOW, We Keep Us Safe," No New Jails NYC, 2019, http://www.drive.google.com/file/d/1dDNc5I-vLsY2eVRXZBNJz2OPbsw5lfT5/view.

31. MTV, "What Now? An MTV/BET Town Hall," YouTube, BET/MTVJuly 9, 2016, http://www.youtube.com/watch?v=BKHcj4EFchI.

32. Ileana Najarro, "Unity National Bank, Only Black-Owned Bank in Texas, Opens Atlanta Branch," *Houston Chronicle*, April 4, 2018, http://www.chron.com/business/article/Unity-National-Bank-only-black-owned-bank-in-12800513.php.

33. Kristen Reed, "Historic Atlanta Bank Sees Spike in Applicants amid Calls to Bank Black," WXIA, July 14, 2016, http://www.11alive.com/article/news/local/historic-atlanta-bank-sees-spike-in-applicants-amid-calls-to-bank-black/85-273141807.

34. Adria Vasil, "TD Facing More Protests over Its Stake in Dakota Access Pipeline," *NOW*, November 30, 2016, http://www.nowtoronto.com/lifestyle/ecoholic/toronto-dominion-bank-dakota-access-pipeline.

35. Mehrsa Baradaran, *The Color of Money: Black Banks and the Racial Wealth Gap* (Cambridge, MA: Harvard University Press, 2017), 9.

36. Martin Luther King Jr., "Letter from Birmingham Jail (August 1963)," *Atlantic*, April 4, 2018, http://www.theatlantic.com/magazine/archive/2018/02/letter-from-birmingham-jail/552461.

37. Congressional Record: Proceedings and Debates of the U.S. Congress, vol. 4, pt. 4 (1876), 44th Cong., 1st Sess., 3967–3974 (3969), http://www.books.google.com/books?id=8KgzSWhR6loC&printsec=frontcover#v=onepage&q&f=false.

38. "Black History Month Freedman's Savings and Trust Company," Oxford University Press Blog, April 22, 2013, http://www.blog.oup.com/2007/02/black_history_m2.

39. John Steele Gordon, "The Freedman's Bank: A Nineteenth-Century Blueprint for the Savings-and-Loan Scandal," *American Heritage* 44, no. 8 (December 1993), http://www.americanheritage.com/freedmans-bank.

40. Garrett Peck, *The Smithsonian Castle and the Seneca Quarry* (Charleston, SC: Arcadia Publishing, 2013).

41. Congressional Record, Proceedings and Debates of the U.S. Congress, 3971.

42. Richard White, *The Republic for Which It Stands: The United States during Reconstruction and the Gilded Age, 1865–1896* (New York: Oxford University Press, 2017), 266.

43. Baradaran, *Color of Money*, 29.

44. Frederick Douglas, *The Life and Times of Frederick Douglas: From 1817–1882* (New York: Christian Age Office, 1882), 357.

45. Peck, *Smithsonian Castle and the Seneca Quarry*.

46. "1888 Capital Savings Bank," Partnership for Progress, http://www.fedpartnership.gov/minority-banking-timeline/capital-savings-bank.

47. James D. Watkinson, "William Washington Browne and the True Reformers of Richmond, Virginia," *Virginia Magazine of History and Biography* 97, no. 3 (1989): 375–398, http://www.jstor.org/stable/4249094.

48. National Parks Service (NPS), "The St. Luke Penny Savings Bank," US Department of the Interior, n.d., http://www.nps.gov/mawa/the-st-luke-penny-savings-bank.htm.

49. Victor Luckerson, "Black Wall Street: The African American Haven That Burned and Then Rose From the Ashes," *The Ringer*, June 28, 2018, http://www.theringer.com/2018/6/28/17511818/black-wall-street-oklahoma-greenwood-destruction-tulsa.

50. Pete Earley, "The Untold Story of One of America's Worst Race Riots," *Washington Post*, September 12, 1982, http://www.washingtonpost.com/archive/

opinions/1982/09/12/the-untold-story-of-one-of-americas-worst-race-riots/e37fc963-71dd-45cc-8cb0-04ab8032bcd2.

51. National Parks Service, *Final 1921 Tulsa Race Riot Reconnaissance Survey* (Washington, DC: U.S. Department of the Interior, 2001), http://www.nps.gov/park history/online_books/nnps/tulsa_riot.pdf.

52. Tim Madigan, *The Burning: Massacre, Destruction, and the Tulsa Race Riot of 1921* (New York: Macmillan, 2001), 174.

53. Alfred L. Brophy, *Reconstructing the Dreamland: The Tulsa Riot of 1921, Race, Reparations, and Reconciliation* (New York: Oxford University Press, 2003), 96.

54. "Tulsa Race Massacre," History, March 8, 2018, http://www.history.com/topics/roaring-twenties/tulsa-race-massacre November 26, 2019.

55. Cori Duke, "1921 Race Massacre Commission to Roll Out Statewide Curriculum for Teachers," KJRH, May 7, 2019, http://www.kjrh.com/news/local-news/1921-race-massacre-commission-to-roll-out-state-wide-curriculum-for-teachers.

56. National Parks Service, *Final 1921 Tulsa Race Riot Reconnaissance Survey*, 44.

57. Brophy, *Reconstructing the Dreamland*, 104.

58. Martin Luther King Jr., "Martin Luther King's Final Speech: 'I've Been to the Mountaintop'—The Full Text (April 3, 1968)," ABC News Network, http://www.abcnews.go.com/Politics/martin-luther-kings-final-speech-ive-mountaintop-full/story?id=18872817.

59. Federal Deposit Insurance Corporation (FDIC), *2019 Minority Depository Institutions Structure, Performance, and Social Impact*, http://www.fdic.gov/regulations/resources/minority/2019-mdi-study/full.pdf.

60. Michael Fletcher, "The Country's Last Black-Owned Banks Are in a Fight for Their Survival," *Washington Post*, February 13, 2015, http://www.washingtonpost.com/news/wonk/wp/2015/02/13/the-countrys-last-black-owned-banks-are-in-a-fight-for-their-survival; Amanda Dixon, "The 15 Largest Banks in America," Bankrate, May 30, 2019, http://www.bankrate.com/banking/biggest-banks-in-america.

61. Daniel Aaronson, Daniel Hartley, and Bhashkar Mazumder, "The Effects of the 1930s HOLC 'Redlining' Maps," (working paper, no. 2017–12, 2017).

62. Rick Rothacker and David Ingram, "Wells Fargo to Pay $175 Million in Race Discrimination Probe," *Reuters*, July 12, 2012, http://www.reuters.com/article/uk-wells-lending-settlement-idUKBRE86B16E20120712.

63. Halah Touryalai, "BofA Coughs Up $335 Million to Settle Discriminatory Lending Case with DoJ," *Forbes*, December 22, 2011, http://www.forbes.com/sites/halahtouryalai/2011/12/21/bofa-coughs-up-335-million-in-unfair-lending-suit-with-doj/#6d54700f6524.

64. Lance Dixon and David Smiley, "Miami Can Sue Big Banks for Predatory Lending, Supreme Court Rules," *Miami Herald*, May 1, 2017, http://www.miamiherald.com/news/local/community/miami-dade/article147851474.html.

65. Federal Deposit Insurance Corporation (FDIC), *2019 Minority Depository Institutions Structure*, 61.

66. Federal Deposit Insurance Corporation (FDIC), *2017 FDIC National Survey of Unbanked and Underbanked Households*, http://www.economicinclusion.gov/downloads/2017_FDIC_Unbanked_HH_Survey_Report.pdf (2017), 18.

67. Deonna Anderson, "Creating a Black-Led Credit Union in Response to Police Violence," *Next City*, May 18, 2018, http://www.nextcity.org/daily/entry/creating-a-black-led-credit-union-in-response-to-police-violence.

68. Adrienne Broaddus, KARE11, Minneapolis, April 6, 2017, http://www.kare11.com/article/mb/news/black-owned-credit-union-potentially-coming-to-north-mpls/429034622.

69. Camille Erickson, "Black-Led Credit Union in North Minneapolis Is 'the Most Important Work' to Drive Economic Vitality," *Twin Cities Daily Planet*, August 3, 2017, http://www.tcdailyplanet.net/black-led-credit-union-in-north-minneapolis-is-the-most-important-work-to-drive-economic-vitality.

70. Morgan Simon, "Will the Real Blexit Please Stand Up?" *Forbes*, November 21, 2018, http://www.forbes.com/sites/morgansimon/2018/11/21/will-the-real-blexit-please-stand-up/#73a1005640e7.

71. Dedrick Asante-Muhammad, Chuck Collins, Josh Hoxie, and Emanuel Nieves, "The Road to Zero Wealth: How the Racial Wealth Divide Is Hollowing Out America's Middle Class," Institute for Policy Studies, September 2017, http://www.ips-dc.org/report-the-road-to-zero-wealth.

72. Candice Owens, "Anne Coulter @ BLEXITLA Full Speech," YouTube, January 22, 2019, http://www.youtube.com/watch?v=256XW5Lbw3w.

73. Brandon Tatum, "BLEXIT BALTIMORE—The Black Community," YouTube, September 17, 2019, http://www.youtube.com/watch?v=LxXahl7lv8I.

74. WCCO Radio Newsroom, "Protesters Interrupt Mayor Frey's 2020 Budget Address," WCCO Radio, August 15, 2019, http://www.wccoradio.radio.com/articles/protesters-interrupt-mayor-freys-2020-budget-address.

75. Jon Collins, "Black-Owned Credit Union Closer to Opening in N. Mpls," *MPR News*, Minnesota Public Radio, December 14, 2018, http://www.mprnews.org/story/2018/12/14/black-owned-credit-union-closer-to-opening.

76. Marielle Segarra, "The Bank Black Movement Gains Traction," *Marketplace*, April 20, 2017, http://www.marketplace.org/2017/04/20/business/bank-black-movement-gains-traction.

77. Marissa Evans and Andy Mannix, "Ousted Director of City-Backed Credit Union Alleges Retaliation," *Star Tribune*, October 5, 2019, http://www.startribune.com/former-minneapolis-credit-union-leader-accuses-organization-of-discrimination/562186952.

78. Peter. Strozniak, "Proposed North Minneapolis CU Organizers Rescind State Charter Application," *Credit Union Times*, December 19, 2019, http://www.cutimes.com/2019/12/19/proposed-north-minneapolis-cu-organizers-rescind-state-charter-application/?slreturn=20191119152756.

79. Fred Hampton, "Power Anywhere Where There's People," History Is a Weapon, Speech given at Olivet Presbyterian Church, Chicago, IL, 1969, http://www.historyisaweapon.com/defcon1/fhamptonspeech.html.

80. SNCC, "Fannie Lou Hamer Founds Freedom Farm Cooperative," SNCC Digital Gateway, http://www.snccdigital.org/events/fannie-lou-hamer-founds-freedom-farm-cooperative.

Chapter 13

1. Terrance Hayes, "We Should Make a Documentary about Spades," Vinyl Poetry, 1, February 1, 2013, http://www.vinylpoetry.com/volume-7/page-4.

2. Elizabeth Alexander, " 'Can You be Black and Look at This?' Reading the Rodney King Video(s)," Public Culture 7, no. 1 (1994): 88.

3. Alexander, " 'Can You be Black and Look at This?' " 81.

4. Alexander, 81.

5. Alexander, 78.

6. Terrence McCoy, "Darren Wilson explains why he killed Michael Brown," *Washington Post*, November 25, 2014, http://www.washingtonpost.com/news/morning-mix/wp/2014/11/25/why-darren-wilson-said-he-killed-michael-brown.

7. Fred Moten, *In the Break: The Aesthetics of the Black Radical Tradition* (Minneapolis: University of Minnesota Press, 2003), 332.

8. Christina B. Hanhardt, *Safe Space: Gay Neighborhood History and the Politics of Violence* (Durham, NC: Duke University Press, 2013), 376.

9. Michelle Alexander, *The New Jim Crow: Mass Incarceration in the Age of Colorblindness* (New York: New Press, 2012), 336.

10. Cathy Cohen, *The Boundaries of Blackness: AIDS and the Breakdown of Black Politics* (Chicago: University of Chicago Press, 1999), 410.

11. Jeffrey McCune Jr., *Sexual Discretion: Black Masculinity and the Politics of Passing* (Chicago: University of Chicago Press, 2014), 224.

12. Moten, *In the Break*, 93.

13. Danez Smith, "Dinosaurs in the Hood," Poetry, December 1, 2014, http://www.poetryfoundation.org/poetrymagazine/poem/249154.

14. Hayes, "We Should Make a Documentary about Spades."

15. Smith, "Dinosaurs in the Hood."

16. Smith.

17. Smith.

18. Jennifer Brody, *Punctuation: Art, Politics, and Play* (Durham, NC: Duke University Press, 2008), 240.

19. Moten, *In the Break*, 13.

20. Jill Dolan, *Utopia in Performance: Finding Hope at the Theater* (Ann Arbor: University of Michigan Press, 2005), 248.

21. Hayes, "We Should Make a Documentary about Spades."

22. First published in *QED: A Journal in GLBTQ Worldmaking* 2, no. 2 (Summer 2015): 177–183.

About the Authors

Editors

Beth Hinderliter is assistant professor of contemporary art history and director of the Duke Hall Gallery of Art at James Madison University. She is co-editor with Noelle Chaddock of *Antagonizing White Feminism: Intersectionality's Critique of Women's Studies and the Academy*. Other publications include *Colonial Wounds/Postcolonial Repair* with Maureen Shanahan and *Communities of Sense: Rethinking Aesthetics and Politics*. Her essays have appeared in journals such as *Journal of Postcolonial Writing, African and Black Diaspora*, *NKA*, and *October*.

Steve Peraza is an assistant professor in the department of history and social studies education at SUNY-Buffalo State College. He earned his PhD in U.S. history from SUNY-Buffalo, specializing in African slavery in global perspective. His research examines slaves' conceptions of law and legal procedure in eighteenth-century Louisiana freedom suits. Other research interests include race and racism in America, the Harlem Renaissance, and the long Civil Rights Movement. He teaches courses in U.S. history, African American history, the African Diaspora, slavery in the Atlantic World, and hip-hop.

Contributors

Lauren K. Alleyne is the author of two collections of poetry, *Difficult Fruit* (2014) and *Honeyfish* (2019). Her work has appeared in numerous publications, including the *New York Times, The Atlantic,* and *Ms. Muse*, among others. Her most recent honors include a 2020 NAACP Image Award nomination for Outstanding Poetry and the longlist for the Bocas

Prize for Caribbean Literature. She is currently the assistant director of the Furious Flower Poetry Center and an associate professor of English at James Madison University.

Shanna Greene Benjamin is a biographer and scholar who studies the literature, lives, and archives of Black women. She has published on African American literature and Black women's intellectual history in *African American Review*, *MELUS*, *a/b: Auto/Biography*, *Studies in American Fiction*, and *PMLA*. Her book *Half in Shadow: The Life and Legacy of Nellie Y. McKay* is forthcoming. She lives with her family in Charlotte, North Carolina.

Dominique Christina is an award-winning poet, author, educator, and activist. She holds five national poetry slam titles in four years, including the 2014 & 2012 Women of the World Slam Champion and 2011 National Poetry Slam Champion. Her work appears in numerous publications and is greatly influenced by her family's legacy in the Civil Rights Movement and by the idea that words make worlds. She is the author of four books and a writer/actor for the HBO series High Maintenance Season 2. Her fourth book *Anarcha Speaks* won the National Poetry Series award in 2017.

Yomaira C. Figueroa-Vásquez is assistant professor of global Afro-Diaspora studies in the department of English and the African American & African Studies department at Michigan State University. She is the author of *Decolonizing Diasporas: Radical Mappings of Afro-Atlantic Literature* (2020), and her published work can be found in *Hypatia: A Journal of Feminist Philosophy*, *The Journal of Decolonization: Indigeneity, Education & Society*, *CENTRO Journal*, *Small Axe*, *Frontiers Journal*, and *SX Salon*. A scholar and organizer, she is a founder of both the MSU Womxn of Color Initiative, the collaborative hurricane recovery project #ProyectoPalabrasPR, and co-curator of the digital/material project Electric Marronage.

Joseph Flynn is the associate director for academic affairs for the Center for Black Studies and an associate professor of curriculum and instruction at Northern Illinois University. His teaching and scholarship focus on the intersection of multicultural and social justice education, Whiteness Studies, media and popular culture, and curriculum. In addition to his professional development work with regional schools and colleges in northern Illinois, Dr. Flynn has published scholarship related to the aforementioned topics, and he co-edited the book *Rubric Nation: Critical Inquiries on the Impact* *of Rubrics in Education* (2015). Dr. Flynn founded the three-day Social Justice Summer Camp for Educators at Northern Illinois University. He also serves as an editorialist on *Perspectives*, a radio program on WNIJ, an NPR affiliate, and as a co-host for the podcast *Mental Illness in Popular Culture*. He is a past-president of the American Association for Teaching and Curriculum. Dr. Flynn published *White Fatigue: Rethinking Resistance for Social Justice* (2018), a book that considers the critical question, why is it a challenge to teach White students about race? The book has been awarded the O.L. Davis, Jr. Outstanding Book Award from the American Association for Teaching and Curriculum.

Jon Henry is a visual artist using photography and text. His work has been exhibited nationally and internationally at *Aperture Foundation*, *Smack Mellon*, *BRIC*, and *Rubber Factory*, among others. His work has been published in *PDN*, *i-D Magazine*, *ArtFuse*, and *JRNL 4*. He has recently been awarded the Film Photo Award (sponsored by Kodak) and En Foco Fellowship (2020) and named LensCulture Emerging Talent (2019).

Jessica Marie Johnson is an assistant professor in the department of history at the Johns Hopkins University. Johnson is a historian of Atlantic slavery and the Atlantic African diaspora. She is the author of *Wicked Flesh: Black Women, Intimacy, and Freedom in the Atlantic World* (2020). She is guest editor of *Slavery in the Machine*, a special issue of *sx:archipelagos* (2019), and co-editor with Dr. Mark Anthony Neal of *Black Code: A Special Issue of the Black Scholar* (2017). Her work has appeared in *Slavery & Abolition*, *The Black Scholar*, *Meridians*: *Feminism, Race and Transnationalism*, *American Quarterly*, *Social Text*, *The Journal of African American History*, *the William & Mary Quarterly*, *Debates in the Digital Humanities*, *Forum Journal*, *Bitch Magazine*, *Black Persp*ectives (AAIHS), *Somatosphere*, and *Post-Colonial Digital Humanities* (DHPoco). Her book chapters have appeared in multiple edited collections.

Derek Conrad Murray is an interdisciplinary theorist specializing in the history, theory, and criticism of contemporary art and visual culture. He works in contemporary aesthetic and cultural theory with a particular attention to technocultural engagements with identity and representation. He has contributed to leading magazines and journals such as *American Art*, *Art in America*, *Parachute*, *Art Journal*, *Third Text*, *Consumption Markets & Culture*, and *Nka: Journal of Contemporary African Art*, where he currently serves as associate editor. Murray is also currently serving on the editorial board of *Art Journal* (CAA) and the editorial advisory board of *Third Text.* Murray is the author of *Queering Post-Black Art: Artists Transforming African-American Identity After Civil Rights* (2016). Murray is also the author of two forthcoming volumes: a single-authored book entitled *Mapplethorpe and the Flower: Radical Sexuality and the Limits of Control* (2019), and an edited volume entitled *Visual Culture Approaches to the Selfie* (2020).

Andrew J. Padilla is an award-winning artist and educator born and raised in East Harlem, New York City. From Hostos to Harvard, Andrew has lectured on Urban Politics across the United States. His work has appeared in numerous publications, including *BET News*, *MTV news*, and *NPR Latino*, among others. His most recent honors include a MacCracken Fellowship and Dean's Doctoral Fellowship at NYU, where he is currently researching the impact of fourth industrial revolution technologies on democratic governance.

Erin M. Stephens is a Black feminist sociologist and staunch advocate for social and institutional change to better meet the needs of marginalized populations, particularly women and youth of color. Her work appears in the edited volumes *Gender in the Twenty-First Century: The Stalled Revolution and the Road to Equality* (2017) and *Women, War, and Violence: Topography Resistance, and Hope* (2015). She is currently the program director for The Beautiful Project, an arts-based collective in North Carolina that uses photography, writing, and care to advance the wellness and representational justice of Black women and girls.

Siona Wilson is author of the book *Art Labor, Sex Politics: Feminist Effects in 1970s British Art and Performance* (2015). Her writing has appeared in several edited collections, including, most recently, *A Companion to Feminist Art* (eds. Hilary Robinson and Maria Elena Buszek), as well as academic journals and art magazines such as *Artforum*, *Art History*, *Art Review*, *Feminist Review*, *October*, *Oxford Art Journal*, and *Third Text.* Recent curatorial projects include *I can't breathe* (2016, the Art Gallery of the College of Staten Island) and *Sexing Sound: Aural Histories and Feminist Scores* (2015, The James Gallery). In collaboration with Oskar Korsár, Wilson was the writer and director of the performance *I Like Feminism and Feminism Likes me* (2020). She is associate professor of art history at the College of Staten Island and the Graduate Center, the City University of New York.

About the Authors

www.ingramcontent.com/pod-product-compliance
Lightning Source LLC
LaVergne TN
LVHW040159080826
844660LV00001B/36

* 9 7 8 1 4 3 8 4 8 3 1 1 5 *